THE
SPECTATOR
ANNUAL

THE SPECTATOR ANNUAL

Edited by Dominic Lawson

Foreword by P.D. James

HarperCollins*Publishers*

HarperCollins*Publishers*,
77–85 Fulham Palace Road,
Hammersmith
London W6 8JB

Published by HarperCollins*Publishers* 1993
1 3 5 7 9 8 6 4 2

Copyright © *The Spectator* 1993

ISBN 0 00 255327 9

Photoset in Trump Medieval by
Rowland Phototypesetting Ltd,
Bury St Edmunds, Suffolk

Printed in Great Britain by
Hartnolls Ltd, Bodmin, Cornwall

CONTENTS

FOREWORD

P. D. James

Those of us who are less than enthusiastic about the secular and commercial celebration of the Feast of the Nativity – it has never been my favourite time of year – have learned to look among the trash and tinsel for our annual consolations. *The Spectator Annual* is high among them. Other once-favourite magazines, good and bad, have died, some after an inexorable decline which makes their demise a happy relief, others suffering a sad, unexpected and more spectacular end. *The Spectator* lives on, thanks to the quality of its editorial staff and contributors and the loyalty and devotion of its readers. It may occasionally irritate or provoke, but it never bores. No one has ever cast it aside in disgust with the comment, 'Nothing worth reading this week.' The journal provides unfailingly for its readers a weekly therapeutic antidote of sanity, eccentricity, good writing and, above all, a blessed absence of that silliness which is the mark of our unfortunate era.

Making a selection of the best weekly offerings for the *Annual* cannot be easy, but we can again expect perceptive profiles of the great and good, and the would-be-great and the less-than-good, political analysis from Right and Left and all points in between, contributions to the Great European Debate, some poetry to reassure us that not all modern verse is merely prose rearranged on the page, and articles, among the best of their kind, about the splendours, ardours and occasional horrors of travel, which no doubt set eager travellers packing their bags but which tend to confirm my timid preference for staying at home. We can expect, too, a selection of the most notable reviews of the year's arts and literature, some kind, some less than kind, but all seriously addressing the work, not merely propounding the prejudices of the reviewer.

I look forward, as always, to a selection of diary entries, those nuggets of good sense, eccentricity and unrepentant prejudice which are as much fun to write as to read, and to familiar names, including Mary Killen's inspired solution to dilemmas of contemporary etiquette which put minor problems of placement and menu-planning in perspective and make me wonder whether my own social life may not be unreasonably restricted and conventional. The *Annual* would be incomplete without Taki's 'High Life' and Jeffrey Bernard's 'Low Life', both equally fascinating to those of us who exist more or less comfortably between the two, and I can confidently expect a selection of the caustic comments of Dr Theodore Dalrymple who seems to attract more than his fair share of society's insoluble medical and social problems. I hope my general practitioner reads him assiduously; it should encourage her to welcome my occasional complaints about the minor decrepitudes of old age with a lively sense of her own good fortune.

In the 1993 *Spectator Annual* we have a picture of the year, its personalities, its art and literature, the concerns of world and domestic politics, and those smaller preoccupations which give a year its particular flavour. *The Spectator Annual* is the one safe present for Christmas given to all our more civilised friends. Regular readers will welcome a beautifully-produced, sensibly-sized compendium of their favourite articles, and those who don't regularly take the magazine will have a sample of what they are missing and may be encouraged to avail themselves of the journal's weekly stimulus, consolation and entertainment. The *Annual* returns as a faithful friend, reminding us of the words of the Apocrypha: 'A faithful friend is the medicine of life.' So welcome, *Spectator Annual 1993*, a palatable tonic to strengthen us for the festive season and set us up for the year ahead.

'POLYGAMY AND HAREMS WORKED'

Candida Crewe

Sir Nicholas Fairbairn tends to go in for the all-over tartan look. His sartorial flourish on a recent television chat show prompted the host to ask if he was planning to audition for a shortcake advertisement. The Tory member for Perth and Kinross, and former Scottish Law Officer, said no, but you wouldn't put it past him. He's no ordinary MP. And it's not only his dress which causes a stir. Each year, his *Who's Who* recreations change: in 1990, he surpassed himself with 'growling, prowling, scowling and owling'. During the recent election campaign, he consistently succeeded in causing his party embarrassment with his outspoken views. The words which prompted particular upset were, 'Why should the bastard child of an American sailor serving in Dunoon have a vote in Scotland even though he's in America, when the legitimate son of a Gordon Highlander born in Daarnstadt who's resident in Carlisle, has no vote or say in Scotland?'

This was not deemed by his colleagues to enhance their cause. At his Westminster office, I asked him if he was enjoying his reputation as a wild man. 'It's not a reputation I've cultivated,' he assured me. 'I was brought up in a family village in Scotland where everyone had the reputation of their own personality. In my view, it's a philosophical and metaphysical duty to be singular and ourselves. I thought we were supposed to be lights, not hidden under bushels.'

So perhaps he could enlighten us about his latest controversy. Why, having written privately and somewhat sycophantically to Sir Edward Heath to congratulate him on becoming a Knight of the Garter, did he then write publicly to the *Sunday Telegraph* to denounce granting of the very same award to the former Prime Minister?

'The *Daily Telegraph* said of this that while one could be rude to one's friends in private, one should be polite to them in public. Well, that's contrary to all I was brought up to believe. I've known Sir E. Heath for 40-odd years. To write and rejoice in what was clearly for him a reason for great satisfaction with himself at last, was the perfectly proper thing to do. But then why can't I say he was a dreadful Prime Minister, and his public behaviour is appalling? The fact that he sent my private letter to the press shows he has no manners. He has grave personality problems, and torment within himself, which he'll never resolve. But there's no reason I can't rejoice with him in private.'

It is hard to establish from where Fairbairn gets his outspokenness. He was born in 1933 – 'the same year Hitler came to power, though he wasn't as good a painter as I am' – and brought up in Scotland (where he still lives). His father was, he says, 'a dipsomaniac, but a psycho-analyst of great distinction, though only interested in listening to the wailings of his patients. I think I've inherited his analytical mind, and my mother's taste and love of art and music, if that's not being too conceited.'

Although he read Medicine, then Arts and Law at Edinburgh University, and became a QC in 1972, Fairbairn knew he wanted to go into politics at the age of 12.

'The 1945 election dealt a real shock to me in that the gardener at my prep school said he was Labour and they were going to wipe out our "type". The concept of resenting those better or worse than oneself was new to me, so upsetting, I was determined to shoot socialism in the brain at noon.' So saying he pressed his forefinger into his forehead like a gun. 'Bonk! After the gardener said this, I even went and got a catapult and put out every window in the Co-op bakery. He motivated me into politics.'

Fairbairn was sitting at his desk. He was dressed in plain cream (that day it was the shoes' turn to demonstrate his sartorial flamboyance, in the form of big square buckles). The paleness of the suit was offset by his almost raspberry-colour complexion. As he spoke, he toyed with a cotton handkerchief, and swigged red wine from a shallow plastic beaker. On the side-table next to some Listermint mouthwash was the bottle. The label read 'Meerlust'.

'That's Dutch for more lust,' he informed me.

This was an opening to talk about Maastricht, I decided. Sir Nicholas recalled the last treaty made in Maastricht in 1944. 'Montgomery agreed the Allies should retreat from the areas of Germany they'd conquered to a line the Russians demanded. It was a disaster. I'm not saying this means anything, it's just an interesting historical coincidence. Attempts to make Europe right and pure by being nice to those who want to divide it in their own interests didn't work the first time. All being called Schmidt and speaking Esperanto *is not* the way ahead.'

The ever growing problem of Europe, he said, was economic migration. 'There's no question at all, if you think about it, that if the people of the British Commonwealth, and all the previous members of the French Empire who still have a right to vote in Paris, all come to the European State, you'll quickly create a situation of ethnic migration that'll create disintegration and intolerance.'

Fairbairn insisted he isn't against immigration *per se*, only if it's uncontrolled. If there's no Asylum Bill, he thinks we will be 'swamped' in 1997, with two and a half million people from Hong Kong.

'They'll just say, "We're here," and we won't be able to say, "Ta, ta, fellows, here's a boat."'

'If an asylum seeker knocks on our door just because he doesn't like these bangs in Sarajevo, well, anyone may as well come to my door and say, "I'm cold out here, a policeman's just been very rude to me, I propose to move into your spare room, and if you don't have one, you can share your room with me, or move out yourself."''

He thumped his fist on the desk to stress his indignation. It was quite a habit with him. On the subject of the Citizen's Charter, he said, 'The concept's good, but it's wishy-washy, and just another opportunity for bureaucratic officiousness!' Thump.

And on John Major's 'classless society', 'It's a ridiculous phrase.' Thump. And on the leadership election which saw to Thatcher's political demise, 'Just to toss her aside with no consultation, it was terrible and fatuous.' Thump, thump, thump.

While on the subject of his former leader, I ventured to ask if he had found her sexually attractive. 'Sexually attractive, no, but certainly bonny', he said, putting on a Scottish accent.

I asked because Fairbairn is known to be exceedingly fond of women, while no great advocate of monogamy. 'Christian monogamy,' he said, 'and its assumption of fidelity, is as fallacious as the Catholic concept of the chastity of priests.'

He first married aged 28 (and had five children, although two died) but divorced 13 years later, and had plenty of girl-friends.

One of them is supposed to have attempted suicide by hanging herself with a pair of stockings from a lamp-post outside his London flat. He says, 'She was certainly depressed, but that story was a gross exaggeration made up by a vindictive Tory MP.' Fairbairn and his current wife married in 1983.

'Are you faithful to her?' I asked.

'I don't think that's an appropriate question,' came the reply. 'But I will say I'm pretty sure polygamy and harems probably worked better. I suppose we have that now, in series as opposed to in parallel. I mean, if you and I were to get married, go to Marbella and screw each other rigid, we'd be throwing eggs at each other on our return. I'd be telling you that you were a stupid bitch, and it'd all be off, we'd divorce, and then marry all over again to someone else.'

Sir Nicholas says we live in a priggish and prim age which doesn't allow for infidelity, especially on the part of those in public life. So why did he remarry?

'I can explain that very easily. I very much wished to marry whom I did, having known her for many years. Unlike the first time, I was conscious of all the problems – of the inevitable tension between men and women who are tied together in marriage, of getting bored of something the minute you get it – so I can now cope with them, as well as enjoy the advantages for which the institution was created. There's no question that one of the attractions of monophysicality is that, apart from the depth of the relationship, you remember when you turn over in bed who you're with, and you don't have to get up at dawn and get out.'

All the same, were temptations now not greater with the larger number of women in parliament? What of them?

'I'm delighted to have more of them in the House of Commons, but they certainly don't give me feelings of femininity – and by that I don't mean beddable. They lack *fragrance* on the whole, they're definitely not desert island material. Maybe, in this day and age with all these hang-ups, they deny their femininity.

'Why has womankind given up the exaltation of herself, that attempt to attract, to adorn, to glint? They all look as though they're from the 5th Kiev Stalinist machine-gun parade. Except for Betty Boothroyd, now she's got style, fragrance. As for Edwina Currie – well, the only person who smells her fragrance is herself. I can't stand the hag.'

With that, he thumped the desk again, and took a final swig from his glass of Meerlust.

4 July 1992

THE RESTRAINT OF ROYALIST MURDOCH

Andrew Knight

Let us suppose that the *Daily Mail* had won the auction for the Morton book about the Princess of Wales's troubles. It nearly did. Until late in the bidding, the *Mail* was the only horse in the race. Indeed the

Sunday Times entered the affair with much agonising only after several of Princess Diana's famous 'friends' had urged the paper to do so. So the *Mail* wins a one-horse race at £200,000, and serialises this slim bombshell for a fortnight with huge increases in circulation on which – unlike the *Sunday Times* – it makes money. (Extra cover price revenue alone does not cover the cost of each extra copy printed of the *Sunday Times*.)

Sir David English, with the Greatest Living Englishman at his side, appears on every box in the land, making a more urbane though no more authoritative fist of it than did Andrew Neil, one of those inconvenient Britons who believe the truth needs no syrup to wash it down. Now: question. Would the world be accusing the *Mail*'s owner, Lord Rothermere, and his 'servile republican editor' of trying to destroy the monarchy – as Rupert Murdoch and Andrew Neil are being accused? Indeed, why has the world not done so as a result of the rapaciously successful *Mail* spoilers which gave the story such supercharged horsepower in the days before Mr Morton's book first appeared in the *Sunday Times*? If a republican plot was behind the *Sunday Times*'s decision to bid, what on earth could have been behind the *Daily Mail*'s?

In their coverage of the controversy, the *Mail* on *Sunday*, the *Daily Mail* itself and their stable-mate, the *Evening Standard*, have justified our serialisation of the Morton book and the right to know the royal revelations contained in it. They called Andrew Neil 'brave' to run it. If the stink of republicanism surrounded the *Sunday Times*, should not a whiff of it cling to the *Daily Mail*?

Let's address the issue of Wapping republicanism face first, starting with me. My colleagues from my *Economist* days probably recall a somewhat gooey monarchist as their editor. I never lost an occasion, with brilliant help from Mr Norman Macrae and Mrs Sarah Hogg, to lay out the full Bagehot catalogue of lapidary phrases praising the dignified monarchy at the apex of Britain's efficient state. I'm sorry to say, but I hold those warm pro-monarchy views to this day, confirmed not weakened by the events of the past three weeks.

Turn then to the more significant figure of Rupert Murdoch. He may have 'been a republican' in youth, as people say he was. I don't know, I wasn't there. What I do know is that over the past two years during the countless times I have talked to him when our first family has been in the news, he has argued for restraint. Long before Diana's lunar month hit us, he was consistently arguing with me and others that, for all his explicit horror of English upper-class snobbery, his suspicion of the British 'establishment', he believes strongly in the institution of the monarchy here. It might not work elsewhere, he says, but since the institution seems to work well in Britain, leave well alone, at least until it doesn't any more (long after we all are gone.)

If this is a conversion since Rupert Murdoch's youth, I guess it has come about from two sources: listening to the readers of the *Sun* and the *News of the World*, and recognising (as many of us did) from Watergate in America and the risks to stability in our country in the late 1970s, that the monarch here holds a crucial reserve power in her hands such as no elected or retired geriatric politico could possibly hold.

In internal discussion, Rupert Murdoch puts a damper on any story that might harm the royal institution. The royal institution, not the royal people. Our two big tabloid newspapers have sat for years on documented stories that could only have harmed the institution of the monarchy. Andrew Neil as editor of the *Sunday Times* gives many royals (particularly the fringe ones) a hard editorial time individually, and has led the charge against the peripheral Civil Listers. Andrew Neil's dislike of the unmeriting British establishment is legendary. But he will tell you very plainly that he is no republican. The *Sunday Times* said as much in plain terms in its strong, unrepentant leader three Sundays ago: the *Sunday Times* 'is not a republican newspaper'.

As for the *Sun*, Kelvin MacKenzie will allow his contempt for snobbery to lash its chief totem in Britain, the Crown. But when I asked him a fortnight ago for his view of Wapping's and his own alleged republicanism, he said: 'Anybody who thinks Rupert is republican is telling an absolute bloody lie, and the more I see of President Mitterrand on television the more it makes me yearn for the Queen.' Any prospect of President Jim Callaghan or President Geoffrey Howe would appal Kelvin MacKenzie, as it would any of the tabloid editors in his shadow. As for the editors of the *Times* and the *News of the World*, they have carried more comment rubbishing their sister paper's scoop than the other way round. *Today's* attitude to the royal family is uncomplicatedly pro.

Worriers about the survival of our monarchy rest their case on its fragility as an institution. Its authority is primarily moral, its standing is wrapped in its mystery, and its little appreciated, and underestimated, power to provide political stability in a crisis in this country would evaporate if it were ever overexposed. Prince Charles himself has argued this, so have my former colleagues at the *Telegraph*, Max Hastings and Lord Deedes, and ardent monarchists like Nicholas Soames MP. They say 'it is not possible to uphold belief in our monarchy unless you show much more restraint. You undermine the monarchy and Britain itself when you intrude into the family and moral lives of the royal firm, when you strip away the mystery of Princess Diana and the family surrounding her, when you harm the inner sanctum of the Queen herself.'

These men are Canute's courtiers. They believe with a genuine, unmistakable, heartfelt patriotism that King Canute will save the foot of his throne from damp by ordering the sea to go back. Canute, of course, knew better, and I side with him in believing the complete opposite. The tide comes in. But it also goes out again, not because Prince Charles, Mr Hastings or Mr Soames shouts at it (Lord Deedes never shouts). They may not believe it, but I and Mr Neil and Mr MacKenzie and, yes, Mr Murdoch are just as patriotic as they are, just as sure that the institutions of this sceptred isle need to survive.

How do institutions survive? They adapt – they constantly adapt. That is a process which, like the evolution of a successful newspaper, never ends. Nothing whatever can be served for the monarchy in Britain by retailing a marital fairy story once every newsroom in Fleet Street and 3,000 other élite London chatterers know for a fact that it is a marital nightmare. That would be 1936 again, but worse.

Was the right way to end this personal fairy tale to prolong the journalistic process of a thousand cuts – the botched post-polo kiss in India, the separate travel logs, the lonely garden at Highgrove, solitary poses before the Sphinx and Taj Mahal? Or should we have published the documented stories of regal infidelities which we hold, deliberately unused, in our safes – and in some cases have actually paid for so that our tabloid competitors may not use them either?

Or was it better to serialise a book that, whatever special pleading (plenty, I suspect) and errors it proves to contain, clearly carried the stamp of being authentic and, at only one remove, sanctioned by Princess Diana herself?

'Sanctioned?' I hear you ask. Let me quote from an undoubted member of the Prince's party (no name: this is not American journalism school). 'What is wrong with this book is that it is just one side of the story. But it is clearly well sourced, yes its sources are excellent, I don't think even Buckingham Palace is bothering to deny that.'

The only crime against any family – our royal one most of all – is the risking of a happy marriage, not the acknowledgement of an unhappy one. 'Where there is a cut there is growth.' My belief is that this family and this institution can grow in standing if they react as a fallible but loving family to Mr Morton's book. Whether serialised in the *Mail* or the *Sunday Times*, the book is a fact. It tells facts of a kind which have afflicted virtually every family in the kingdom, directly or at little distance. People now recognise the family they see. After the

*'In my time, such schoolyard disputes would be
settled with a handgun.'*

years of fairy tale that grew up artificially round George VI's little girls
this is a new situation, but not necessarily a bad one.

Why, then, the fuss? Of course because it is Diana, it is Charles, it
is 'the royals'. But also, of course, because the story has involved, once
again, 'Murdoch'. The neurosis of the London liberal intelligentsia
(intelligent but far from liberal) about Mr Murdoch is the subject for
another article one day. Enough to say here that for anybody who
works for him, as I do, the demonology round his name is weird when
it is not laughable.

Mr Murdoch has a long history of offending one after the other of
Britain's entrenched establishments. And, now, one of his character-
istically strong, individualist editors has serialised a book which,
despite its all too obvious partisanship and distortions, contains a 'true
story' and 'ends the speculation'. That, as history will relate, was the
right thing to do.

4 July 1992

ARCHITECTURE

THE LATE BIG JIM

Gavin Stamp

The unexpected death of James Stirling leaves me with a sense of loss, for criticising his architecture has sustained me for almost a quarter of a century. I feel strangely diminished by the departure of this enemy. Although we never met, messages were relayed to me that if he ever encountered me he would punch me on the nose. My crime, of course, was to disagree with the British architectural establishment that promotes careers and recommends knighthoods and to suggest, in this organ and elsewhere, that Stirling was a deeply flawed architect who did not deserve all the praise heaped on his work. That he was a creative artist of considerable originality I do not doubt, but architecture must be more than the production of seductive images of buildings in glossy journals. It also involves a responsibility to the client and users of a building, and in this James Stirling was singularly deficient. But *de mortuis nil nisi bonum*: the question I must address is whether functional failures should prevent a very talented artist from being regarded as a great architect.

In his touching tribute to 'Big Jim' in the *Independent*, Mark Girouard notes how 'young fogies, at the mention of Stirling's name, turned crimson . . .' I fear he means me. Yet, when I first encountered one of Stirling's masterpieces, I was, in fact, predisposed to like it. In 1968, as a second-year Cambridge undergraduate and after a year spent, enjoyably, working in a Neo-Classical library by the great C. R. Cockerell, I was looking forward to experiencing Stirling's brand new History Faculty building. Like Mark Girouard (who, I think, influenced me), I saw its angular, aggressive forms made of engineering brick and cascades of patent industrial glazing as a creative protest against blandness and mediocrity – analogous to the vigorous work of mid-Victorian Goths like Butterfield and Teulon reacting against Georgian good taste.

How cruelly was I disappointed! I soon realised that Stirling's masterpiece was a brute. The library was not comfortable to work in: the three giant coloured fans which powered the much-vaunted air circulation system vibrated too much to be turned on; the structure leaked and the lecture rooms were almost unusable owing both to noise and to the heat generated through the single-skin external glazing. The pseudo-industrial aesthetic was a fraud. Above all, the details were coarse and crude. Here, it seemed to me, was the work of an architect who was only interested in being avant-garde, who simply did not care how his creation was used and had no interest in the details which humanise architecture and raise it to the level of high art. Eight years after it opened, John Casey gave me the chance to write about the building in the *Cambridge Review* and so contribute a tiny counterpoint to the professional hagiography of Big Jim; eight years after that, all the external tiles were stripped off the building and the University seriously considered demolishing it altogether. In the end, only economics dictated refurbishment instead.

It is not an exaggeration to say that this experience of one of Big Jim's masterpieces formed my whole attitude to architecture – perhaps Stirling's real crime was to make me into a fogey. Today I hope I am more tolerant and I find myself seeing the point of, if not actually liking, much of the more considered architecture of the 1960s. I recognise that all architects make mistakes, even great ones, and a really beautiful building can succeed as a monument despite functional failings – as with the Sydney Opera House. But I still must make two qualifications with regard to Stirling. First, I remain unconvinced that the History Faculty was as wonderful an object as the architect's admirers maintain. The structure is miserable in scale externally and the overall glass roof sags between the extended wings. It is altogether a feeble thing in comparison with the earlier and celebrated Engineering Building at Leicester University – a really remarkable, dynamic composition influenced by Russian Constructivism designed (I think significantly) when Stirling was in partnership with James Gowan. Mr Gowan once told me that he was amazed that Stirling continued with the same problematic pseudo-industrial style in two more projects despite its inappropriateness.

But, more to the point, the failure of the History Faculty was not an isolated case but part of a pattern: coarse, thoughtless detail which demonstrates a contempt for the human user was all too evident 20 years later in the Clore Gallery. Stirling seemed to make the same mistakes over and over again. The Leicester building was once memorably described by Martin Pawley as 'a heap of oxidising geometrical junk'; the Florey Building for Queen's College, Oxford caused such problems that it was closed to visitors and became the subject of lengthy litigation; the Southgate housing at Runcorn New Town has now been partly demolished.

Yet Stirling had genius – at building images that photograph well. I went to see Runcorn shortly before the end: it was grey and drizzling; there were burnt-out cars lying around and the enclosed concrete staircase towers stank of urine. Yet, as I lifted my camera, I knew that these forms would look dramatic and powerful in the resulting colour slides. They did. It was Stirling's ability to supply such images for books that resulted in his admirers, who are legion, claiming international greatness for him (usually without seeing the buildings for themselves) and that the absence of commissions in his native land after the 1960s was a national scandal. But what sensible client would go to an architect with such a record? It would be vanity to suppose that anyone was influenced by the handful of critical articles I wrote: the record spoke for itself.

Big Jim's serious claims to greatness rest, I think, on one building: a seminal building of its time which stands, significantly, not in Britain but in Germany. This, of course, is the Neue Staatsgalerie in Stuttgart, which I found myself praising in *The Spectator* of 1 October, 1988. It is the supreme product of the architect's remarkable shift from industrial and space-ship imagery to a creative reinterpretation of Neo-Classicism. This, at Stuttgart, was combined with an extraordinary plan which resulted in powerfully resonant pure forms and voids faced in stone. I still think the work is flawed – it has no proper façades and is full of gimmicks – but it is memorable, haunting and genuinely popular. Remember that television advertisement for Rover cars, which was filmed in front of this masterpiece by a 'britischer Architekt'? For once, a Stirling building was well made – by Germans. *Vorsprung durch Technik*!

But I do not think this promise was sustained. When the opportunity came to build in London, at the Tate, the resulting Clore Gallery proved to be a vulgar assembly of crude clichés with little relevance to its purpose of housing paintings by Turner. As for the over-scaled office block designed for Lord Palumbo to replace eight listed buildings in the City of London, few of Stirling's admirers can find much to say in its favour. We must hope it is never built, though I fear Lord Palumbo has a penchant for realising the designs of dead architects. Nevertheless, I now sincerely wish that Stirling had won the National Gallery Extension. Unlike the pretentious conceit that now smugly addresses Trafalgar Square, the Stirling building would have been properly monumental and provided a coherent rectilinear plan.

So I shall miss Stirling. He was a big man, in every sense; a captivating maverick who could always be relied on to surprise. Despite his arrogance and his indifference to the necessary practical aspect of his profession, he was at least in the central tradition of European architecture in that he was interested in shape, form and colour – unlike those other much-vaunted knighted architects who seem to think architecture is a matter of structure, services and technology: pipes, wires and gaskets. Although he never said he was a Glaswegian because he was brought up in Liverpool, I see that Scottish newspapers are now claiming Stirling as one of the many great architects that Scotland has given to Britain. Perhaps he was; perhaps I was always wrong – except I still do believe that a responsible architect both creates beautiful, powerful forms and is concerned with detail and practicality – as were those supreme Glaswegians: Thomson, Burnet and Mackintosh.

So I think I prefer to leave the question of whether Stirling was a great architect for posterity to answer. It is just sad that I will not now meet him and so will never know if he would have punched me or not.

4 July 1992

VERSE

Alan Dixon

When everything important
is going to pot
it might be a good thing
that verse is not

(important I mean),
to those who matter,
keeps healthy and slim,
sees others fatter.

Verse has a way
of not giving a hoot
for the economic forecast
and the ten gun salute.

May it go on forever
not wasting ink
on what our betters
expect us to think.

4 July 1992

POP MUSIC

TOUPEE OR NOT TOUPEE

Marcus Berkmann

The rehabilitation of Elton John has been remarkable to observe, a return to critical and public favour that even the distinguished singer-songwriter himself must have been surprised to experience. Although never exactly on his uppers – he may have spent a lot of money over the years, but he has stashed away even more – his great days were generally considered to have passed. Nonetheless, his 1990 album *Sleeping With The Past* sold three and a half million copies around the world and *The Very Best Of Elton John*, which cannily followed it up a few months later, sold seven and a half million. Now, it is said, Elton John's records, tapes and CDs account for three per cent of all records tapes and CDs sold worldwide. His new album *The One* (Phonogram) has even had a few good reviews.

What can explain this sudden burst of creative energy? Why, after years of churning out substandard material, has the man that no one at all calls Reg Dwight finally started writing good tunes? Some have ascribed his return to form to a settled personal life. Others have pointed to the unusual gap between albums – it's three years since the last one, an eternity for someone of Mr John's prolific gifts. To me, though, the explanation is clear – so clear, in fact, that you can actually see it on top of the his head. The silly hats have gone, apparently for good. For Mr John, long the most trichologically challenged of rock's great stars, has suddenly developed a full and lush head of hair.

How he has obtained it has of course been the subject of much fevered speculation. Sewn in, grown in, driven in with steel rivets – no one knows for certain, although £14,000 is what it is alleged to have cost. Some people even claim to have seen it move during Mr John's recent Wembley concerts, and suggest it may be alive. But whatever it may be, the remarkable effect it has had on its host cannot be denied. Rock music may be kind to those afflicted by other unfortunate conditions – drink, drugs, cheeseburgers – but traditionally it has had remarkably little time for baldies.

Think of Paul Simon. Though still successful as ever, the angst-ridden New Yorker has been losing the battle with his hairline for many years and, according to reliable reports, is now something of a domehead. So much so, indeed, that he is rumoured to have employed someone on tour specifically to look after his toupees. And you thought it was all his own hair? It may have been once, but it ain't any more.

But at least Simon makes good records, which has undoubtedly saved him in the eyes of his predominantly ageing audience. For Gary Numan, though, baldness has proved a disastrous career move. It's all right stomping around in a black leather jacket and daft make-up pretending to be a robot if you look the part, but when you hair departs for pastures new, the illusion tends to suffer. Numan too has adopted a jet black syrup for public life, but his record sales have never recovered.

More sensible, perhaps, is the hat approach. Elton John, of course, took the whole headwear motif to unusual lengths, but more recently we have had the pleasure of seeing U2's guitarist The Edge adopt a large hat, apparently to conceal a cranium with increasingly reflective qualities. Bruce Springsteen's old collaborator Little Steven, by way of contrast, usually sports a red, patterned bandana, thus revealing as little of his hair as possible – rather conveniently as it happens, as there isn't an awful lot to reveal.

In fact, only one rock star has taken baldness on and beaten it: the multitalented Brian Eno. Realising early on that his reputation as a wayward genius would only be enhanced by swift hair loss, Eno has gone bald with a vengeance, and is now generally acknowledged by his fellows to have a brain of titanic proportions. But he is the exception. As we see Elton bouncing up and down at Wembley, and his unruly schoolboy mop bouncing up and down with him, we can observe a man whose career has been brought back from the very brink – and at the cost of just £14,000. Some might regard this as an outrageous sum to spend on personal vanity. I'd call it a bargain.

11 July 1992

'MY CENTURY HAS A CLEANER BOTTOM'

Hardy Amies

My year, 1909, was in the first decade of the century. Now we are in the last. The 20th is my century. It doesn't seem long. Three times brings us to William and Mary. Six times more to William the Conqueror.

I was just born an Edwardian, and ladies on the District line wore Edwardian dress until 1914. Then we followed my father to his army camps. On 11 November 1918 a thousand day-boys and I cheered our heads off in the playground. War rations were enough to avoid hunger. But there was disgusting marrow jam in brown cardboard cartons.

A Daimler was hired to move us to a farmhouse on rhubarb fields ten miles east of Barking. There was neither gas nor electricity. I boarded at an ancient grammar school just gone public. We were given a bath night once a week. My century has learned to wash. There are more bidets around. My century has a cleaner bottom.

The motor-car became part of our body by the Twenties. My mother died before the second world war without ever having had a refrigerator. My father longed to earn a thousand a year as this was the seal of success. My younger brother was a mongol who did not die until his 60th year. Only in about the last ten years did we have help with the expense of a boy who could never be left alone. My century has learned to look after such things. Whenever I have seen the National Health function, in the countryside especially, it fills me with admiration.

My century has travelled enormously. I was sent to France in 1926 for the last of my summer holidays while at school. Next year I left school to take up an 'au pair' job at the English school in Antibes.

People were just beginning to sunbathe. The big hotels at Cannes and Nice were closed in summer. Winter was the season. Hotels in Juan-les-Pins were opening in the summer. My century has sunbathed too much. Skin cancer in old age is the price we pay for youthful folly. A leather-textured and -coloured skin looks seriously common.

In Paris, I worked in the office of custom agents. The London basket filled with parcels from cloth merchants would arrive next morning at the Court dressmakers in London. I had my foot in the door of a dress house. I travelled home at Christmas, steerage, from Dieppe to

DOLDRUMS 10 MI
DUMPS 12 MI
ENNUI 26 MI

'I guess we've entered the winter of our discontent.'

Tilbury. The next year I went to a Lutheran parsonage in a small town on the Rhine. I got work at a wall-tile factory. I studied German fiercely and became assistant manager.

I stayed two and a half years in Germany. My 21st birthday was celebrated on 1 August, the same day the French tricolour was lowered on the fortress of Ehrenbreitstein, 1930. The occupation of the Rhineland was over. I went back to England.

My German boss gave me as a parting gift an air ticket from Cologne to Brussels and then on to London. It was Imperial Airways and the seats were wicker armchairs. Several people were discreetly sick into bags.

I wanted to work in Europe but ended up in Birmingham. My mother left the Court dressmaking business in which she had worked for ten years, when war broke out. She kept in touch with the proprietors and several of the staff. I did too. But with never a thought of entering the business.

Suddenly there came an offer to run a fairly recently established bespoke tailors, women's tailoring business, the designer manager of which had left to start his own business. The owners had been my mother's employers.

The shop specialised in tailoring: in what ladies still called 'coats and skirts' but which by the young rich were known as 'suits'. I now see that the 'suit' has truly been the ladies' gear of the century. Based on a man's jacket, Chanel did it in the Twenties: her successor Lagerfeld is still doing it. Hundreds of thousands of women all over the world are wearing versions of men's jackets, made in real or imitation wool, over matching skirts or even printed silk dresses.

Success came to me slowly but steadily. The Coronation of George VI in 1937 brought American buyers to London *en route* for Paris. We made better suits than did the French. I am good at planning tailoring. The placing of buttons and pockets, added to good proportions of the body of the coat, is as important to me as fenestration in a house.

I moved to London. I became friends with fashion journalists and went on into the fringes of the *beau monde*, but slowly – I was intelligent enough not to be pushy. I learned the lingo. But I am surprised to remember that I was invited to a party given in the old Carlton Hotel for the Prince of Wales and Mrs Simpson by Mrs Beatrice Cartwright, an American hostess. 'Molyneux made the dress especially for tonight. It's awful. You should always copy things out of the collection.' I was learning fast.

My century has seen the rise of a huge industry based on ready-to-wear clothes for men and women. Sport has become a bigger influence than elegant living. Taste is not required.

In my century we won two wars. In the second there was created an organisation called Special Operations Executive. Its role was to encourage and strengthen subversive resistance movements in countries occupied by the enemy. It organised and sometimes took part in sabotage: big bangs. It was hated by the Secret Service (M16) and its protective sister M15. I became head of the Belgian Sector. Belgium was the most heavily guarded part of Europe. We parachuted agents into the Ardennes with radio equipment – I fear often into the arms of the Germans who had penetrated the secret armies we were trying to support. I was successful in keeping the exiled Belgian government happy. They had to prove that they were trying to help. They were preparing for their come-back after victory. I made five parachute jumps, just to prove I could do it: not behind enemy lines but into an airfield near Manchester. I was made a lieutenant-colonel and was allowed to demobilise myself, deeply distressed by Churchill's call for unconditional surrender. I had got used to thinking of my old friends in Germany as my enemies. I know that most intelligent Germans had seen the horror and the vanity of their leaders and were longing for a truce.

In 1945, I collected some capital from friends. I took a lease of a house built by Lord Burlington in 1735 and badly damaged by a land-mine which fell on Savile Row in the Blitz. I gathered a staff of tailors and seamstresses, and of saleswomen who had treasured their address books from before the war. We had no cloth, so we cut brown paper into what became new models. The war was a long time dying. In February 1946 American buyers came over before we were ready with a collection. They bought everything. New York was hungry for Euro-pean clothes.

We attempted to make London into a centre of fashion, imperti-nently comparing it with Paris. By specialising in English suits, we, for a season or two, became part of the European scene. But Paris quickly reformed its industry of cloth merchants, flower-makers, embroiderers and armies of nimble-fingered workers, and drew back into its arms the chic rich and discerning of Europe and later the world. In my century, England lacked financiers who liked and understood fashion. It lacked the support of a scent industry backed by the rose and lavender fields of Grasse.

My century saw long skirts disappear from the streets – not during the 1914–18 war but in the Twenties, culminating in 1926. It was then that they were shorter than they ever had been, just around the knee. They never went above the knee until recently. Women have usually only accepted a difference of an inch from one year to another. I cannot see this, my century, ending with long skirts. I think it will all settle down around the knee rather than round the ankle or the crutch.

The reign of the short skirt was rudely interrupted by that of Dior and his New Look. It was a time of beautiful clothes and plain access-ories. It ultimately had to change because it did not take into account the power of sport.

My century is ferociously interested in sport. Young girls dress like sportswomen. Matrons look as if they played tennis or golf. All go to the gym. The Queen, whose custom came to us as early as 1950 when she was still Princess Elizabeth, has always made it clear that she wished to be dressed as correctly as possible, with hat, gloves and handbag. It seemed like a kind of exquisite politeness, but it looked strange next to the hatless Mrs Jackie Kennedy.

I asked my brilliant friend and contemporary, Enoch Powell, at one of his 80th birthday parties, to tell me what was the most exciting thing that had happened to him in his life. 'Flying to Australia,' he said quickly. I have flown there about 20 times. The journey has no fears for me. I am now pretty clear as to the shape and size of the earth.

It is now evident that I think that my century is a pretty stunning one. I do not wish to knock it. But I can't let my fellow inhabitants of the globe get away with everything. We went to the moon. (No one talks any more about that. I can't remember the date.) We created Concorde to fly to New York. Rather feeble arrangements to fly Concorde to Australia quickly petered out. Too expensive.

Travel abroad has brought new tastes into the mouth of my century. With these sensations came an interest in cooking. One of my *Egerias* – ladies I consult about manners they have been brought up to respect – admits that they were not allowed to discuss food at table. They are happy to do so today.

When it isn't food, it's gardening. My century has seen the arrival and the triumph of the garden centre. The Chelsea Flower Show is an annual Great Exhibition. Let us rejoice. Gardens do not make revolutionaries. It would be a good idea to encourage those Serbs and Croats to take to growing roses.

In my century, inflation has truly become inflated. To give examples is to encourage bores. I am fascinated by the statements of politicians that they have plans to control inflation. Looking at my century, I can see that a man now demands for his work many more things than he did when I was born. He requires a centrally heated house, a garden, a television set, a motor-car and holidays abroad. Washing-machines are as common as water-closets. To truly stop inflation you would have to ban all advertising.

I ask my *Egerias* for their favourite developments in my century. 'The elimination of fog.' In second place they reply, 'Television, the companion of maiden ladies in the country.' Early in my century one snatched a crystal with a cat's whisker. Now television is the voice of my century.

This autumn I shall go to Sydney. At meal-times, listening to the classical music channel, I shall think of the Revd Sydney Smith: 'My idea of heaven is eating pâtés de foie gras to the sound of trumpets.' Only in my century can you do just that at the height of 30,000 feet.

18 July 1992

LOW LIFE

BROUGHT TO BOOK

Jeffrey Bernard

Last Monday the noble biographer Graham Lord announced that he had finished the book, to be called *Just the One*. He has delivered the last three chapters and in about ten days' time we shall be able to see something in print. I look forward to that event with considerable trepidation, as Graham has told me that I won't like the book since so many people have been so bitchy about me. Women mostly, of course, but there are also men like Richard Ingrams who stand in the butts with itchy trigger fingers only too keen to snipe at a man who likes to gargle. That comes as no surprise. He already had a go at me in the television programme *The Obituary Show* before inviting himself to my birthday lunch party at the Groucho Club, which was a convenient freebie for him.

What did surprise me was to be told by Graham that my third wife, Jill, my daughter's mother, has also had a boil which has been festering for 20 years and he has, it seems, managed to lance that. It puzzles me not a little, then, that she should have invited me out to Majorca to see her last month. Come to think of it, there were a couple of occasions there on which she spoke to me a little in the way in which sergeant-majors address raw recruits. At any minute I thought she might have called me 'you sloppy, dirty little man'.

But I was actually amused to hear that the old Fleet Street virago who, when reviewing these collected columns in the book *Low Life*, called me 'as beguiling as a Nuremberg rally' has taken a few more pot shots. Anyway, I would far rather be compared to a Nuremberg rally than a summer's day. Another woman has said that I ruined her marriage, which is quite simply not true. No woman in her right mind would jeopardise a happy marriage by going to bed with me, but have any women got a right mind? After 30 years and three large gins she still maintains that I am a shit. Now a shit is somebody who makes trouble and misery with aforethought and intention, whereas my misdeeds are accidental happenings and merely the result of having been in the wrong bar or bed at the wrong time, say most days between midday and midnight.

What is amazing is that after ten months of really hard graft – Graham has interviewed nearly 100 people and written 400 pages – he is still talking to me. I fear his live-in lady may not be. Oh dear, have I ruined another marriage? Graham has worked like a dog on *Just the One* and he says the task is likely to turn him into a teetotaller. Not before the book launch party, hopefully, where I expect to see Richard Ingrams arrive for a free glass of mineral water.

What I shall miss reading are the comments some women could have made who flatly refused to talk to Graham. I take it they are simply ashamed and embarrassed to have known me and I on my part am not particularly proud of my past promiscuity, so boo to them. One of them, a well-known actress, could have played the shark in *Jaws*. She is an absolute ringer. Another, also an actress, has a reputation to protect. So have I, which is why I shall not name her. Oh the self-importance of fading stars. Never mind, they will be black holes one day.

18 July 1992

DIARY

Dominic Lawson

A major-general retires and, with the aid of a lump sum army pension, buys some lovely farmland and a house in Kent. Some years later, Margaret Thatcher and François Mitterrand decide that a tunnel across the Channel is one thing they are both prepared to promote. The major-general's farmland, by now devoted to setaside (another great EEC brainwave), is in the wrong place at the wrong time. In order to provide for the putative extra traffic, the M20 is to be extended across his land – neatly bisecting it, in fact. But the motorway planners are no fools. Building the road a few hundred yards away from the house itself means that they are not required by law to make an offer for it at market prices. But they are allowed to make a compulsory purchase of the strip of farmland on which the motorway is to run. Now it is running, and from the front door of the house the noise is stunning, even if the view no longer is. The geese which used to swim in the artificial lake, now on the verge of the motorway, can no longer stand the noise, and spend their summers somewhere quieter. Soon British Rail get in on the act. They plan to build part of the Kentish section of the new London to the Channel Tunnel rail link on much the same land. But they, too, are canny enough to place the track sufficiently far from the house – more than 200 yards – to avoid the legal require-ment to make a bid for the major-general's house. Then, at last, the old soldier's luck turns. A property developer decides that the infras-tructural links around the old farm are – or will be – so good that the place would make a very successful golf-course. To the major-general's surprise and pleasure, the developer makes a fair bid for all the farm-land not owned by either the Ministry of Transport or British Rail. He is even prepared, should the general and his wife agree, to buy the house itself, and turn it into a clubhouse. He pays a small sum of money for the option, to show he is serious, and makes a planning application to the local council of Maidstone. This proposal, you will not be surprised to hear, is the one bit of construction which the authorities are not prepared to nod through. Twice they block the proposal to turn the desecrated farmland into a golfcourse. Shouting above the roar of the traffic, they proclaim the area one of natural beauty, an accolade that the Ministry of Transport's planners can rarely have received. So the retired couple are stuck. Even if they were not my parents-in-law I think I should be very angry about this. Once, in this country, retired generals who served their country well were given land by a grateful nation. Nowadays an ungrateful nation takes their land – and their rights – away from them.

25 July 1992

THE REDUNDANT MALE

James Buchan

At Llantrisant, a place in South Wales where men used to wrest coal from a tight-fisted earth, there is a factory called Race Electronics. I went there one day in March with John Major on a campaign visit so tedious, artificial and futile it seemed an affectation: this was the day when the photographers mutinied in the back of the campaign aircraft, warned John Major they'd all be out of a job if he didn't do something more interesting and the Soapbox took shape and began its progress into history.

I wasn't thinking about John Major that day. I was staring through a window-pane at 500 young women seated in blue uniforms at a moving assembly line. I thought, through this screen of glass and pained gallantry, that I'd understood something: that long after the boys had gone swinging down their valley with their songs and beer and contact sports, their pathos and labour-market rigidity, the girls would still be there, filling printed circuit boards for Swedish satellite television receivers at £3.90 an hour. I thought: This, as much as John Major, is the future of South Wales and of Britain.

In the last 20 years, the British labour force has grown by 3.2 million people. Of these, 90 per cent were women. What this means is that women took many of the new jobs, and displaced about 1.3 million men from work. In the next ten years, even if the economy doesn't give up the ghost, the labour force will grow very little. Of the few new jobs, the Department of Employment expects eight or more out of ten to go to women.

As for the present, men and women are being swept wholesale out of work, but women appear to be holding on better. The figures are a little manky, but by putting together the Department of Employment's monthly count of people claiming unemployment benefit and its annual Labour Force Survey, you get the impression that male unemployment is rising half as fast again as female. This is despite the very severe recession in those service trades – retailing, banking etc. – in London and southern England which employ a whole lot of women.

The men of Britain might be forgiven for thinking that the threat to their jobs comes not from Polish miners or Indian steelmakers but from the lovely creature across the hearth-stone, the Englishman's delight and comfort and nemesis.

That is not the overture to a *Spectator*-like blast at Englishwomen and a demand that they get back home and attend to their slapdash housework, noxious cookery, perfunctory love-making and delinquent childcare. There are reactionary passages in this article but this isn't one of them. All things being equal, it is in all our interests that women find jobs in the paid economy: the ability of the millionth woman is much higher than that of the 12-millionth man; she will create more wealth and make us all better off. (My first job was in Saudi Arabia, where women are excluded by custom from almost all paid work and where the sloth, corruptibility and incompetence of my work-mates passed all description.) As for British housework, child-care and sex, these have long been contracted out, at least in the higher social classes.

What interests me is this. Most of the new women's jobs have been part-time. In effect, British women have made a Faustian bargain with British business. To feed their families or escape the hysterical boredom of the British household, many married women or single mothers have offered their ill-paid, part-time and unprotected labour to business people desperate to reduce fixed costs in the face of slumping product markets. These women, who have often had to put children out to the care of strangers, are unwitting agents of the deflationists led by John Major and Norman Lamont who, by subordinating policy to the exchange-rate mechanism of the European Monetary System (but not, alas, to the emollient elements of German labour contract or the European social charter), are trying to bring British wages grinding to a halt.

This chivalrous policy has a little way to go. Money wages were still rising earlier this year – if not at the 10 per cent rate just before Margaret Thatcher was toppled in 1990, then at least at 6½ per cent. But there are burning straws in the wind. In my neighbourhood, which is Camden Town in north-west London, the wages for unskilled males have collapsed because the employers of last resort (the local authorities) are either bust or contracting out services to companies that are sifting brutally through an army of long-term unemployed men. In the whole United Kingdom at the end of April, there were 700,000 men who had not worked for more than a year and, barring a miracle, their number will increase to over a million by next year. Strong men, once the glory of British society, are now its problem, unwanted even as street-sweepers or foot-soldiers. (The Home Office appears to believe that there is no connection between the number of unemployed males and the incidence of theft. The Field Report of 1990, whose argument is very refined, holds that property crime and male unemployment are both *symptoms* of falling personal consumption.) We are still a long way from Bedford-Stuyvesant in Brooklyn, New York, say, where men have fallen out of the legitimate economy and women struggle to bring up children unaided. But the British labour market is slowly disintegrating and with it the British household.

British men have had it coming. If they had not barricaded themselves into superannuated manufacturing and production industries, behind outworks of trades unionism, high wages and low productivity, the crash would not have been so drastic; all the free capital would not have migrated into services, and part-time work (in effect, married

'Ah Smith, now you remember how we
guaranteed a job for life?'

women) would not have so cannibalised full-time. When I entered this
dying world in 1980, returning from Saudi Arabia to join the *Financial
Times*, I was surprised by how little work British men did. There were
parts of the building where I'd come on somebody chain-smoking at a
typewriter, and parts of the day (six to eight in the evening, if I remember) where everybody appeared to be doing something; but most people
did nothing, either absolutely or through typing up news budgets,
bothering foreign correspondents, holding chapel meetings, discussing
strategy at department lunches etc. Understandably, some people
found it more interesting to be drunk for at least some of the day. I
myself did nothing for 11 months, and in the 12th wrote a detailed
survey of the Fijian sugar industry (now, unfortunately, somewhat
superseded). Even as hoarded labour, I feel privileged to have seen this
old masculine economy as the shades of twilight were falling.

   For this was also a period of the most profound change in the nature
of unpaid female labour. Housework is a valuable economic activity
which, if it were fully commercialised, would add between a fifth and
two-thirds again to GDP, depending on how you measure it*: certainly
it's a business worth Lord Sainsbury breaking the Sunday trading laws

to capture. By the early 1980s, housework and cookery had become mechanised to the point where even women with children could go out and take part-time, jobs without leaving utter chaos behind them. Since 1971, the number of women employed part-time in the paid economy has gone up from 2.8 million to 4.6 million.

The result was that when the manufacturing and mining industries collapsed in the early 1980s and male employment fell by up to 25 per cent in South Wales, round Birmingham, on Merseyside and the Tyne and Tees, except in the most traumatised districts women could come to the rescue of their men. Later in the 1980s, the economy boomed briefly, and many of the men were taken back in much less secure jobs and having spent their savings; even the long-term unemployed, the men most short of skills, luck and good health, found in 1988 and 1989 that they could get jobs; and the older men simply quit. (My grandfather was still taking the train to an office in London at the age of 70. No old man does that now.)

This picture is reflected all over western Europe, but smaller, as in a series of receding mirrors. Some tables that the OECD will publish later this month show that the rates of participation in the paid economy for women between the ages of 25 and 34 rose by 23 percentage points in the United Kingdom, 15 in western Germany, 20 in France etc. between 1972 and last year. Everywhere male employment crumbled at the edges: my subjective impression that no Frenchman lifts a finger after 55 has considerable empirical support. What is odd about Britain is that so many women already have jobs and that they've held on to them as the latest wave of recession has crashed through the labour market.

I have lots of theories. First, the heavy or heavyish industries employing men (such as defence or construction) are still being hit harder than those employing women: things will even up when, for example, the clearing banks peer at their gaping balance sheets, panic and lay off staff. Second, women are more docile as well as cheaper. Third, men are too inflexible about the kind of jobs they take. (This may be true, but in conversations at my local Job Club, in Georgiana Street, Camden Town, I got the opposite impression: a 58-year-old ex-shipbuilder unemployed for ten years will always find it hard to compete as a part-time juggler/dancer at £110 a week.) Fourth, because unemployment benefit is paid to heads of households men cannot afford to take the part-time jobs that their wives or other men's wives can. In other words, a welfare system designed to buttress the Beveridgean family – male breadwinner, little wife, couple of children – is actually demolishing it.

The risk is that British men will riot, as they did when they were thrown out of work or couldn't get work in the early 1980s. But – notwithstanding the recent unrest in Bristol and Burnley – Britain has changed since then. Riots are done by young men. In the early 1980s, a rising population of young men smashed into a falling number of jobs. This time, the weak birth-rates of 1973–79 mean that relatively few young men will be reaching working age over the next few years: 25 per cent fewer in 1994 than in 1983. It will be a tame as well as flexible workforce.

Theoretically, if the labour market works properly, male wages will fall and ex-dustmen will be taken on as trainee beauticians at £60 a week. The labour market will have achieved flexibility. It will be a market dominated by short-term, unprotected, ununionised, insecure, low-paid and unmotivated labour without employment rights where, as Winston Churchill once said, 'the good employer is undercut by the bad, and the bad employer by the worst,' and children will see little of their mothers. Wages and prices will, presumably, be in free fall. Devaluation, except of an entire society, will have been avoided.

*OECD Economic Studies, No. 18/Spring 1992 goes into this.

25 July 1992

DIARY

P. D. James

Mr Mellor should, of course, have remembered the advice of Arthur Hugh Clough:

> Do not adultery commit,
> Advantage rarely comes of it.

There is, however, something particularly unedifying in our present outbreak of public morality. What is important in deciding whether the minister is suited to his job is the ability, enthusiasm and intelligence he brings to it. It may be reasonable to suggest that his moral standards are relevant to this ability and that we, the electors, have, therefore, the right to a lively concern in the details of his private life. But even if this is true, where do we draw the line? Some people might argue that the sins of the flesh are among the least important, distressing and embarrassing though they are to the husband or wife concerned. But adultery, surely, is a private grief. And what of the minister (if such there should ever be) who is brutal to his subordinates, uncaring of his aged parents, unkind to his children, given to kicking the dog or ungenerous and neglectful of his wife, even though the marriage remains intact? Are these delinquencies also to be exposed, even though they would hardly sell newspapers, and the man judged unsuitable for high office? I am intrigued by some of the press comments about the Mellor case. One columnist suggested that the offence would have been less heinous had the woman concerned been intellectually and socially more Mellor's equal. Does this mean that adultery is condoned if it takes place in a five-star hotel with a woman who is beautiful, rich, intelligent and high-born, but is judged reprehensible if it takes place on a mattress in a sleazy flat? Is a colleague or secretary more acceptable as an illicit partner than an actress? Would the press be less judgmental if the actress in this case had been a star of the South Bank and in work? And what about prominent people who are not ministers? It could be argued that a newspaper proprietor occupies a position of very considerable power. Are we entitled to demand that he, too, is kind to his children, aged parents and animals, considerate to his subordinates and faithful to his wife? I would find this scrubbing around to discover fresh scandals to bring a man down less distasteful if newspaper editors had been as diligent in seeking out and exposing the delinquencies of Robert Maxwell, the former owner of the *Sunday People*.

Hitting on a title for a new book is always important and sometimes not easy. I find that I either know the title even before the book is started or have great difficulty when the writing is finished in deciding what the novel shall be called. It is always depressing to work with a provisional title, a sure sign of problems ahead. Some writers are better at the art of titling their books than others, and a good title is easier to recognise than define. Titles which come to mind are *The Trumpet Major, All Passion Spent, The Lord of the Flies* and *A Handful of Dust*: all reasonably related to the story or theme of the novel concerned, yet memorable in their own right. The most damning indictment of a bad title is the comment 'I liked the novel but I can't remember what it is called.' My greatest difficulty in finding a title was with *Innocent*

Blood. This was originally to be called *The Blood Tie* since it dealt with the relationship between an adoptive girl and her natural mother. Just before publication, my publishers discovered that the title had recently been used and, although there is no copyright in titles, no writer wants to duplicate another's idea, quite apart from the risk of confusion. All alternative titles suggested by me or my publishers here or in America had either been recently used or seemed cumbersome, inappropriate or contrived. With the book ready to go to press things were becoming desperate, when I remembered that my American publisher, a Roman Catholic, had great success in finding lost objects by intercession to St Anthony, and thought that he might as well provide a title which, if not exactly lost, was certainly mislaid. So I said one night what I hoped were the appropriate words and awoke in the morning with the title *Innocent Blood* virtually on my lips. My publisher expressed no surprise that I had been successful, merely remarking that he paid heavily for St Anthony's services whereas I, a Protestant, had received them for nothing.

1 August 1992

THE NEW BULLY OF THE BALKANS

Noel Malcolm

Salonica

You begin to notice it the moment you arrive on Greek soil. If you land at Athens airport, you can find crude posters declaring 'Macedonia is Greek' in the customs hall. If you are crossing by land from the former Yugoslavia, you will find the passport control booth covered with stickers making the same point, some of them in English more hysterical than grammatical: 'Macedonia is Greece Since Ever'.

Inside the country, the barrage continues. Posters fill the windows of shops and offices: 'Greeks, awaken! Beware of the conspiracies of the great powers and the neighbouring states!'; 'An end to the provocations of Skopje!' In Florina, a town close to the former Yugoslav border, one building on the main square flies a large banner reading,

'Macedonians shed their blood for Greece!'; the graffiti on a building up the road say, 'Freedom to the Greeks of Northern Macedonia' and 'Macedonia is One and Greek'. Glancing at the print-out on a computerised bus-ticket, I found, in the space where you might expect 'Have a nice trip', the statement, 'Macedonia was and shall be Greek'. Never outside the communist bloc have I had such a sense of an all-pervading and unanimous campaign, in which all levels of public life are mobilised to whip up popular feeling. If one adds the world-wide campaign run under the cover of the Greek Tourist Board, it must be the most expensive publicity campaign in Greek history.

It is also the silliest. Only fear for my personal safety has prevented me from emending some of those graffiti, changing them from 'Macedonia is Greek' to 'Greek Macedonia is Greek'. Other bits of Macedonia, self-evidently, are not. Throughout the last two centuries, 'Macedonia' has been a geographical expression: it refers to a whole region, which in 1913 was divided between Greece, Bulgaria and what became Yugoslavia. The part which Greece obtained was named 'Macedonia' by the Greek authorities. The part which Yugoslavia obtained was named 'the Republic of Macedonia' in 1946; the people who lived there had already been widely referred to as 'Macedo-Slavs', and their language as 'Macedonian', for decades. When the people of that Yugoslav republic voted for independence last year, it was not surprising that they wanted their new state to be called 'Macedonia' – they had no other name.

But at this point the Greek government claimed a kind of copyright on the word, on the grounds that Alexander the Great, that well-known representative of the modern Greek state, had used it first. (This way madness lies: modern political geography is not and cannot be mortgaged to ancient history. One might as well complain that the borders of modern Germany do not correspond to what Tacitus meant by 'Germania'.) Initially, the Greek government did also have some reasonable objections. A handful of extreme nationalists in Yugoslav Macedonia did make speeches about 'liberating' the part of geographical Macedonia which is now in Greece; and the draft constitution for the new state did speak ambiguously about 'caring for' the interests of Macedonians who lived beyond the state's frontiers. A high-level commission of jurists from the EEC asked for amendments renouncing any territorial claims against neighbouring states. These were duly enacted, and the jurists recommended immediate recognition. But Greece still blocked it; and at the Lisbon summit at the end of June, the EEC resolved never to recognise the new Macedonian state so long as its name contained the word 'Macedonia'. This was a triumph for

Greek obduracy, a surrender to Greece's maximal demands – ruling out any compromise solution along the lines of 'Slav Macedonia', 'North Macedonia' or even 'Skopje Macedonia'. (The Greeks refer to it only by its capital city: 'the Skopje Republic'.)

It would take the pen of a Swift or an Orwell to explore all the ramifications of this. More than a million people who have spent their lives thinking that they spoke Macedonian, that they read Macedonian literature and watched Macedonian television, are now to be told, at the whim of 12 people lunching in Lisbon, that they speak some nameless thing which may eventually be called 'Skopjan', or possibly 'Central Balkan'.

We are dealing here with the strangest and yet in some ways most typical of all Balkan states – a state with a profound neurosis about its own sense of identity. I refer, of course, to Greece. Much has been written about the problems of ex-Yugoslav Macedonia, and the potentially catastrophic consequences of the EEC's destabilising policy towards it. But little is ever written about the root cause of the problem: the neurotic nature of Greek nationalism.

One of the ways in which Greek attitudes reveal themselves as typically Balkan is in this wilful confusion of modern politics and ancient history. (Compare the Serbian line on medieval Kosovo, or the Rumanian obsession with Roman Dacia.) But the appeal to ancient history is vital to the Greeks precisely because it is their way of arguing that they are utterly unlike the riffraff peoples of the Balkans. Their unbroken descent from Plato, Aristotle and Demosthenes sets them apart; theirs is a higher civilisation, a higher destiny. They have nothing to do with the messy history of the Balkans north of their ancient and immemorial border (established in 1913 and 1919).

This approach to history requires skimming rather selectively over the thousands of years when there was no such thing as a national Greek state. The early Slav invasions, which reached far into the Peloponnese and left settlements which spoke Slav well into the 15th century, are preferably ignored. So, too, are the influxes of Albanians which settled many parts of eastern and central Greece at the invitation of Byzantine, Catalan and Ottoman rulers. In the early 19th century, the population of Athens was 24 per cent Albanian, 32 per cent Turkish and only 44 per cent Greek. In the early 20th century, Salonica was 60 per cent Spanish-Jewish, 18 per cent Turkish and 18 per cent Greek. Things have changed since then, of course. The population exchange with Turkey in the 1920s got rid of nearly 400,000 Turks and assorted Muslims; and Kurt Waldheim's fellow-officers during the war ensured that Salonica is now a thoroughly Greek city. But just changing the people was not enough. In the mid-1920s, nearly all the Slav, Vlach or other non-Greek place-names were suppressed. Even personal names were not exempt. One Greek Slav told me that his father, whose name was Boris, had been instructed by the local officials that he must change it to a proper Greek name: the choice they offered him was between 'Pericles' and 'Byron'.

The consequence (or rather, the basis) of these policies is that Greece is that rare thing, almost unknown in Europe, a country with no national minorities. They do not exist: the Greek government says so. For such a phenomenon to be found in the Balkans of all places is indeed a miracle – a sign that Greece is certainly not like other countries. Sitting at a café in a Slav village near Florina, in northern Greece, surrounded by people talking in the Slav Macedonian language, I pondered this minor miracle. 'They say we don't exist,' said one of them; 'but tell me, do I look like a ghost?'

How many of these Slavs still live in Greece is not known. The 1940 census registered 85,000 'Slav-speakers'. The 1951 census (the last to record any figures for speakers of other languages) put it at 41,000; many who had fought on the losing side in the civil war had fled, but other evidence shows that all the censuses heavily underestimated the Slavs' numbers. The lack of a question on the census-form is not, however, the only reason for their obscurity. They are a brow-beaten population whose culture has been and is being suppressed. Within Greece, there are no newspapers or radio broadcasts in their language (which, being the language of the 'Skopje Republic', is officially not recognised as a language by the Greek government). One group of these Slavs has started a small monthly newsletter, with an estimated readership of 10,000. But they have great difficulty finding a printer (even though it is in Greek), and they say that if copies are sent through the post they tend to 'disappear'. 'Even if we find a sympathetic printer,' one told me, 'he's usually too scared to take the work: he's afraid of losing all his other contracts, or perhaps of getting bricks through his window.' Another group has applied for permission to start a cultural society in Florina; the application has been turned down, on the grounds that it is 'anti-Greek'. They are not even allowed to sing songs in their language: the last time this happened, at the village festival of Melitis two years ago, proceedings were broken up by the police.

A few bold individuals have taken their case to human rights conferences at Helsinki, Copenhagen and Moscow. I talked to three of these people, each of whom had encountered certain career problems on his return to Greece. Hristos Sideropoulos was a forestry worker living

near Florina; soon after his return from Copenhagen he was told that
he was being transferred to a distant island off the west coast of Greece.
Not wishing to abandon his wife and children for months at a time,
he refused the posting, and was sacked. He has been unemployed ever
since. His friend Stavros Anastasiadis owns a small trucking company.
On his return, he was told that his regular contract with a local firm
was being terminated; other contracts proved strangely hard to find,
and his trucks now stand idle. And the grave and dignified Archiman-
drite Nikodemos Tsarkinias, who also testified at Helsinki, showed
me a peremptory letter from his bishop telling him that he must leave
his parish work and withdraw into a monastery.

The public hysteria over the 'Skopje Republic' certainly does not
help. The weekly nationalist-extremist newspaper *Stohos* ('Aim' or
'Target') now issues regular personal threats against these individuals
and their friends, listing names and addresses; its more general articles
on this subject carry titles such as 'Cut Off Their Heads'. *Stohos* is
not a typical paper, of course (it refers to Slav Macedonians as 'Skopje
gipsies' and to Turks as 'Mongols'); but it is widely available at news-
stands in northern Greece, and there is a curious continuity between
its views and those of public or quasi-official figures. When I attempted
to discuss these issues with Professor Konstantopoulos, director of the
Institute of International Public Law in Salonica, I was assured that
the so-called Slavs were just bilingual Greeks and that their second
language was not a real language but a mere *patois* ('the "idiom"', as
Stohos sneeringly calls it). 'Why can't they have a newspaper in their
own language?' I asked. 'They don't want one!' shouted the professor.
'Some of them do want one,' I said. 'Two or three people – paid agents
of Skopje!' he roared. He showed me a crude propaganda-sheet
demanding the 'liberation' of Greek Macedonia. 'You see,' he thun-
dered, 'these are the views of the Skopje government!' The corner of
the sheet was stamped, in Cyrillic: 'People's Liberation Front'. 'Why
do you say these are the views of the Skopje government?' I asked.
'This was issued by an extremist émigré organisation – I might just as
well show you some Greek extremist pamphlet claiming that Skopje
belongs to Greece.' His anger was cataclysmic. 'So you try to make
excuses! If you want to make excuses, that is your affair! *Qui s'excuse,
s'accuse!*' A few minutes later, he assured me that 'secret figures'
revealed that 18 per cent of the population of Yugoslav Macedonia are
Greek – a piece of ethnographic nonsense so gross that even *Stohos*
might blush to print it.

The Greek Slav Macedonians are caught between the hammer and
the anvil of Greek policy on minorities: assimilation or expulsion. To

'He's suffering from Ides.'

see successful assimilation in action, one has only to visit the Vlach region in the Pindus mountains of northern Greece. The Vlachs, who speak a language closely related to Rumanian (with a little practice the two become mutually intelligible), have a population of perhaps no more than 50,000 in Greece, and have seldom sought any kind of political nationhood in modern times. (The one exception was a short-lived fascist 'Principality of the Pindus' set up with Italian help during the last war: most of its supporters either died in battle or emigrated.) At the annual festival in one remote mountain village I found the square decked from end to end with Greek flags; all the Vlachs I spoke to seemed either puzzled or offended when I asked whether they thought that being Vlach made them somehow less than completely Greek.

Most modern Greek writings about the Vlachs claim that they are 'pure Greeks', descended from ancient Greeks who just happened to acquire a Latinate language when they did military service for the Romans; and most Vlachs believe these highly improbable claims. The current issue of *Ellinismos* ('The Greek Race'), a middlebrow magazine devoted to the discussion of Greek ethnicity (can you imagine a magazine actively concerned with English ethnicity?), devotes four pages of dismal pseudoscholarship to this argument; and one recently published Greek book about the Vlachs gives a list of words in the Vlach language borrowed from Greek, and concludes in all seriousness that Vlach is 'a Greek dialect'. Under these conditions and provisos, Vlach culture is allowed to continue: there are songs, festivals, cultural societies and so on. The Vlachs are the good boys of Greek nationalism, and that is their reward. But at the same time their language is dying; it is hard to find anyone under the age of 40 who can speak it, and within two generations it will have disappeared off the face of the Greek fatherland.

The 100,000 Turks of western Thrace, on the other hand, have a much stronger sense of ethnic identity. Yet in the eyes of the Greek state they are not Turks at all; they are 'Greek Muslims', a religious minority, not an ethnic one. When Dr Sadik Ahmet, a surgeon who stood for parliament in 1989, referred in a campaign leaflet to 'the Turkish minority', he was sentenced to 18 months in prison for using the word 'Turkish'. Books and newspapers from Turkey are strangely unavailable in this, the neighbouring area of Greece. Anyone who wanted to read such things would have to go and live in Turkey instead – which is, it seems, the long-term aim of the Greek policy.

When I visited Dr Ahmet at his surgery in Komotini, six hours east of Salonica by slow train through the heat-scorched foothills of the Rhodope mountains, I found him surprisingly up-beat. 'Things have improved in the last two years,' he said. 'For a start, Turkish farmers can now get tractor licences.' (The Turkish population is mainly agri-cultural; though they have tractors, they have not been granted licences in the past. This gave the local police a hold over tractor-driving Turks – a classic example of the 'legal limbo' technique favoured by east European régimes.) Two things seem to have brought about the recent improvements: Dr Ahmet's election as the local MP, and a blistering New York Helsinki Watch report in 1990, entitled *Destroying Ethnic Identity: the Turks of Greece*. This was the most critical human rights report on an EEC country ever published – until, that is, this summer's Amnesty report on torture and ill-treatment in Greek prisons and police stations (many of the case-histories in which just happen to concern Turks, Albanians and other non-Greek victims).

But not everything is rosy in Western Thrace. The new Greek elec-toral law will prevent Dr Ahmet from being re-elected next time, and when he loses parliamentary immunity he may face another deferred prosecution. And the long-standing policy of driving these Turks out of Greece continues; more than 500 of them were stripped of their citizenship last year while travelling abroad, and were refused entry. But the best way to get rid of an agricultural population is to deprive them of their land. More than 3,000 acres have been confiscated for various public projects in the last ten years, and there is now a plan to seize 15,000 acres of farm-land which at present support 20,000 Turks) for a new 'open prison'. Some of these Turks might be forgiven for thinking that they live in a kind of open prison already – 'open', that is, in the unusual sense that they are encouraged to leave it and never come back.

Fear of Turkey is, in the long run, a greater stimulus to neurotic Greek nationalism than the Macedonian issue. The fall of the communist bloc has badly damaged Greek self-esteem: whereas ten years ago Greece was a vital bulwark of Nato, today that role seems unimportant, and it is Turkey that is emerging as the strategic power-base of the whole region from the Balkans to Central Asia. Hence the psychological importance for Greece of the EEC, as a Turk-free top table. 'Maastricht,' trumpets a Greek government television advertisement every night, means equal status [or "equal honour": *isotimi*] for Greece in Europe!' – a statement either meaningless or mendacious, and all the more powerful for that. Personally, I have found that whenever I have long conversations with EEC politicians or officials, there always comes a point when they say, 'Between you and me, I can't understand how we ever let Greece in.' With its peculiar brand of paranoid nationalism, Greece's foreign policy is now the biggest single impediment to any sensible EEC policy in the Balkans; and if the Greek public mood intensifies any further, it may threaten not only the future of ex-Yugoslav Macedonia but the territorial integrity of Albania as well. Amid all the discussions about the procedure for new members to join the EEC, has anyone thought of a polite way of inviting one member to leave?

15 August 1992

IF SYMPTOMS PERSIST . . .

Theodore Dalrymple

Like Lord Justice Butler-Sloss, Dr Marietta Higgs and all right-thinking people, I am against the sexual abuse of children, though it has fleetingly crossed my mind that the complete extirpation of such abuse from our green and pleasant land will perhaps prove rather difficult. Indeed, the very attempt to do so by the Torquemadas of our social services might on occasion result in more harm than good.

Last week I was called to see a man who had suddenly become convinced that 'they' were after him. He had barricaded himself and his family into his house, and would answer neither the door nor the telephone. Less than a fortnight before a pair of social workers had called at the house and declared that a denunciation had been received from an unnamed source to the effect that the man had been sexually abusing his daughter.

The daughter was taken away and subjected to torture (for such is the correct characterisation of an interview with the unctuously compassionate bureaucrats of care). Nevertheless, she refused to confess to her father's crimes and was reluctantly returned home. The fact that the family had previously been a close-knit one was regarded as especially suspicious by the social workers; and the community in which the man lived, being a small one, soon got to hear about the accusations.

Never of strong character or intellect, and unable to disperse the Kafkaesque miasma which now enveloped him, the man went mad and was carted off to the local asylum. Could a guilty conscience have made itself plainer?

During my own infrequent moments of paranoia, I have wondered whether child sexual abuse was not an invention of social workers to prove their indispensability to the welfare of society. I discovered how unworthy a thought this was when I visited a department of social services three days ago. While waiting, and having exhausted the deeply condescending posters on the wall of great blacks in history, produced by the Racism Awareness Unit's Education and Development Bureau, I turned to the internal telephone directory. Here are the positions held by the first 25 of the 80 people on the list:

> Child Care Planning Manager, Supplies Manager, Secretary to Assistant Director of Quality Assurance, Secretary to Service Development Section, Quality Assurance Manager, Informations Systems Support Assistant, Customer Services Manager (Quality Assurance), Operational Support Manager, Service Development Manager, Secretary to Resources Development Manager, Quality Assurance Research Manager, Research Officer (p.m. only and not Thursdays), Information Systems and Technology Manager, Secretary to

Assistant Director of Personnel, Principal Planning
Manager, Computer Information Systems Organiser,
Senior Personnel Manager, Secretary Quality Assurance Section, Secretary (part-time) to Quality
Assurance Manager, Administration Manager, Administrative Support Officer, Principal Service Development Manager, Secretary to Assistant Director Family
Social Services, Secretary to Operational Support Manager, Assistant Director of Quality Assurance.

I realised at once, of course, that Social Services need no *bonne
bouche* like the sexual abuse of children to occupy their time. Indeed,
they require no external reality at all. They live in a truly solipsistic
world of awareness and sensitivity groups, mutual support meetings
and courses on the changing role of social services in a multicultural
environment. The wonder is that they can spare a few moments from
their busy schedules to drive my patients mad.

15 August 1992

DIARY

P. D. James

Apparently there are now as many counsellors as there are patients
suffering from Aids. I'm sure all of them are giving useful help, but
some illnesses are certainly more fashionable as well as more terrible
than others and I wonder how many arthritics receive counselling
while waiting for their knee or hip replacements. The police are counselled after dealing with fatal road-accidents, as are the survivors of
mass disasters and the bereaved, and since counselling has now apparently become so traumatic the counsellors themselves need counselling, a sequence which could go on almost indefinitely. I prefer not
to believe a recent report that a primary school teacher is prepared to
reintroduce competitive games providing there is counselling for the
losing side. Should unsuccessful athletes at Barcelona be counselled, I
wonder, and if so, individually or on a group basis? Counselling is

certainly a growth industry, and I wonder whether this is because in a secular age people no longer seek solace from a priest or minister, or whether it reflects our greater isolation and loneliness and our inability to communicate with those closest to us. During the last war, there was no counselling as far as I remember, either for the bereaved or those bombed out, or for returning prisoners of war, although some of the latter, particularly those who were prisoners of the Japanese, might perhaps have benefited from it. But it must surely be difficult to accept counselling from someone who hasn't himself or herself experienced the trauma. This is why support groups, such as Cruse for widows or Alcoholics Anonymous, are helpful: at least the people who join know what they are talking about. One of the worst tragedies human beings can experience is to lose a child, but if this happened to me I don't see what help I could get from the visit of a stranger whose children were alive and well. At the heart of it all seems to lie our modern belief that life is intended to be pain-free and that when it isn't something ought to be done about it. Could this be part of the reason for the tragic rise in young suicides: the belief that to be miserable is not only unnatural but somehow wicked? Perhaps one of the greatest gifts we can give to our children is the knowledge that some unhappiness is inseparable from being human, and the strength to cope with unhappiness when it comes. But perhaps counsellors would say that is precisely what they are trying to do.

15 August 1992

A HAM THAT CAN'T BE CURED

Jani Allan

George Alfred Carman QC is the most feared criminal barrister in the land. Physically, he resembles a small bewigged ferret. When addressing the judge, little, pointed, pink hands make Uriah Heep gestures. 'Of course, my lord. I humbly submit, my lord,' he says. 'I am in your lordship's hands.'

If the truth be told, the judge is more often in *his* hands. One of

Carman's accomplishments is being able to bully a judge while letting him believe that he is making the decisions. That is what happened in my case. The phrase that I will forever dread is, 'I am in your hands, Mr Carman,' since it inevitably preceded the jury being sent out and Carman indulging in one of his endless legal arguments, the *sequitur* of which would be a piece of my evidence being ruled inadmissible.

While sucking up to the judge, Carman contented himself with shooting poisonous glances in my direction, impaling me on the flames of his blow-torch blue eyes.

It is said that the 63-year-old Carman had an adolescent flirtation with priesthood before being called to the Bar. (It was during this period, apparently, that he lost most of his Blackpool accent.) It is difficult to imagine Carman indulging in a flirtation of any description. Thrice married (he admits to only two wives in *Who's Who*, though under cross-examination I have every faith that he would be able to explain the memory lapse), these days he lives alone in a 'flet' in the Temple. Outside the courtroom, a bleached blonde, a score or so years his junior, loitered about loyally. While Carman chain-smoked efficiently, she mainly busied herself with investigating the contents of one of those large Louis Vuitton bags similar to those favoured by the concubines of rich, powerful men.

It is said that Carman practises in front of a mirror before a case; a ham that can't be cured. One has serious doubts whether he could ad lib breaking wind after a bowl of baked beans. But, while it is difficult to imagine Carman being swept away by the grand broom of passion, it is easy to speculate as to the grounds for his two divorces: mental cruelty, perhaps?

'I put it to you, Ursula. You are a dangerous and accomplished liar who feels no remorse at leaving the cap off the toothpaste tube,' etc. etc.

If a jury does indeed consist of 12 persons chosen to decide who has the best barrister, it has to be said that Carman wins hands down. That the 'evidence' provided by his client's – Channel 4's – witnesses was, I believe, as fishy as a trout in milk, if hugely entertaining, was no impediment to Carman. Carman's dictum is roughly the same as that I remember from teacher training college: 'Tell them what you're going to tell them, then tell them, then tell them what you've told them.'

Thus: 'Tell us what you saw, Miss Shaw.'

Miss Shaw: 'A large white bottom.'

Carman: 'A large white bottom?' Theatrical pause. 'A large. White. Bottom. So you saw a large. White. Bottom . . . ?' *Protracted pause.*

Rolls reptilian eyes about the courtroom. 'And where was this [*lip curled in distaste*] large. White. Bottom?'

As a technique it is crude – meatcleaver rather than scalpel – but highly effective. 'Killer' Carman is an appropriate sobriquet for this 5' 3" barrister's bovver boy.

When he is on less solid ground and the edifice of 'fact' that he has laboriously built up threatens to disintegrate, as happened when my barrister, Charles Gray QC, produced the lock through which he proposed to invite Miss Shaw and the jury to peer in order to prove that it would have been physically impossible to see what she claimed to have seen through a keyhole, he retreats smartly into technicalities.

When the lock appeared Carman bounced to his feet. 'My lord,' he simpered, wringing his small, pink hands, 'we all know how perilous it is to invite the jury to become involved in experiments of this nature.'

In the 13 days that the trial lasted Carman did as much bouncing up and down as a member of the Harlem Globetrotters. Enter the witness box Dori Weil, my clinical psychologist. Carman leaps up to object. Jury file out. Statement from Eugene Terre'blanche arrives in which he pointed out that one of Carman's witnesses was working for South African National Intelligence. Carman leaps up to protest most strongly. Jury file out. And so on.

In addition to the impressive catalogue of sociopathic crimes of which he accused me, but somewhat less widely reported, were Carman's attacks on my political stance.

To this end he embarked on a leisurely trawl through a selection of columns I had written for a South African publication.

'You described Nelson Mandela as the Chocolate Redeemer,' he said, affecting utter disbelief. 'The Chocolate Redeemer?' He enunciated half-a-dozen syllables. The court tittered. 'The Jailed. Martyr . . .'

I pointed out that Mandela was tried and found guilty of high treason. Besides, the description was, in fact, one of Dr Mangosothu Buthelezi's.

'Hnnnnh,' said Carman unpleasantly. He is not, strangely, particularly eloquent. Carman's equivalent to the Seles grunt is possibly more off-putting because of the unpredictability with which it is employed. In the middle of Miss Linda Shaw's cross-examination, just as she had taken refuge behind her Charles II hairstyle, sobbing rhetorically 'How long is this nightmare going to go on?', he sounded a *fortissimo* 'hnnnh!' which startled even my phlegmatic solicitor. Further into the cross-examination he – for some reason – brought up the fact that I had described Winnie Mandela's wigs as looking as though they had been bought from a vending machine. Carman glowered.

*'When father died, he was all over the front page
of the newspaper.'*

'What about Neil Kinnock?' He then rounded on me. 'You called
him an arch pillock.'

I said I felt no further elaboration was necessary. More titters in
court. When he attempted to bully me with the charge of being a racist,
I realised that he is not a particularly sophisticated political animal.
He earns his money by the sweat of his brow-beating. Carman's preferred script relies on ritual humiliation of the deeply personal kind.

A stolen diary that I had written in 1984, which, Carman assured
the judge, had 'appeared mysteriously' by courier one minute after I
was in the witness box, was manna from a muck-raker's heaven. Since
Carman found the notion that the entries were in the main fantasy
adjacent to preposterous, one must presume that he has never heard
of Nancy Friday's best-selling book of women's fantasies, *My Secret
Garden*. But armed as he was with the stolen diary, for the three and
a half days I spent in the witness box my feelings were close to those
I would have facing Waqar Younis on a cricket pitch. My response to,
'Would you commit adultery with a married man?', which I took not
to mean in the imperfect subjunctive, provided Carman with the hangman's noose.

In the end the jury were in Carman's small, pink hands. With each
day their 24 eyes became more glazed in appearance. No doubt the
result of dreaming of large. White. Bottoms.

22 August 1992

PANTS ON FIRE

Sir: Jani Allan's attack on George Carman, QC ('A ham that can't be cured', 22 August) was an outrageous outburst of personal spite even by the standards she has now made her own.

Your readers will form their own view of the respective characters and reputations of Ms Allan and Mr Carman. A jury who studied Ms Allan's demeanour and evidence over 13 long days in court came to the unanimous conclusion that she was a liar. In other words, let me remind you: we won; she lost.

Ms Allan's remarks about the judge in the case must be a matter for those responsible for the administration of justice. The clear implication that Channel 4 and George Carman came to court with untrue evidence, however, is a disgraceful suggestion for which you have no foundation whatsoever and which I flatly reject.

Liz Forgan
Director of Programmes,
Channel Four Television,
60 Charlotte Street,
London W1

Sir: In her interesting *apologia pro testimo nium suum* Jani Allan tells us that she understood George Carman's question 'Would you commit adultery with a married man?' not to mean in the imperfect subjunctive. In other words, she thought she was only being asked about her future conduct and not about anything which might have happened in the past. I don't believe her. Nor, it would seem, did the jury.

Malcolm Knott
New Court Chambers,
Temple,
London EC4

29 August 1992

DIARY

John Mortimer

For at least 15 years of my adult life I was concerned in divorcing people, not personally, but as a barrister. Warring husbands and wives would drag up every possible and wounding accusation against each other, and no holds appeared to be barred. They would charge each other with talking too much ('nagging'), or too little ('indulging in long periods of sullen silence'), of being uninterested in sex ('wilful refusal of conjugal rights'), or being over-amorous ('excessive sexual demands'). Every form of love-making, apart from the missionary position, could be stigmatised as 'perverse practices', and we spent many days in court trying to decide exactly who threw the fish-slice at whom in 1946. When the bottom of the barrel was being scraped for matrimonial misdemeanours and sexual habits were being described in detail, I find it hard to believe that child abuse, had it happened, would not have figured in some hundreds of cases, and yet I cannot remember it doing so. Now, it seems, the divorce courts hear of little else, and American custody cases, including Woody Allen's, are filled with these allegations. As Judge Katherine McDonald of the New York Family Court has complained, such issues are almost impossible to try and possibly 'spurious claims' are extremely hard to substantiate. I can't make up my mind if child abuse, like sex, only came in around the time of the Beatles' first LP, or if it's the allegations that started then.

As for Woody Allen and Mia, I hope the world can soon return to enjoying their talents and ignoring their private lives. I wrote a film with Mia Farrow in it long ago and I thought her enchanting. She did have, in the Sixties, a tendency to sit on the floor wrapped in some ethnic garment and, looking up to the ceiling, say things like, 'Mozart, wherever you are, I love you, Mozart.' But she could be extremely funny, especially about Frank Sinatra's bedroom floor, which was apparently covered with an elaborate model railway. Woody Allen I found enormously gloomy, despite the fact that he had enjoyed a lifetime of success and some of the most beautiful women in the world. I disagreed with him when he said comedy was less important than tragedy. Comedy, he thought, didn't deal with the big background. 'What's the "big background" like?' I remember asking him. He answered, perhaps after an appalled glimpse into the future, 'Horrible!'

One of the most admirable qualities of Australians is that they speak their minds on [animal welfare] matters. I heard from a judge's wife how on one chilly winter night in the occasionally draughty Sydney Opera House an attractive middle-aged lady was wrapped in a fur coat. 'Do you realise how many animals had to die for that coat on your back?' a politically correct young person asked her. 'Yes,' she said. 'And do *you* realise how many animals I had to sleep with to get it there?'

29 August 1992

BOOKS

A PHENOMENON NOT A GENIUS

Anita Brookner

TROLLOPE
by Victoria Glendinning
Hutchinson, £20, pp. 551

Let us begin with the almost unbelievable statistics. Imagine a man so attuned to business, or perhaps simply to activity, that he began his writing day at five in the morning (latterly at four) and finished it by breakfast time, after which he would go to his work at the Post Office. This Post Office work involved almost constant travel to places near and far, and immense physical exertion (he was easily capable of walking 24 miles a day). Imagine the writing thus undertaken to be as regular as a metronome, each word on each page of 250 words counted and accounted for as the work was in progress. Imagine this procedure as being less of a rule than an intimate workmanlike satisfaction. Imagine the ensuing prose (for he had no compensating fantasies about art) as being 'entirely free from alterations and additions,' according to his friend Frederick Pollock: 'It seemed to have flowed from his pen like clean liquor from a tap.' Imagine a man capable of completing one novel on a certain day and starting another on the next, as Trollope did with *Dr Thorne* on 31 March 1858, and *The Bertrams*, begun on 1 April. Imagine this feat being performed in the course of a sea journey to Egypt, the regular and regulated output only interrupted by visits to his stateroom to be sick. Imagine writing 19 novels between 1860 and 1871. Imagine the three very greatest – *Phineas Finn, The Eustace Diamonds*, and *The Way We Live Now* – being produced in less than a decade.

This lucid but always unpoetic activity ('gross fertility', according to Henry James) was achieved with an ease which seems to us utterly mysterious. Nor did Trollope make anything of it. In *An Autobiography* he praises his own regularity of production, adding, 'I have never fancied myself a man of genius, but rather as an honest workman', comparing himself to a shoemaker. The comparison was valuable. 'Think about your business as a shoemaker thinks of his', is the advice the Duke of St Bungay gives to the Duke of Omnium. Nor does Trollope consider his obligation to write as he does a burden. In these days of literary prizes and Arts Council grants it is a corrective to read his views on the life of a novelist. Writing, he says, 'requires no capital, no special education, no training, and may be taken up at any time without a moment's delay'. He is the most expert of witnesses in his own defence. *An Autobiography* is essential reading for all those who aspire to put pen to paper.

But it does not explain the peculiar charm of the novels, which, oddly enough, do not convey the impression that the author was a man or genius. These novels were written to charm, to instruct, to please (and to make money). So easy is the style, so inexhaustible the characterisation, that one accepts them without question, not as being true to life but as being true to the conventions of the novel. In many of them the same theme is repeated, with agreeable variations: a young man will declare his love for a blameless girl and will then go off and become ensnared by an artful and superior woman, before returning at the end to his true love, as Frank Greystock returns to the faithful Lucy Morris. In the meantime the snares of this world will be represented by those clever women – Lady Glencora Palliser, Lizzie Eustace, Mme Max Goesler – with whom Trollope has a great deal of sympathy. These lively women offer a great temptation to young men, like Phineas Finn, who have their way to make in the world, and it is only the honourable and dull Plantaganet Pallisers who would groan at their impetuosity. Trollope could create a male charmer – and Burgo Fitzgerald and Phineas Finn are the genuine article – but it is his portraits of women which particularly appeal to the English reader. It is not insignificant that John Major admires Lily Dale, although I would rather he had gone for Mme Max.

The author of these novels (47 of them) was a bluff, coarse, noisy, and generally dishevelled person, 'the dullest Briton of them all', according to Henry James. That he became such a person, combining physical ugliness with the sweetest of affections, affections which are palpable in all his writings, was something that could not have been foreseen. The son of a depressive father and a highly adventurous mother, he remembered the bitterness of his deprived early years with a strength which was never to be diminished by the passage of time. He particularly disliked his failure of a father, who sent him to Harrow and to Winchester to suffer poverty, beatings, and a feeling of inferiority at being excluded from the 'social paradise' enjoyed by wealthier, luckier and more graceful boys. Yet these painful years were to be vanquished by the great success and popularity of his maturity. He writes of easy people, in easy circumstances: there are to be no Dickensian victims and martyrs. Yet, in his greatest novel, *The Way We Live Now*, and in the character of Melmotte, Jewish speculator and crook, he is able to sympathise with the man and even to admire him. The scene in which Melmotte gets up 'on his legs' in the House of Commons and makes his blustering and disastrous speech contains the seeds of his own early humiliation. It is the finest thing he ever wrote.

It was fortunate, and no doubt fortuitous, that Trollope followed in the footsteps of his mother rather than his father. Frances Trollope, an inveterate chancer and a fearless traveller, wrote 41 books herself, starting her day's work at four and joining the family for breakfast at eight. In addition to being industrious she was an accomplished social climber, and in the days of her fame and prominence was able to dine with Metternich and converse with Louis-Philippe. In the intervals she was a fond but more or less absent parent, preferring her elder son, the finicky Tom, to bearish Anthony. The family was enormous: relations crowd the pages of Victoria Glendinning's altogether excellent biography, much as they must have crowded the author's life. But this large family became a solace to Trollope, and it may be assumed that it went some way to overlaying memories of his own unsatisfactory parentage. In old age Frances Trollope became anxious for Anthony's love. He gave it, but distantly.

Readers of this splendid book will do well to master the intricacies of Trollope's family life. They would also do well to commit to memory the 47 novels, the five volumes of short stories, and the capacious travel writings. Victoria Glendinning does not make the mistake of searching for symbols or for hidden agendas, or for adducing theories about Trollope's intimate psychology. It may well be that the man is as transparent as his writing, having successfully internalised, overcome, and dismissed his earlier conflicts. She does mention Proust's theory that the life lived in writing and the life lived in society are two disparate entities, that it is the inaccessible *moi profond* which produces the books. Apart from this she is as sensible as Trollope was himself. This is a first-class account of a writer more phenomenal than he was ever to appreciate. No doubt he would have dismissed many of the claims one is tempted to make for him. Victoria Glendinning treats him with affection and respect, and thus does him full justice.

29 August 1992

HIGH LIFE

JOHNNY'S BUSTED FLUSH

Taki

Gstaad

My spies tell me that Johnny Bryan is angry as hell with me for having written that he and I once raised hell for days and nights on end together. This surprises me because I did not go into details, nor reveal anything of a sensitive nature. After all, I've been accused of many things but not of kissing and telling.

But speaking of kissing and telling, my guess is that Johnny Bryan is now considering whether to sell his story to the press. As far as I know, Johnny is out of pocket, paying out for what the taxpayer didn't for Fergie's frolics. One way he could recoup is through a sale of what he knows. And the only man he trusts, Nigel Dempster, just happened to be staying with me last weekend. What follows is speculation on my part, because the Greatest Living Englishman kept his cards very close to his chest throughout.

Here is the gossip columnist *par excellence* receiving calls from abroad on my telephone, and I wasn't even allowed to answer my own phone in case it was Bryan ringing. He even swore my cook and maid to secrecy, and I hate to think what he promised to the mother of my children, but none of them would talk. When I finally threatened to invite Ross Benson to stay, Dempster did admit that he and Bryan were talking.

Which to me means as follows. Johnny will obviously try and retaliate against those he believes set him up – namely Buckingham Palace. But such a tale will not sell. What will sell like proverbial hot cakes is his story about Fergie, the Fergie-loves-Johnny saga. In my not so humble opinion the Fergie-loves-Johnny tale would go for £400,000, the Johnny and Fergie versus Buckingham Palace story a mere £75,000.

Bryan is a busted flush now that his love affair with Sarah Ferguson has been exposed. My guess is that he has already run up about £50,000 in lawyers' fees, starting with Carter-Ruck, my own nemesis. To pay the lawyers he might decide to spill the beans, which in turn would signal the end for him in Britain. But not necessarily in America, the place I advised him to go last week because there is no difference *chez* Uncle Sam between celebrity and notoriety.

Having said all this, I wish him well. He's truly between Scylla and Charybdis this time, so he had better get some good advice. People like Latsis can afford royal company, but not Johnny. Needless to say, royals should not be allowed to run around with rich foreigners – especially Americans, who might exploit their royal links. Mind you, in Bryan's case he's the one that got exploited. He was doing some social climbing, not having understood that Fergie was not exactly social climbing material. In fact, the contrary. Nigel Dempster and the *Daily Mail* are being sued by the Paddy Dodd Nobles because the GLE called them Dodd Nobodys on account of the airs he claimed they put on when next to Fergie.

Everyone involved in this ludicrous situation comes out a fool. Fergie's friends emerge as superficial, glitzy and most of all extremely stupid, Bryan as an ass for thinking he could fool one and all and then believing that the royals dealt him a lousy hand. Even the Queen is proved wrong. She should throw everyone off the Civil List and tell

them to stop acting like Taki and, if they refuse, exile them to Malta
or Mykonos – preferably the former as I swim off the latter.

29 August 1992

HOW VAINLY MEN

Laurence Lerner

Here in the garden, hiding from the future,
Between the cranesbill and the clematis,
The peonies shedding petals everyday,
The sun my only guest, the pyrocanthus
Putting forth hundreds of tiny golf balls,
Plenty of things are going on; but no-one
Is buying toothpaste, or getting divorced,
Or catching a bus that knows where it's going.
Various questions are not being asked – for instance
How is my bank account, or my daughter's marriage?
Will my lecture be well received, will the students
    listen?
Am I taking early retirement, or being promoted?
What did Tom say to Dick about Harry – or was it
    me?

The golf balls have burst into cloudscapes
Of whipped cream; and the peonies
Died into pools of blood. It's a kind of future.
Last week somebody won an election,
Someone else shot a man. Here in the garden
The foxgloves are climbing their stalks; each morning
They've got a bit further.

29 August 1992

WHY CAN'T HE KEEP HIS YELLOW TOES TO HIMSELF?

Auberon Waugh

On Tuesday of last week, the Office of Health Economics, a body funded by the pharmaceutical industry, published a report saying that national spending on health care will rise to more than £40 billion next year, which it wrongly supposes to represent £640 per man, woman and child (in fact it represents £702 per head); which sum will divide into £35 billion spent on the National Health Service, £5 billion on private health. If this £35 billion is divided between the 56,972,000 men, women and children in Britain, it might suggest that we each spend £614.34 on the NHS every year. In fact, NHS charges bring in the best part of £1 billion, which reduces the taxpayer's subsidy to £34 billion, or £596.78 per head if all heads paid tax and if they all paid the same amount of tax.

In fact, of course, by no means every man, woman or child in the country pays any tax at all, and taxpayers all pay different amounts. After playing around with a calculator I reckoned that my personal contribution to the National Health Service was somewhere between £8,000 and £9,500 per annum, for which, so far this year, I had made precisely one visit to my local GP.

So it was with a slight sense of grievance that I returned, alone, to my flat in Hammersmith at 11.30 on the evening of Tuesday, 25 August, after dining with friends in a Korean restaurant. On arrival, in response to some irregular promptings, I went to the lavatory to defecate and was somewhat alarmed by the colour of what emerged. Attributing it to the unfamiliar Korean food, I went to bed and composed my thoughts for the morning.

The OHE Report, whose purpose, as revealed by Professor George Teeling-Smith, the director, is to urge another £10 billion annual expenditure on health, representing 5p on the standard rate of income tax, avers that death in middle age has been much reduced by the arrival of the National Health Service. That seems laudable, although it also points out that life expectancy – 73 for men, 78 for women – is now seven years longer than in 1948. Is that necessarily a good idea?

Hidden within those figures are hundreds of thousands of miserable, lonely 80- and 85-year-olds in poor health and failing awareness, tens of thousands of human vegetables, officiously kept alive for months, even years, being turned like an omelette twice a day, insensible, on a drip. Nobody would wish to be kept alive in those circumstances. The only purpose of these unfortunates is to fuel the great NHS employment juggernaut.

At a quarter past two in the morning, visited by the same irregular promptings, I went to the lavatory and was more irritated than alarmed to find that I had produced about a quarter of a pint of fresh red blood out of my bottom. The irritation was due to the fact that I realised I would have to do something about it. I could not blame the Korean *kimchi* (a delicious sort of pickled cabbage) and go back to bed. All my plans would be thrown out. I was to be collected at eight in the morning by a New Zealand television company to discuss the royal family's problems. At ten I had an important board meeting for an old people's magazine with which I am connected. At one I had the annual Literary Review Grand Poetry Prize lunch, and then I had to do an evening pilot television programme for the new Wogan show, *Friday Night*. One does not like to let down Terence, from whom one has received nothing but kindness over the years . . . none of which was easy to unscramble at a quarter past two in the morning before going into hospital.

My lack of alarm was probably due to the fact that I felt no pain, no discomfort, even a faint pride in my achievement. No icy hand gripped my heart. To the extent that I thought of death, I found myself contemplating it with a strange equanimity. I took a minicab to the Charing Cross Hospital, reminding myself of Betjeman's lines:

> The man who smiled alone, alone,
> And went his journey on his own
> With 'Will you give my Wife this letter,
> In case, of course, I don't get better?'
> Waits for his coffin lid to close
> On waxen head, and yellow toes.

No sooner was I admitted to the casualty ward than I entered an enchanted land. Dozens of people were around at 3 o'clock in the morning, all friendly, good-humoured and efficient, none of them remotely bossy or patronising. I was told I would have to wait an hour before being seen, which seemed perfectly reasonable. If the NHS kept spare capacity to treat every new admission immediately, it would

have to employ the nation's entire workforce, instead of only half of it.

After I had proudly produced another half pint or so of blood they went and woke up the assistant registrar to look at it. There being no other beds available, he put me in something called a High Dependency Unit – not quite as grand as intensive care, but second-best thing. For most of the time, four highly qualified staff nurses looked after four beds, one of them empty, with an array of technological equipment like the cockpit of an airliner.

This, again, was an enchanted land. After a few hours the bleeding stopped, rather to my disappointment, and next day I was moved to the endoscopy ward to be endoscoped. Even there, everybody was cheerful, kind and efficient. Here, although the corridors are disfigured by the usual Nazistyle injunctions against smoking, ashtrays are also supplied for those who choose to disregard them.

In short, the whole vast milling employment racket is a taste of heaven on earth. After the endoscopy, through which I slept like a baby on some mild tranquilliser, I was told that there was nothing wrong with me; my symptoms, which had cleared up of their own accord, were only to be expected in a gentleman of my age who prefers a high-protein diet.

It goes without saying that three-quarters of the money spent on health is money wasted. In the course of those two and a half days, I probably received my £596.78 worth. As to the other £8,500 which our crooked tax system requires me to contribute towards everybody else's health, what would I spend it on if I were allowed to keep it? More Korean meals, of course, more protein.

The NHS may be a shocking waste of money, but if it can produce

little corners of happiness and goodness like this – self-contained cities
of pleasant activities within the great despairing one of London – then
it must be a worthwhile cause.

5 September 1992

WHO WILL PUNISH
SERBIA'S CRIME?

William Tribe

Sarajevo

The anguish that has been visited Sarajevo on this city – this totally
innocent city – this is, I think, beyond the power of words to convey.
But life has to go on, and does go on, though pedestrians are felled by
snipers' bullets or teenagers taken apart by exploding mortar shells, or
a young woman's brains spilled on the steps of her apartment building
or whole families snuffed out by direct hits on their homes. We are
all unwashed and undernourished and no longer know the names or
dates of the days, but women still dress well and keep their poise,
and people still smile and enjoy a joke, and we all laugh at *'Allo 'Allo*
on television – perhaps inordinately so. I burst into tears the other day
when an Argentinian friend played me *Evita* – something I had not
heard before. 'Don't cry for me, Argentina' – it was a voice out of a
forgotten world of feelings. It is as though, in the reduced trickle that
personal life has become, the unexercised ordinary emotions must
seize every rare excuse to be used. 'A wonderful time for a love affair,'
a friend said recently. I thought this a figment drawn from books and
films. But then a girl I hadn't seen for a month threw her arms round
me in the street, and I discovered how wrong I was. The sexual emotions at such a time have a heightened painful sweetness, like the
infinitely tender soothing of a bruise.

It is not just the physical misery or the danger or the fear. It is the
emotional pain. Many weeks ago whole segments of the new city,
where the majority of people live, were cut off from the centre by
Serbian barricades, and at the same time the sabotage of the central

post office put half the phones in the city out of action. This meant that families, relatives, lovers and friends were and remain cut off from each other. Terrible stories reached us of what the Chetniks – the Serbian irregulars – were up to in these inaccessible suburbs, applying every method of terror to 'ethnically cleanse' what Dr Kanadzic's Serbian Democratic Party (the SDS) has deemed must become 'Serbian Sarajevo'. There can be few people here who have not been living for months with the anguish of not knowing what has happened to dear ones not more than two or three miles away. One girl I know has for four months had no news of her mother who lives only 300 yards from the offices where she and I work. They are Muslims – she has reason to fear. The capricious Chetniks, or their SDS masters, have occasionally released groups of people, hundreds at a time, who turn up in the centre with a few pitiful belongings – refugees in their own city from flats which have not, for the most part, been destroyed or even in many cases looted, but have simply been stolen from them because they are 'not wanted' in 'Serbian Sarajevo'. These and other escapers bring the stories: murder, torture, rape. I am in normal times a university teacher. Most of my students, generation after generation, are girls. Can you imagine my fears?

From the beginning, I have been cautious about the atrocity stories because I know they are a natural product of the propaganda of war, especially civil war. Temporarily, I work as a translator for the government, and many of these cross my desk. I think I can spot the obviously manufactured ones, and occasionally I have refused to be party to what I regard as the propagation of obscenity for its own sake. There are psychopaths and virulent Serb-haters on our own side who enjoy laying on the horrors. But somehow the authenticity of the small stories begins to confirm that of the greater ones.

Jasna Karaula is one of my oldest and dearest friends. We all sat one afternoon in the quiet breathing peace of her little house on Gorica. 'You don't have to talk about it, Jasna.' 'I must, Bill, I must.' She had gone to stay with her sister and widowed mother in the airport settlement and got trapped by the barricades. The phone went dead on the day of the reported massacre of 40 people in the next street – 17 June.

The only hope was that the three of them were in the mass deported (how can you be 'deported' in your own city?) to the Kula restaurant outside town which the Serbian side uses as a clearing house for 'ethnic' undesirables.

Pandemonium roused them at dawn that dreadful day. Armoured personnel carriers were firing point-blank into the house entrances and at the windows of non-Serbian flats. They fled to a back room and so survived the wrecking of their own home. A Serbian neighbour guided this shooting. 'He was a friend. He mended my car free of charge three months ago. We used to drink coffee together.'

With their staircase neighbours they sheltered in the cellar, and were hauled out countless times to be questioned at gun-point by what appeared to be a series of totally disconnected Chetnik bands. A Muslim youth was singled out. 'What's your name?' 'Samir.' Without a word, the man kneed him in the groin, stuck a knife in his side, then slit his throat. 'Right in front of my eyes, Bill! They carry their knives blade upwards in their belts – ready for throats.' In a vain attempt to staunch the flow they all got covered in the boy's blood. Then the Chetniks marched the boy's father away as he shouted, 'Let me at least bury my son!' Later they learned he'd been summarily shot.

It was now that the three Croat women began to pass off the boy's mother – who was catatonic with shock – as an aunt. About the massacre Jasna knew nothing except that in the daylight hours of the two days and nights they spent in the cellar they heard men's voices crying in the street, 'Don't!' 'Please don't!' On 18 June the Chetniks disappeared and the Yugoslav army came. They behaved 'correctly', but set up a machine-gun nest in the front garden, and in the morning asked for coffee. In the interval the only Serb in the group, an elderly pensioner, went out to speak to the soldiers.

When Jasna's mother went out with the coffee she found him dead across the threshold with his throat cut. No explanation, and they dared not ask. The four women were bundled into a van and driven to Ilidza where an officer questioned them. 'What are you?' 'For some reason,' Jasna said, 'I stuttered and said "Catholics". God knows what I thought that would achieve.' She explained that they had a relative nearby. Could they stay with him? 'Yes, Croat rubbish, you can go!' Ilidza is SDS-controlled, so they were still prisoners. A Serbian Orthodox priest sneaked them out by car to the Sarajevo lines a fortnight later. 'Better not ask me questions. I do my best to help.'

How can these things happen, why should they be allowed to happen to ordinary people who until five months ago lived ordinary lives in a city as ordinary as any in the world? Or was it? It was a city of desperately increasing social problems, but one in which the violent-crime rate was low and where a woman could walk at night without fear of being molested. Let me tell you something about this raped 'new city' of ours – the Sarajevo that never appears on the picture postcards – the names of whose districts – Grbavica, Hrasno, Otaka, Alipasino Polje, Mojmilo, Vojnicko Polje, Dobrinja – are now synonymous with outrage. This vast complex of high-rise concrete boxes where people live like ants in tens of thousands of tiny flats represents the flimsy achievement in about 40 years of a level of prosperity unknown to any previous generation, but which is skin-deep, imitative of, but far from equivalent to, the mass prosperity of the West. There is little private capital. When these people lose their possessions, they lose all that they have painfully accumulated over years of earning less in a month than a British labourer earns in a week. For even the minority of better-off there is still the same complete investment in moveable property. This gives the dimensions if not the depths of the tragedy, but because its authors – Karadzic, Koljevic, Plavsic and the rest of the SDS leadership – are of precisely the same *milieu* and know exactly what they do, it gives the dimensions, if not the depth, of their callousness.

But was not Sarajevo a city of acute ethnic tensions, an impossible amalgam of mutually intolerant peoples and creeds which the Muslims were trying to hijack into the fundamentalist camp? No, never. First, there *are* no 'peoples', no 'ethnic groups' here. It is a communist lie. Generations of my students knew no differences amongst themselves, though some might have been aware of tedious prejudices in their parents – much as an English Catholic might not like the idea of his daughter marrying an English Protestant. Even this analogy is not quite exact, since the English Catholic would have to be agnostic or atheist, as most English 'Protestants' are. Serbs, Croats, Muslims, Montenegrins are the same people speaking the same language with the same general culture. The varieties of dialect, custom and 'mentality' across at least the Serbo-Croat-speaking territories of former Yugoslavia are no greater than you would expect in any European country of comparable size. There were a few lunatic-fringe nationalists of one ilk or another as there are in Britain, but as in Britain they were regarded as jokes. Bosnia-Herzegovina was Yugoslavia-in-miniature, and proved that the Yugoslav idea worked.

Second, these 'Muslims' must be the least *Moslem* of any of the world's nominal adherents of Islam which, it is worth remembering, is as much a social order as it is a religion. A distaste for pork, a preference for running water instead of toilet paper, the habit of saying 'Merhaba' by way of greeting and of leaving one's shoes at the door, the survival especially in country districts of certain minimal traditions in domestic architecture, furnishings and dress, and a distinctive tradition of personal names, do not add up to very much except to something innocuous and charming. The Koranic prohibition of alcohol is absolutely unobserved except amongst the small minority of self-consciously religious; and except amongst them, there is absolutely no sexual puritanism. No doubt there are imams who would sweep all the freedoms away and subject the society to the rigours of Shariyat law, just as there are priests of the Churches who would take us all back to the Middle Ages, but they cut no ice. And who is more 'fundamentalist' than those that regard these people as a stain on 'Orthodox Christendom' and would banish or exterminate them simply because their ancestors adopted the faith of a conqueror who came and went long before anyone now alive was born?

The root of the Yugoslav crisis does not lie in the clashing 'national' myths or their cynical manipulation by power-greedy politicians – although these two things are its main agents and manifestation – but in the fragmentation of the country which the communist régime carried to extremes in the last 20 years of its existence. Six republics and two autonomous regions meant six (or eight) parliaments, six (or eight) bureaucracies, six (or eight) economies, even six (or eight) communist parties in a country smaller than France. We lived and moved about inside the country as though these internal boundaries didn't exist, but the consciousness of 'ethnic' difference was never allowed quite to drop out of people's minds because the régime increasingly felt the need to divide in this way in order to rule. The 'national key' – the maintenance of a proportional balance between members of the 'constitutive nations' – was everywhere applied. Even top communist party officials, even federal prime ministers, were selected on the principle of 'national' rotation, and in my university department an ideally qualified applicant for a post could be rejected on the grounds that too many of us would then be of his 'nation', and an inferior but 'nationally suitable' candidate elected instead. It was all supposed to be very fair, but in fact kept something entirely artificial unnecessarily alive. But the fatal flaw in the system was that, after Tito died, it allowed the kind of incompetents and nonentities – who, by elbowing and shoving, could achieve power in the federal units – to become the brokers of the country as a whole. It was these big fishes in small ponds who gave tottering 'communism' its *coup de grâce* from within. It was they or their kind who brought the 'national' parties to power on an anti-communist ticket but on a far more esssential demagogic appeal to an 'ethnic' mysticism which was purely Yugoslav-communist in spirit. Now, from being regarded as merely eccentric, it became actively disreputable for free spirits to declare themselves 'Yugoslav' by nationality. Now we entered an Alice-in-Wonderland world in which pundits could solemnly declare that for centuries the 'three constitutive peoples' of Bosnia and Herzegovina had spoken three languages, the Serbs Serbian, the Croats Croatian, and the Muslims something they weren't sure how to name – 'Bosanski' and 'Bosnjacki' were both entertained.

Now it became possible for Karadzic to say that his task as SDS leader was 'to teach Serbs to be good Serbs', for Tudjman to speak of the undesirability of two 'peoples' as 'different' as the Serbs and Croats living together, for Karadzic to declare that the children of 'mixed marriages' – 30 per cent of the total in Bosnia and Herzogovinan last year – were 'bastards'.

The power base of a 'national' political party, as of an 'ethnic' republic, can only be 'ethnic' identity, and if that identity has no attributes but nominal religious allegiance, you can only justify your position by violence of some sort – violence to nature and common sense, violence to the Yugoslav idea or the ultimate violence of land-grabbing and war, 'ethnic cleansing' and genocide. Ordinary Yugoslavs' consciousness of the wholeness of their country, which had always transcended administrative divisions and politicians' squabbling, was violated by the Slovenian and Croatian secessions.

But fatally the Serbian response was a violence of quite another order – on the basis of a false identification of Yugoslavianism with only itself, a utilisation of the might of the disenfranchised Federal army to grab territory and eliminate populations, and viciously and venomously to destroy whatever it considered non-Serbian. 'Smash it to bits,' the monstrous Vucurevic said of Dubrovnik when someone objected to the desecration. 'We'll build a better one – in a thousand years it'll be old again!' In one short year, a country – but far more than merely a country – has been irreparably lost.

Even if the Serbian cause were just – which it is not – it would have utterly disqualified itself by the methods it has chosen to use. Civilians get hurt in all wars, but here the war on the Serbian side is calculatedly and exclusively against civilians – to kill them in sufficient numbers to make the remainder flee, so that whole territories are abandoned to Serbian occupation and the demographic map altered for ever. I do not think this should even be called war – it is terrorism on a scale unprecedented in Europe since the Nazis. Shame on the western world for not intervening, and greater shame on those who would equate the two sides, find excuses for the Serbs, and dare to suggest that the solution lies in persuading the victim to parley with his tormentor.

And third, I know of no one here who is not convinced, as I am convinced, that what the West needs to do is something very small, simple, cheap and easy. An army whose strength is only in its armour, which has lived fat and easy for 45 years, which has never been tested against an equal opponent, which concentrates on shooting point-blank at civilian targets, can have no fighting spirit. Chetnik bands who specialise in cutting helpless throats and looting homes after the army has done its work, or under the protection of its guns, are not capable of being anyone's opponent. A few quick air strikes, and those cowardly bullies will take to their heels and run like rabbits for the Serbian border. Let them go!

It will be sufficient punishment for Serbia to have to contend with its own murderous soldiery on home ground. There is no need to enforce a political settlement. International commissions will no doubt help the Bosnian government in its hour of need to rehabilitate the refugees, to feed and clothe and succour the population of a devastated land through the cruelties of the Balkan winter we are all beginning so much to dread. There will be a need to investigate the mass crimes, the pogroms and orgies of killing which have happened in the Drina valley and elsewhere, and the concentration camps. And if possible the authors of it all must be brought to justice. But all this is for the – albeit near – future. What is needed now, immediately, is to stop the crime. The West could do it in 48 hours.

William Tribe has for the past 26 years taught English at Sarajevo University.

12 September 1992

DIARY

Max Hastings

It has been a prickly summer at the *Telegraph*. Week after week, we have found ourselves debating some new instalment of the question: if it's all over the front pages of the pops, how should we respond? The 'it' at issue has been principally royal, but with a long string of supplementaries provided by the likes of the National Heritage Secretary. Broadsheet papers rarely break stories about private lives. But all of us face a dilemma, once a story about a public figure has been published elsewhere, in determining how far we fail our readers if we do not then follow it. I decided to carry no reporting in the *Telegraph* about the odious Morton book on the Princess of Wales. Even some of our best and most thoughtful executives believed I was wrong, and argued that my policy made the paper seem foolish. Today, I have no regrets. The tabloid reporting of the Wales marriage makes lager louts look like gentlemen. There was no dilemma about the saga of the Duchess of York, once the collapse of her marriage was officially acknowledged, and her erratic behaviour seemed a matter for legitimate discussion. I hesitated for some hours following the publication of the *People's* story on Mr Mellor. Once he made a public statement, we followed the pack, and reported his vertical difficulties, although we omitted some of the horizontal details. In the past six months, Fleet Street has moved the frontiers of coverage of private lives, and especially royal lives, a long mile from where they have stood historically. It is unlikely that they will ever be rolled back.

Today there is a large school of journalism, native but not exclusive to Wapping, not all tabloid practitioners, who sincerely believe the world will be a better place when everything about everybody is known and published. I dissent. There are large areas of human affairs which benefit from, and indeed depend upon, privacy, secrecy, discretion – call it what you will. A measure of hypocrisy is the cement of life, and protects many innocent people from harm. Nor does this only apply to individual privacy. British government is indeed far too secretive. But I support the view that nobody can run anything – a ministry, a business, a newspaper – without maintaining the confidentiality of a host of discussions, meetings, expressions of opinion. Some of us strongly resist the view that revelation must, in itself, be a good thing. When Andrew Knight was chief executive of the *Telegraph*, I admired much that he did, and remain lastingly grateful for his role in making me editor of the paper. But I could not stomach his recent article in *The Spectator* claiming that the *Sunday Times* has done the royal family a service, by serialising the Morton book. Andrew sought to argue that opening the windows and letting the light into the sorry saga will ultimately be good for them all. His words choked me. I would have been more respectful had he simply written: 'Royal gossip is the best proven route to boosting newspaper circulations. This company is not in the business of making moral decisions which may adversely affect its profitability.' All newspapers, including our own, struggle through the minefield of moral dilemmas, groping uncertainly for the truth with frequent errors of omission and commission. I do not think privacy legislation is workable. The remedy, about which nobody is optimistic, can only lie in a change of attitude by the news-paper-buying public. But the notion seems wretchedly mistaken, that the world will be a better place when the press can Tell All. A lot – yes; all – no.

19 September 1992

HENRY HANDEL RICHARDSON
Doris Lessing

Ethel Richardson decided to test the contention that it is easy to see when a book is written by a woman. She wrote *Maurice Guest* as a man, and proved her point. She has often been claimed as a great writer, and I think she is. For years I was asking Australians here what they thought of her, but they said 'Who?' When I went to Australia and asked reading people, they sometimes had heard of her. She is caught sight of in Literary Departments. The trouble is, her three major books are so unlike each other, and the same set of phrases will not do to describe them all. Each asks for a different kind of approach.

The easiest to come at is *The Getting of Wisdom*, about a girls' boarding school in Melbourne. She described it as a 'little book', writ-ten as a relief after the 11 years' slog of *Maurice Guest*, but surely her tongue was in her cheek. It is a coldly angry, contemptuous novel. She knew her compatriots do not forgive criticism, and cut excelling people down to size – their own. I think she was doing what she had learned at school. 'Laura grew very sly . . . a regular little tactician.' 'She pocketed injuries . . . played the spaniel to people she despised . . .' 'Laura began to model herself more and more on those around her; to grasp that the unpardonable sin was to vary from the common mould.' This was the wisdom that had to be got at boarding school, in order to survive. She had the disadvantage of being a poor girl from a poor country place, competing with richer girls. This and the violently emotional life of these schools is her subject. There is a small but unforgettable scene of the poor women teachers for whom to teach in this sixth-rate place at all was probably a defeat, reading Ouida and joking feebly about marrying the first man who asks them, but they know they will soon

'You wait ages for one – then several come at once!'

be old and alone and poor. H. G. Wells and others called this novel a masterpiece. It belongs on the shelf with the classic school novels.

Her first novel, *Maurice Guest*, was a bold book then for man or woman writer. It is about erotic obsession. Reviewers were quite upset. It is set among music students in Leipzig in the 1890s. Most will be music teachers, but many are there because of the freedoms of bohemian life, an escape from the tedious proprieties of the time. Maurice is an ordinary young man, but he falls in love with Louise Dufrayer, an archetypical sex woman, lazy, sluttish, dishonest, and unscrupulous, from moral inertia. She is a slave to the one real talent in the town, a 'genius' in the 19th-century manner. Women – naturally – do not see her fascination, but a man describes her like this:

> Believe me, there is more thought, more eloquence, in
> the corners of a beautiful mouth – the upward look of

two dark eyes – than in all women have said and done
since Sappho.
Do you really think man asks soul of a woman – with
such eyes and hands as those? There is only one place
for him and that is on his knees before her.

This is said to Madeleine Wade, an Englishwoman who is all admirable qualities, a daylit woman, to whom everything Louise stands for
is contemptible. Comedy; high comedy. And social comedy too: there
is a landscape thick with subsidiary characters: landladies, warring
prima-donna music teachers, tavern keepers, Americans 'doing'
Europe, girls wanting husbands, people who love the aromas of 'art'
and who think the life of cafés and salons is what art is. And embedded
in this, the relentless tale of self-destructive passion. Louise could
easily be one of Dostoevsky's masochistic women. This novel has been
claimed by many for the gallery of the great, and it belongs there. It
is unputdownable, unforgettable, but if it is a good read no one could
say it is an easy one, for it is too painful.

And now the three volumes of *The Fortunes of Richard Mahoney*. If
tragedy is a great character brought down by inner weakness, then this
is not a tragedy, yet it has the effect of one, because if the hero is not
up to the role, he nevertheless stands in for England, Europe, the Old
Country's values. This is Europe on trial and Richard Mahoney makes
a poor showing. He is clever, book-loving, full of touchy pride and
prickliness, and takes his stand on being a gentleman, not a claim to
make Australians like him. Yet many do, and admire him too. What
he yearns for is to be well-off and respected, to have cultivated friends
and properly brought-up children. Twice he succeeds, starting from
nothing, but an inner enemy, invisible to him if not to others, forces
him to depthcharge his own success. He ends up very poor, mad, and
dependent on a wife whom he has always patronised for being too
earthy and practical.

Lucky for him that she is. Mary Mahoney is one of literature's great
women, though her qualities are not likely to be admired by feminists.
She married her Richard, moth to star, aged 16, and for ever after
subdued her needs and wishes to his. She loved him. That this author
could create the awful Louise Dufrayer, and then Mary Mahoney,
shows her range; and, too, the simple-minded Maurice Guest and the
contradictory complexities of Richard Mahoney. This is another novel
dense as a plum pudding, 19th-century in feel, slowmoving, con-
templative, while we watch fates and destinies reveal themselves.
People who enjoy Trollope would find themselves at home here: the

same sense of quiet and patient irony, the same understanding of weakness.

If one may read *Maurice Guest* to know what it was like to be part of the musical life of Germany in the 1880s, then *The Fortunes of Richard Mahoney* are as much a history of the early days of Victoria: the gold fields of Ballarat, the infancy of Melbourne, the small towns and villages just holding their own in the bush. And if we read Patrick White at least partly to find out what Australia is like now, then Richardson provides the same service for the past. They have a good deal in common, for in both there is the same feeling, as if a hand were stretching out to encompass more than is possible for it. Australia the continent, the deep alienness of it, the difference of it, seems to mock Patrick White's people, and so it does the people of Ethel Richardson.

These wonderful novels, with the exception of *The Getting of Wisdom* (Virago, £5.99), are out of print. One has to marvel at the fortunes of writers and of books.

19 September 1992

'WILL A LION COME?'
MEMORIES OF EVELYN WAUGH

Richard Acton

My parents, John and Daphne Acton, were friends of Evelyn Waugh from 1936 until the writer's death 30 years later. I knew nothing of him in the earlier years (I was born in 1941), but after the second world war our vast family emigrated from England to Southern Rhodesia, today's Zimbabwe, and in 1958 and 1959 Waugh paid us two memorable visits. The following year I stayed with him in Somerset.

Waugh in middle age has been portrayed as jaded, but the Waugh we saw in Rhodesia was usually amused and always stimulating. At times, certainly, he was bored, but for the most part he was in good spirits. Not only did he make us laugh, but he laughed himself a great deal.

In 1936 Waugh was 32, and famous. He had marooned himself in

Shropshire to work on a travel book, *Waugh in Abyssinia*. My parents then lived in Shropshire at Aldenham Park. My father's sister, Mia Woodruff, brought the writer over that April, and Waugh wrote to my mother: 'I absolutely loved my visit.' Soon after that, Waugh came for another weekend. On the Sunday afternoon, my father proposed that they go for a walk. My father was immensely proud of a great crested grebe which nested on our lake – the Shore Pool – and he wanted to show the grebe to Waugh. The latter was violently opposed to the plan. Alcohol had flowed that day and Waugh objected that 'the poisons ought to be allowed to settle'.

My father won, and my parents set off, dragging their reluctant guest with them. Eventually the party got to the Shore Pool and sighted the grebe. Waugh was furious at its inadequacies and gave vent to his feelings: 'It's a pathetic bird, a miserable bird, a wretched bird.'

A few months later Waugh began *Scoop*, and the grebe became immortal. William Boot, the hero, first appears while he is writing a weekly nature column called 'Lush Places'. William is in despair over an article on badgers. His sister, out of mischief, had substituted 'the great crested grebe' for 'badger' throughout his piece, and William had received indignant complaints from his readers. One nature lover

> challenged him categorically to produce a single auth-
> enticated case of a great crested grebe attacking young
> rabbits

– and so William's adventures begin.

Sent to Africa to report on the war in Ishmaelia, William is a hopeless war correspondent. As the book reaches its climax, the grebe has become a god. William, in a slough of despond, bows his head:

> 'Oh, great crested grebe,' he prayed, 'maligned fowl,
> have I not expiated the wrong my sister did you?'

The grebe answers William's prayer, and as a result, William gets the 'scoop' of the title.

But even this mockery of the grebe did not appease Waugh's fury over the infamous walk with my parents. Twenty years later he wrote *The Life of Ronald Knox*. Contempt for the great crested grebe smoulders in Waugh's pointed description of the Shore Pool, '. . . a lake which has afforded pleasure to ornithologists'.

On one of Waugh's visits to Aldenham, my mother's younger brother, Hedley Strutt, was a fellow guest. After dinner, Uncle Hedley

beamed and said: 'I am going upstairs to see Nanny.' Waugh was riv-
eted. 'Why is he going to do that?' he asked. My mother explained that
Nanny Galer, who looked after my sister Pelline, had been Hedley's
nanny and that, although now in his early twenties, Hedley still doted
on her. Waugh showed such interest that my mother believes the episode contributed to the bond between Sebastian Flyte and his nanny
in *Brideshead Revisited*.

The friendship continued to grow. My father, whom Waugh later
described in one of his books as 'a light-hearted, sweet-tempered, old-
fashioned, horsy young man,' adored roulette. Waugh accompanied
him and my mother to Ostend so that my father could indulge himself
at the casino. When Waugh was to remarry, he brought his fiancée,
Laura Herbert, to meet my parents at Aldenham.

The second world war ended such weekends, and after the war my
parents sold Aldenham and bought a farm called M'bebi, 25 miles from
Salisbury (today's Harare). There they settled with their family of six
children, which by 1954 had grown to ten.

Evelyn Waugh re-entered my parents' lives when Ronald Knox –
Ronnie to our family – died in 1957. Ronnie was an eminent priest
and scholar, and had entrusted Waugh, a Catholic convert, with his
biography. During his eight years at Aldenham, Ronnie had translated
almost the entire Bible. As my mother had known Ronnie so well,
Waugh flew out to Rhodesia in early 1958 and spent a month cross-
examining her at M'bebi.

My first glimpse of Waugh was striking. My father's idea of dressing
for dinner after his business day in Salisbury was to remove his jacket
and come into the drawing room in open-necked shirt and trousers.
We boys wore khaki shirts and shorts and had bare feet, often streaked
with mud from the farm. On the evening Waugh reached M'bebi, I
came straight from the dairy and wandered into the drawing-room
barefooted and dressed as usual. A vision greeted me of a short, stout,
red-faced man wearing an immaculate white dinner jacket, a garment
I had only seen in films. When my mother introduced us, he glared at
me. Shamed, I rushed off, put on socks and shoes, combed my hair,
and reappeared. Evelyn Waugh had arrived.

After dinner my father waved airily down the passage which
stretched the whole length of our vast bungalow. 'You see, Evelyn,
it is like a ship with cabins on each side,' he said. To us children,
M'bebi was simply home, and we were amused by Waugh's description of its eccentric features, which he recorded in a letter to Ann
Fleming:

Children were everywhere, no semblance of a nursery or a nanny, the spectacle at meals gruesome, a party-line telephone ringing all day, dreadful food, an ever present, tremendously boring ex-naval chaplain, broken aluminium cutlery, plastic crockery, ants in the bed, totally untrained black servants (all converted by Daphne to Christianity, taught to serve Mass but not to empty ash-trays). In fact everything that normally makes Hell, but Daphne's serene sanctity radiating supernatural peace. She is the most remarkable woman I know.

True, our ash-trays were in much use, as many of us chain-smoked cigarettes. Waugh added to the overflow by constantly smoking huge cigars. I was now, at 16, officially allowed to drink alcohol. But Waugh astonished me by drinking beer at breakfast. We children concluded that this was because he found our family so stunningly boring.

Although only 54, Waugh made a pantomime of being an old man. His chief prop was an enormous ear-trumpet, which he laid in front of him at meals. At lunch one day, the conversation turned to vocabulary. For reasons which are beyond me, I announced that I had a large vocabulary. This was too much for Waugh. His eyes blazing, he picked up the ear-trumpet and put it to his right ear. Omitting to make me repeat myself, he said: 'My dear boy, you only know about 200 words.' I still cringe when I hear the word 'vocabulary'.

Waugh was diverted by all of my sisters, who used various methods to make an impression on him. Catherine, two years my senior, determined to get on Christian-name terms with him. For somebody with her charm, this was not a very difficult task. But she made certain of it by bellowing 'Mr Waugh' towards the ear-trumpet at the end of every sentence. Eventually he gave in. 'Won't you call me Evelyn?' he suggested graciously.

My little sisters, Mary-Ann and Jane, decided that what our guest needed was entertainment. Waugh would sit trying to read his book, but found it impossible, as the little girls danced before him in varying degrees of dress and undress. Waugh produced coins to persuade them to go away. But he never forgot their dancing and he ever after referred to them by the collective nickname 'the nautch girls' – Indian dancers.

Waugh was especially entranced by my sister Jill, known as Tickey. He conceived a plan that she should marry his eldest son, Auberon. His letters to my mother for years are full of Jill. 'My love to all your hordes, especially Tickey.' After she had had an operation on her toes, he demanded furiously, 'Why have you cut off Tickey's feet?' Then he complained of a photograph 'showing dear Jill in a very bad light. Young Auberon is not so keen & wants a nautch girl instead.' He was only to abandon his dream in 1961, when Auberon got engaged.

Twenty years earlier in England, Waugh had lost the battle of the visit to the great crested grebe. Now in Rhodesia he won the battle to visit my married sister Pelline. My mother had pointed out that Pelline could not travel, as she was heavily pregnant and had three tiny sons, so Waugh insisted on going to see her instead. My mother urged that this was an impractical scheme, as Pelline had only three modest bedrooms.

But Waugh was adamant, so my mother packed him, Father Maxwell (the 'ever present, tremendously boring ex-naval chaplain'), and her five youngest children into our Volkswagen bus and drove the 100 miles to Pelline's house. Pelline's entire family huddled in one bedroom, Waugh had another, Father Maxwell the third. My mother slept on the sofa and her children in the bus. After dinner, Waugh grew bored and went to bed early. He took a formidable sleeping draught of paraldehyde, and soon terrible snores penetrated the thin ceilings and bounced off the tin roof. His roars woke my three-year-old nephew, Denes. 'Will a lion come?' he asked his parents.

Early in his visit to M'bebi, I showed Waugh the schoolroom which housed most of our books. Examining the shelves, he kept laughing. He was amused by the haphazard way that some great classic stood next to a book he dismissed as rubbish. I had always thought our books perfectly well arranged, but his laugh was so infectious that I found myself laughing with him.

Drinking tea on the stoep (as we called the verandah at M'bebi), my mother and I talked to Waugh about literature. I was reading *Mansfield Park* at school and asked him what he thought of Jane Austen. 'Very complete,' Waugh nodded. My brother Charlie and I adored P. G. Wodehouse, and Waugh thought well of our taste. He quoted a sentence from Wodehouse: 'I could see that, if not actually disgruntled, he was far from being gruntled.' No other author could possibly have written those words, Waugh emphasised with a chuckle.

My innocence at 16 emboldened me to ask Waugh some direct questions about his own books. When I had read *Brideshead Revisited*, it had struck me that Sebastian's mother, Lady Marchmain, was – like my mother – a beautiful Catholic peeress. So I blurted out: 'Is Lady Marchmain based on Mummy?' Waugh, who had the highest opinion of my mother, but not of Lady Marchmain, burst out laughing.

My next question was more successful: 'What was the most difficult thing you ever did as a novelist?' I asked. Without hesitation, Waugh said: 'Turn a woman into a man.' I persisted: 'Who was the man?' 'Beaver in *A Handful of Dust*,' Waugh replied. Catherine and I had always laughed together at Beaver, the villain of the book. He had no personality and no job, but sat by the telephone hoping for invitations to meals. He was called 'London's only spare man'. Catherine had a fantasy that when I left school I might become Salisbury's only spare man. Now we knew that the model for Beaver was a woman.

The sequel to this story came 30 years later. I had read an article about *A Handful of Dust* by Auberon Waugh. He explained that Beaver, who wrecked the hero's marriage, was based on a man called John Heygate who had wrecked his father's first marriage. I wrote to Auberon and told him of the conversation I had had with his father. He replied:

> What you say rings a tiny bell. I believe that I may have heard my father say that . . . Baby Jungman . . . was at one time London's spare girl, waiting on the end of a telephone. It is possible that he shifted this one characteristic on to Heygate. If so, it might have been a double revenge, as he had been in love with Baby Jungman at one time. A curious idea.

Waugh went back to England in March 1958 and at Christmas that year my mother proudly sent a family photograph to all her friends and relations. Waugh's response was biting:

> I say, what a photograph! I have been telling my family how pretty you all are & now you send them this very disillusioning group. Not like human beings at all.

Waugh's nostalgia for M'bebi was evident when he wrote: 'It was touching to see the stain of the red earth of M'bebi on your letter', and he duly returned in March 1959. This time he made a sponsored trip to east and central Africa an excuse to spend a fortnight with us. The fruit of this second expedition was *A Tourist in Africa* (1960). Here he describes his first day back at M'bebi:

> The teeming life of the house, as in a backstreet of Naples, rages round me from dawn to dusk, but I remain in my chair, subject to interrogation, and the

performances of conjuring, dancing, and exhibitions of
strength, but for one day at least immovable.

Much of Waugh's second visit was taken up with sightseeing. He,
my mother, Father Maxwell and a young tycoon friend set off by car
to see something of Rhodesia. The conspicuously red faces of Waugh
and Father Maxwell inspired my father to christen the group 'the Lobster Quadrille'. All went well until they got to the magnificent Zimbabwe ruins. At their hotel, the manageress insisted she had only one
room with a bath. Waugh insisted that four rooms with baths had been
booked. Their voices grew more and more heated, and the manageress
sought to clinch the argument. In a tone suggesting that they take
their business elsewhere, she said: 'We like our guests to be happy.'
Waugh trumped her with, 'I shouldn't think that happens very often.'
My mother, as usual, resolved the matter – Waugh got the room with
the bath.

During the Lobster Quadrille tour, Waugh found a way to tease our
luckless chaplain, Father Maxwell, who summed up his intellectual
life in the words, 'I read people, not books.' The priest, as his figure
attested, enjoyed a glass of beer, and he was particularly fond of a cold
Castle, Rhodesia's leading brew. At their first stop, Waugh asked Father
Maxwell what he would like to drink. 'A co' Cussell,' Father Maxwell
replied, with his heavy Manchester accent. From then on, every time
they ordered drinks Waugh would triumphantly add: 'And a co'
Cussell.'

But if Waugh mocked the man, he treated the priest with respect.
After his son had been appallingly injured in an accident, a grateful
Waugh wrote to my mother: 'Please thank Father Maxwell awfully for
saying Mass for Bron.'

Waugh had the virtue of generosity, which at times rewarded him
materially. At the end of his second visit to Rhodesia, he gave a fine
dinner party at a Salisbury restaurant in honour of my 19-year-old
sister Catherine. After his return to England he reported gleefully: 'My
income tax man passed the bill for Catherine's Portuguese wine as a
necessary literary expense.'

A special joke was born over The Life of Ronald Knox, which came
out in 1959. Waugh dedicated the book to Katharine Asquith and my
mother. Mrs Asquith, whose guest Ronnie had become when we emigrated to Rhodesia, read the book in proof. She wrote to my mother
that it was a masterpiece. My mother in turn wrote to Waugh. 'Katharine says the book is a masterpiece.' From then on, Waugh always
referred to the book in his letters to my mother as 'Masterpiece', and

turned the joke into a bibliophile's treat. On publication, he sent my mother two copies. In the ordinary edition he wrote: 'This for bottom shelf.' He inscribed the special edition: 'For Daphne with my love and gratitude from Evelyn. This one is for the top shelf.' The title page read: 'The Life of the Right Reverend Ronald Knox . . . A MASTERPIECE by Evelyn Waugh.' He had had this volume specially printed for my mother. My brother Edward is now its proud owner; my mother, seeing me green with envy, presented me with the 'bottom shelf' copy.

My mother's brothers, and indeed my father, had gone to Cambridge; my mother's friends had gone to Oxford. She was more impressed by the education of her friends than her relations. So, in 1959, she persuaded me to try for Trinity College, Oxford. Waugh joined in the plan, and on a visit to Oxford sought to insinuate me into Trinity. He reported to my mother:

> I told the President how lucky he was to be getting a
> promising scholar like Richard. He said: 'Yes, I hope
> very much he gets in.' Not an absolutely satisfactory
> answer.

I will never know if Evelyn Waugh influenced the result, but I managed to pass the entrance exam. I wanted to tour Italy and France before going to England, so my mother asked Waugh if he could suggest any friends to entertain me on the continent. Complaining, as usual, about my Rhodesian accent, Waugh pointed out some of my other inadequacies: 'Poor chap, he has lived among bungalows and skycrapers and won't know the difference between Classic, Gothic and Baroque.' As to hostesses in Europe:

> I don't see Richard being at all easy in cosmopolitan
> society – e.g. Nancy Mitford or Diana Cooper or Pam
> Churchill. He must get some English polish before we
> put him into circulation.

He sensibly concluded: 'Richard shall take Europe very slowly and humbly.'

After some months on the continent in the first half of 1960, I arrived in England. Masses of English people had stayed at M'bebi and, as a naive 18-year-old, I expected reciprocal invitations to flow. They did not. However, Waugh came up trumps, and promptly asked me to stay at Combe Florey. I had a happy weekend there. Auberon told me about

*'Tell me! Is it really my drinking that concerns
you, or is it that another non-returnable is about
to pollute the environment?'*

Oxford, and I told his mother about our Jersey cows at M'bebi. Waugh
talked of people and books, expressing particular admiration for the
work of Muriel Spark. I played chess with Auberon, and there was a
dinner party for relations on Saturday night. On Sunday, I went to
Mass with the Waughs.

We had a conversation at lunch Sunday about thank-you letters. I
loathed writing letters and asked in a voice of despair if I had to write

and thank for the weekend. Laura Waugh kindly said 'no', Evelyn Waugh firmly 'yes'. He went on to suggest possible topics for my letter, and made me rock with laughter. After much discussion, he concluded that it would be best for me to make some uncontroversial remarks about the weather and the Sunday sermon.

I did write a thank-you letter, and Waugh wrote his own letter about the weekend to my mother:

> I asked [Richard] with the promise that there would be a house-party, but one by one the other guests chucked & took ill, and in the end he was alone. He was a pineapple of politeness. The last year has transformed him from a Rhodesian schoolboy into a pre-1914 under-graduate. His accent has almost gone, his spots entirely . . . How cleverly he disguised his boredom, which must have been acute.

I was not in the least bored at Combe Florey, but I was, as always, daunted by my host. Having lost my watch, I was terrified of being late when the family set out for Mass on Sunday. Waugh discovered me pacing the hall ages before the appointed hour. He wrote to my mother:

> [Richard] has no watch and is disconcerted by English habits of punctuality.

Catholicism was Waugh's conviction, writing his craft. His one com-munication to my father which survives shows to perfection his mas-tery of succinct prose. He knew that in Rhodesia my father sorely missed the roulette wheel. From Monte Carlo he sent him a picture postcard of the casino. The message consisted of one word: 'Homesick?'

From the time he was engaged on *The Life of Ronald Knox*, Waugh made pithy comments to my mother about his work:

> When I am writing a novel I know all about my charac-ters and what they are doing when they are not on the stage. I just record what seem the most interesting incidents. I am rather doing that with Ronnie.

When the book came out, he wrote:

> The reviews have been jolly decent to me. A few beasts,
> notably Graham Greene, have been beastly about Ron-
> nie. It is selling like warm cakes . . .

He had nothing good to say about *A Tourist in Africa*:

> I am trying to write about my African jaunt. It is hard
> going because I can only be funny when I am com-
> plaining about something, and everyone was so decent
> to me.

And when the book was published he wrote:

> I've sent you a copy of Pot Boiler because it would have
> been impolite not to, not in the hope of causing any
> pleasure or interest.

Waugh's next book was *Unconditional Surrender* (1961), the final
volume of his war trilogy. He complained to my mother:

> Midwinter past and here I am stuck in my novel longing
> for Monte Carlo and Umtali and Kashmir but I can't
> move until the book is finished. I interrupted it to trans-
> late a little life of La Veuve Cliquot (paid in champagne)
> and can't get started again.

But ultimately he took pride in the book:

> I can't remember, did I send you a copy? If I didn't, I
> am very sorry & will send you one at once. It has some
> funny bits.

Then he started the first (and only) volume of his autobiography, *A
Little Learning*:

> I am toiling & tinkering away at an autobiography. The
> trouble is that I am (genuinely) not interested in myself
> & that while my friends are alive I can't write candidly
> about them.

Later, he was less negative:

> I have finished the first volume of an autobiography.

No 'Masterpiece', but it has some comic bits, ending
with an unsuccessful attempt at suicide at the age of
21.

The last letter from Waugh to my mother was in January, 1964. The
Queen had just made my father a Companion of St Michael and St
George. Waugh wrote:

> I was much amused to see that the Queen had decorated
> John for services to Rhodesian agriculture. As I remem-
> ber it he served a (foreign) company manufacturing bags
> out of imported materials. Surely someone has been
> pulling the royal leg? I am jealous . . .

He ended his letter: 'All love to you & Jill & the CMG and the nautch
girls.'

Evelyn Waugh died on Easter Sunday, 1966, at the age of 62. To the
world at large he was a ferocious literary lion. We were lucky; to our
family, he was much more than that. He was warm and generous and
stimulating and funny. When I think of Evelyn Waugh, I remember
how I held him in awe when he roared, but above all I remember his
infectious laugh.

19 September 1992

DIARY

Max Hastings

In the past week, we have all had cause to think a great deal about
principled resignations, their merits or otherwise. I have heard ministers and advisers muttering about 'the futility of ritual sacrifices'. I
disagree. It seems an absolutely sound principle of all commercial and
political affairs that, if matters go wrong enough, somebody must be
seen to pay a price. One of the strongest reasons for doubt about the
management of the clearing banks in the past decade has been their
reluctance to conduct ruthless executions at the top when disastrous

errors have been made. A few years ago, I received a personal note from a bank chairman, whose resignation we had demanded in the *Daily Telegraph*, asking with obvious bitterness, 'What have I ever done to you and yours that you should now allow your newspaper to behave in this way?' Plainly, he felt deeply aggrieved that he should be faced with ending a long career in disgrace, when he himself had no personal knowledge of the appalling errors committed by subordinates. I was impenitent. If a scandal is of sufficient magnitude to have brought discredit upon an entire institution, then one or other of the men at the very top should surely go. Reluctance about resignation from high office stems partly, plainly, from horror of losing the chauffeur and Covent Garden tickets, but often also from a misconceived concept of courage. It is remarkable how often ministers and tycoons persuade themselves, conveniently, that it will be heroic to withstand the media pack baying for their blood. Yet Sir Thomas Dugdale will always have a small but honourable place in British history, as the last minister to resign for his civil servants' follies. Lord Carrington also commands deep admiration, not only for the fact of his resignation after the Falklands débâcle, but for its manner. He did not hesitate for a moment. There was no undignified, desperate attempt to hang on. He simply saw what honour and dignity required, and did it. Modern practice, refined under the present Government and in the City, is to conduct a protracted grapple with the hangman before being dragged kicking and screaming to the trap. Sidney Carton would have found them contemptible.

26 September 1992

ANOTHER VOICE

HUBRIS, NEMESIS AND SINGING IN THE BATH

Charles Moore

'My wife said she had never heard me sing in my bath before,' said Norman Lamont, all smiles, in Washington at the weekend. This statement had no possible public interest defence. It was a completely unwarranted and distasteful intrusion into Mr Lamont's privacy, no less so for having been committed by Mr Lamont himself.

There is nothing intrinsically wrong with Mr Lamont singing in the bath. He may, for all I know, do it very well, and such behaviour could indicate amiability and *joie de vivre*, qualities which Mr Lamont does in fact possess. But it was something over which he should have drawn a veil. I was a fellow guest of the Chancellor in a house in France last year. One evening he imitated an owl very amusingly. But if he had done the same thing and blown mimic hootings in the course of one of his flurried public statements in the past few days, one would have felt uneasy. So with the story about the bath. Future histories of the most absurd of all sterling crises will say in the index:

Lamont, Norman

– puts up interest rates on Wednesday p.91
– puts up interest rates again on Wednesday p.92
– takes pound out of ERM on Wednesday p.93
– sings in bath p.94

It won't look good, any more than 'Nero, Emperor – fiddles while Rome burns p.17'.

Mr Lamont's little confession must have been designed to do two things: to convince a doubting public that he is a charming and relaxed man, and to persuade Euro-sceptics that he is one of them, who, freed from his previous shackles, will fight their cause. I doubt if it will do either. If, for the last two years, you have been paying about £300 a month more mortgage interest than you need have done because of the Chancellor's policy of ERM membership, you may feel that if he is so happy to be shot of the thing, he might have thought of doing so before your house was repossessed. If you are a Tory MP whose opposition to the policy has caused you to be chastised with scorpions and, worse, with government whips, you will not be impressed by Mr Lamont's late conversion. *You* are fully entitled to sing in your bath and let the world know about it. *He* may only splash and warble behind sound proofed doors.

The bath remark is only a small example of a syndrome common to most of the prominent members of this Government – an inability to see what they look like to other people. One detected it in David Mellor when he said that the press should stop causing pain to his family. One detects it, in fact, in almost every pronouncement of David Mellor. One has seen it again and again since 'Black Wednesday', or, as Bruce Anderson, a pathological sufferer from the syndrome, calls it, 'the day John Major won the next election'.

That day brought the collapse of the economic policy of two years in the space of a few hours, exposing the chief ministers as fools. Their first response was to hide completely, leaving Sir Norman Fowler and poor Tim Smith to squeak and gibber on the television. Their next was to act as if they had made no mistake. Mr Lamont spoke of 'continuing the policy'. Mr Major's only remark was that it had been 'a very good Cabinet', and out came the very good Cabinet, John Patten tossing his hair and grinning and John Gummer scampering along to keep up and grinning too in an important sort of way and Mr Lamont attempting a slightly more statesmanlike grin. They were, in press lobby parlance, 'trying to tough it out'; a better phrase for this Government would be that they were weaking it out. What right, any normal person asked, had they to smile?

Then came the recriminations. Instead of talking to the nation, admitting the gravity of the crisis and asking for patience until the new policy was put before the House of Commons next week, Mr Major rang round editors to say how beastly the Germans had been and how it was all jolly unfair. Confronted with the suggestion that Mr Lamont might resign, the Prime Minister indicated that they were all in this one together and let it be known that at the Cabinet meeting he had asked each minister individually if there should be any resignations and all had said, *mirabile dictu*, that there should not. To Mr Major this might look like an impressive display of unity and a demonstration of collective Cabinet responsibility. To anyone else it looks like a group of naughty boys agreeing not to tell. Since every policy, by convention, is Cabinet policy, the logic of Mr Major's line is that there can never be a resignation on the failure of a policy. It is a doctrine of collective Cabinet irresponsibility.

Now the French have said 'yes', and Mr Major has courageously pointed out in the *Evening Standard* that the majority was 'wafer-thin', and so we all need to 'reflect on the consequences'. He goes further. He is calling a summit 'to take a profound look at where Europe is going'. It is very important to be at the heart of Europe, but on the other hand it is impossible since our currency cannot stand it. It is vital to follow the disciplines of the German economy and benefit from Mr Major's close friendship with Dr Kohl, but on the other hand those disciplines appear to have strangled us, and Dr Kohl, by Mr Major's implication, is a treacherous bastard. The Prime Minister is almost speechless with self-contradiction.

The solution towards which the Government is groping is a whips' solution. The people who think Mr Lamont ought to go are chiefly those who opposed the failed policy. He must stay, they are told, because he *really* agrees with them, and if he goes they'll get someone who doesn't. It is he, after all, who has said that we can now have an economic policy framed for British conditions and in Britain's interests. But all this only compounds the syndrome I am describing. Mr Lamont and those trying to keep him do not see what he looks like. He looks absurd and unbelievable. For the past two years he has hinted that he did not like the policy, but he has implemented it. Since the new policy is forced on him by circumstances it scarcely matters whether he likes it. Michael Heseltine would have to follow the same policy if he were Chancellor. (One would like, for base reasons, to watch him compelled to do so.) If it were true that the Chancellor chosen by Mr Major to replace Mr Lamont would do the wrong thing, what message does that convey to the doubters about Mr Major's trustworthiness and judgment of men? As for the new 'policy for Britain's interests', the implication of the phrase must be that we had the opposite before. It is as if a doctor said, 'I've decided to stop trying to make you ill now, and will try to make you better,' and was then surprised and hurt when the patient said he'd rather be treated by somebody else.

None of the main players seems to realise that he is on stage, that politics is a drama. It has hubris, nemesis and catharsis, not hubris, nemesis and singing in the bath. The actors have their exits as well as their entrances.

26 September 1992

NOT A PRETTY PICTURE

Jeffrey Bernard

Last week I read the proofs of Graham Lord's biography of me, *Just the One*, and I have been feeling not a little depressed ever since. This is not Graham's fault, who has worked very hard and done a good job,

'What a fantastic view!'

it is just that it is not a nice story, not a pretty picture. I must have been mad to have looked forward to it. I wasn't daft enough to think that everybody Graham interviewed would be lovey-dovey about me – I wasn't even that myself – but some of it still came at me like a bucket of cold water in the face when I read it in the sober light of day. Being as vain and self-preoccupied as any man, I thought it might be required reading for me from cover to cover every day for the rest of my life.

I shall be interested to see what the book looks like when it comes out – it is illustrated – and then it shall be kept closed for ever after. Was Dorian Grey in the habit of looking at his revolting portrait? I wouldn't know since I have never read the book. I would guess that he took the odd peek at it. I was happily surprised, though, to discover that a couple of ex-wives and the odd ex-girlfriend had been fairly pleasant about me, although even they couldn't remember much beyond the fact that I had blue eyes when they met me. (I have just looked at them and they have faded like an overexposed water-colour. What with the pink in them now they remind me of Sir John Astor's racing colours.) Of course, to me, the book reads like an obituary without pulled punches: I wasn't 'convivial', I was as pissed as a rat. And it should be required reading for any boy stupid enough to think that a glass of whisky will make him an instant Jack the Lad.

Anyway, when I finished reading *Just the One* it occurred to me that now I live with a potted palm tree I have arrived at an anticlimax. Or maybe it is a climax in disguise. There are, of course, a few things that are mildly irritating to me and that is only to be expected. Yes, I have ignored my sister in the past and I do now because I have never liked her and I couldn't suddenly feel any warmth for her when she was certified years ago, just as I wouldn't feel sudden affection for somebody who was diagnosed as having cancer. It would just make one think a bit. I do that all right.

It has also stirred memories and muddied a pond which I thought was becoming clearer. I had nearly obliterated my memories of the horrors of early family life but they have been brought back to the surface. My brother Oliver's forthcoming autobiography, *Getting Over It*, also slightly depressed me for that reason. I used to argue with Frank Norman that his being taken into a Dr Barnado's home was a blessing in disguise but he would have none of it. Nevertheless it can be a terrible thing to be a child and discover that you have inherited a mother. And as for my daughter, Isabel, she came round last week to see me and read a chapter or two which opened her eyes a little. She wasn't shocked but she didn't exactly laugh. But now that she is 22 years old it won't do her any harm. I wish I knew more about my father, whom I strangely miss although I never knew him when he died and I was only seven.

I see now that what I have said looks very much like self-pity but I am not much given to that nowadays since I see that it has all been rather absurd. What Graham Lord's book has done has been to rekindle some guilt and remorse and that is my own fault. Remorse is horribly negative, as is envy, and I was surprised to read an under-current of envy in some of my friends and enemies that Graham interviewed.

How anybody can envy a faintly breathing cadaver is beyond me.

Oddly enough, the book has a comparatively happy ending when Graham Lord writes of the opening and run of *Jeffrey Bernard is Unwell*. Was it really such a nightmare up until then and did Keith Waterhouse simply invent me? I shall never know. But I can't help smiling at a remark made by a woman in the book who says of years ago that I wasn't very good at cuddling because I got so instantly randy that it led to closer contact. And that is meant to be a put-down? Those were the days.

26 September 1992

A WORD ON BULLYING

John Whitworth

The English are good folk to go among;
Tractile, unused to violence of the tongue,
Their natural aggression is inchoate:
But Scots are hard, hard men. A Scottish poet
Is still a hard, hard man and lets you know it.

Be nice to people; they'll be nice to you –
My English lesson but it isn't true.
Better to learn the butcher-bird, the Shrike
That sticks his enemies up on a spike,
Better to learn pre-emptive counterstrike

And love your enemies as I love mine:
I treasure him, my own, my Valentine,
Valentine Tudball – this exultant Jock
With the amazing handle, thought to mock
My name, and turn me to a laughing-stock

Why did he? Why? You snivelling hypocrite,
Because he *could*. Eh Whitworth? Worth a wit?

Eh Shitworth? Worth shit all? Bang on, sweet slanger,
My handsome Valentine, my bold haranguer,
My stormtroop darling and my doppelganger.

26 September 1992

ANOTHER VOICE

DOES ONE HOOT OR DOES ONE NOT?

Auberon Waugh

Last week *The Spectator* printed a complaint about this column from a correspondent in Bruton, North Somerset, called D. C. Barker, who took exception to a piece I wrote in the issue of 5 September 1992, using an indisposition I had briefly suffered to illustrate a short sermon on the National Health Service.

'I hope I am not being churlish if I say that I do not find his [AW's] bottom a particularly inspiring subject for contemplation,' wrote D. C. Barker before proceeding in sterner tones: 'Even less did I care for the vivid account of recent melancholy events occurring in that region of his body.'

It would be easy to sympathise with D. C. Barker and say 'there, there'. But I am afraid that future accidents of the same sort will almost certainly be reported just as conscientiously. Too little happens in a columnist's life for any of it to be wasted. A few years ago I devoted a whole page to the story of how I had nearly (but not quite) kissed an unknown young woman in the Underground, on the lips, through absent-mindedness. Was D. C. Barker inspired? I do not know. You can lead a horse to water, but you cannot make it drink.

By the same token, I was interested to learn in last Wednesday's *Guardian* that my colleague Germaine Greer has recently had a reportable experience. She nearly (but not quite) had a motor accident in a country lane. The incident is soon told. If one disregards all the usual stuff about how the other driver was on the wrong side of the

road, passing on a blind corner etc. etc., what happened was that Dr
Greer saw a lorry coming towards her and stopped in good time to
flash her lights at its driver. As he drove past, he made a V-sign at her.

That, then, is the essential incident. More dramatic than my nearly
kissing a strange young woman on the Tube, but less so, perhaps,
than my experiences in the Charing Cross Hospital last month. All
motorists have occasional near-misses. I have superstitiously refrained
from drawing attention to my own, but if I were truly desperate for
something to write about – what we hacks call a McKay situation –
and could think only of a near-miss like Dr Greer's, followed by a rude
sign from the lorry driver, I would probably use it to illustrate the
rudeness and aggressiveness of the New Briton, apportioning the blame
equally between Shirley Williams and Mrs Thatcher, who appear to
have produced Andrew Neil between them . . .

Greer, being Australian, is not concerned with our class war. Writing
for the *Guardian*, which has not allowed any but the same old ideas
and opinions to be expressed for the last 25 years, she probably felt
she had no choice but to discuss the lorry driver's two-finger salute as
part of the Sex War. It does not seem to have occurred to her that
the poor fellow was suffering from social deprivation, powerlessness,
government cuts etc. Instead, she asks herself whether his gesture was
part of a reported anti-feminist backlash.

She might have had a point. I have noticed that New Brits on the
road are especially loathsome in their rudeness to women, making free
use of the c-word, which, in its use by men to insult women, surely
separates whatever is left of our concept of the gentleman from the
subhuman New-Brit oaf. But I generally attribute this especial rudeness to the New Brit's cowardice, rather than to his hatred of women.

Greer similarly pooh-poohs the idea of an anti-feminist backlash,
attributing the lorry driver's behaviour to traditional male brutality.
But first she must wring as much as possible out of the incident.

'Let's be quite clear about what the two-finger salute means,' she
wrote in Wednesday's *Guardian*. 'It means a digit up your vagina, a
digit up your rectum. Fuck you *and* bugger you. I shrugged it off, of
course. Such insults are commonplace, after all, but their real meaning
should be registered.'

Well, perhaps it has that meaning in Australia, but nobody with whom
I discussed the matter had the faintest idea that the derisive V-sign
(which is made at men as much as at women) carried any such anatomi-
cal implications, and I don't believe it does. Greer, however, uses this
'sadistic reaction' on behalf of the driver to repeat every moan in the
feminist's litany – that husbands are frequently pardoned for murdering

wives who irritate them, that contraception does not leave women in control of their reproductive destiny because IUDs and contraceptive pills are unsatisfactory (I was reminded of the famous apothegm of Evelyn Home, agony aunty of *Woman* magazine in the great days, that the best contraceptive is 'No'), that many women do not have as much sex as is their right ('Female sexuality still depends upon male demand') or always enjoy it as much as they should when they do:

> The kind of sex that leaves women pregnant is not the
> kind that gives them the most intense pleasure, but it
> is the kind they usually get.

Once again, I am afraid that Dr Greer must speak for herself. All this may seem a long way from her Real Fright and Horrid Experience in a country lane, when a lorry driver made a rude gesture at her after she had flashed her lights at him. The thought occurs to me that the lorry driver might have been trying to apologise to her. I do not know – I do not speak to these people, either, if I can help it – but I met some woman or other about ten years ago who assured me that lorry drivers were often the salt of the earth . . .

Greer's résumé of the feminist position, prompted by the rude lorry driver, takes in the significant moan that 'where once we struggled for the right to work, we now have a duty to work to service the family debt'. It is on that area that I would urge her to muse further. For the rest, her repetition of familiar moans about male bias and hatred of women might support the impression that the women's movement is running out of vitality. We can always trade insults, as the *Times* has babyishly invited us to do, but that is not what I mean by the Sex War, nor by hatred of women. No doubt there has been a backlash of the lorry-driver sort against feminism, but it is not significant. A more significant reaction – one could call it a backlash, but it is slower and more-purposive than that – may be seen in New York, in the emasculation (or at any rate impotence, when confronted by women) of New York men, and their adoption of homosexuality despite the gravest discouragement on grounds of health. Lesbian growth is obviously part of the same thing. The key text for our times may not be the lorry driver's ambiguous gesture to Greer in a country lane, but the *Sun* reader's other injunction, blazoned on his rear window: *Hoot if you've had it today*, or *Honk if you've bonked*. Does one hoot, Germaine, or does one not?

3 October 1992

SPORT

TIGERISH TO THE END

Frank Keating

A dozen years ago, I innocently plonked myself and my clobber down on a seat which was surprisingly free in Adelaide's crowded press box, that charming, splintery row of desks which gently rake up from the mid-wicket boundary. Australia versus the West Indies. I was a touch late and Vivian Richards, in all his swaggering grandement, was already ripping into a fuming Dennis Lillee and Lenny Pascoe.

I bid a 'good day' to the hunched, bald and scrawny ancient beside me. The face looked not unlike that Trog portrait of old Beaverbrook as a wizened prune. He answered my greeting with a momentary glance of appalled disdain from his watery spaniel's eyes and he just growled a sneering, throat clearing 'garrumph'. I had quickly realised why the seat had been empty.

Out in the middle, Richards's string of extravagant strokes continued to scatter the seagulls and pepper the pickets. The throng was awestruck. Not my neighbour. He just garrumphed or sighed, totally unimpressed, as each sumptuous retort exploded off the West Indian's bat.

Why should he be moved by this young foreign 'slogger'? Anyway, Lillee can't bowl for toffee. As for the Australian fielding, well, even groaning sighs failed him there, and he buried his head in his long, purply-veined, parchmenty-skinned old hands. The younger generation would get no change out of him.

He was, of course, Bill O'Reilly, of the *Sydney Morning Herald* and cricket's immortal hall of fame – 'the Tiger', whose death at the age of 87 was announced on Tuesday. In 27 Test matches up to the 1939 war he took 144 wickets at 22 apiece with an always aggressive, fast-spitting, leg-break mixture – and then became an equally fast-spitting, truculent and unmissable pamphleteer of the back pages.

Bradman considered him the best bowler of his time – 'to hit him for four would arouse a belligerent ferocity, almost like disturbing a hive of bees'. Cardus thought he was better than Barnes as the bowler of the century because O'Reilly's repertoire included a hissing cobra-strike of a googly. (Sir Neville put this point to Barnes once: 'It's quite true, I never had the googly,' admitted Barnes, then, after a pause and a twinkle in the keen steely eyes, he added, 'I never needed it.') I never saw O'Reilly bowl, of course, but have enough old sepia newsreel on video to get the message.

He approached the wicket with no nonsense, no finery – all venom and malevolence. Just like his journalism and his views on modern cricketers. Robertson-Glasgow described his run-up as 'a sort of fierce galumph, the right forearm working like a piston, at delivery the head ducked low as if to butt the batsman at the bowler's end onto the stumps.'

On the Tiger's two tours to England, in 1934 and 1938, he topped the bowling averages both times with over 100 wickets. His last Test against England was at the Oval and Hutton's 364. He was, apparently, the only Australian fielder not to shake young Hutton by the hand. 'I had 364 reasons for not doing so,' he said afterwards.

The last thing I ever read of O'Reilly's was a few weeks ago in the new book *Len Hutton Remembered*: 'What do I remember of the 364? I remember that I did 13½ hours of hard yakker out there and bowled 85 overs. Nowadays they get big money for bowling ten, and if they bowl over ten they're thrown out of the union.'

Tigerish to the end. A true great has been caged at last.

10 October 1992

THE SECRET AGENDA OF GENDER

Barbara Amiel

In the past 20 years, our society has gone a good way towards becoming a matriarchy. Just as it was not necessary for there to be a male sovereign in the days of Queen Elizabeth I for that society to be organised along patriarchal lines, so it is entirely unnecessary for there to be a majority of women appeal court judges, Cabinet ministers or policemen for this society to be on the road to matriarchy. All that is required is for our institutions to be governed by the needs of radical feminism and for social engineers to carry out the agenda of radical feminists. And just as I, being a supporter of liberal democracy, would fight a patriarchy, the fight now must be against matriarchy. I wish our Prime Minister was on board, fighting against radical feminists in

domestic policy, rather than avoiding trouble by sending danegeld and
having his ministers implement the radical feminist agenda.

Feminism was for many years a respectable and worthy descendant
of the classical liberalism that flowed from the Scottish Liberals to the
framers of the American constitution. So long as feminism was in
pursuit of equality – equality of opportunity, equality before the law
– it was a movement to which one gave one's whole-hearted support.
The notion that the state and its laws would not encourage sanctions
or prescriptions against any individual on the basis of gender or indeed
race or homosexuality was a worthy goal, and one we reached.

But soon feminism developed less respectable tendencies. Extreme
feminists could not say to the Lord Chancellor or the Prime Minister,

'Look, we abhor your society with its naïve liberalism and old-fashioned notions of individual liberty or heterosexual families. We want power to modify your rather outdated notions of blindfold justice, and fairness in the workplace.' Instead, they used a sleight of hand: they substituted the notion of group parity for equality and muddled up the two ideas. The result is that all our notions of fairness, equality and liberty have fallen down.

This, actually, is the key to where the women's movement went off the rails from enlightenment to reaction – and George Jonas has documented this in his book *Politically Incorrect*. First, Jonas says, there was a foolish tolerance for stretching – in the way of all prejudices – perfectly rational ideas to absurd and irrational limits. Second, there was a willingness to make a pact even with the devil for the immediate purpose of women's advancement, and to dismiss all other considerations of fairness, equity, aesthetics, national interest, civil liberties or commonsense as 'negligible' if they seemed to hinder the 'cause'. But third, and most important, was to identify the cause itself as no longer the fair and equal treatment of human beings who happened to be women, but as the advancement of the status of women as a *group*.

It is important to understand that equality for the individual – as in equal opportunity or equality before the law – is a classic liberal ideal, while parity for a group is at best a political and at worst a profoundly reactionary notion. Equality stresses that any qualified human being may become an engineer, plumber, prime minister or jet pilot, regardless of gender, religion or race, while parity maintains that a proportionate number from each group *must* achieve such positions regardless of merit or utility. The belief in parity is based to some extent on a genuine error – the view that any disparity in society has to be the result of discrimination – as well as the cynical politician's view that when disparity makes some people restless it should be eliminated, even at the expense of freedom and fairness. By choosing parity over equality as its main goal, the women's movement embarked on the tortuous path of having to make its own thinking as prejudicial and nonsensical as that of any genuine male chauvinist.

The notion of group parity was quickly adopted by every other special interest group – ethnic groups, blacks, homosexuals. There was a curious symbiosis between government and special interest groups about this illiberal idea: the notion of parity enhanced the power of both. Enforcing it was a means of giving a statist government more power and regulatory authority, and the special interest groups more funding, more scope. So quietly, without much fanfare, we buried the notion of equality. We stopped being colour blind and gender blind –

indeed even justice itself now peeks from under her mask to see if the witness or defendant is female, in which case evidentiary rules and procedures may be modified to protect her. When I asked the Lord Chancellor, Lord Mackay, about this, he explained to me that while he still believed in the level playing-field of justice, we 'had to make up for past disadvantages'.

Group parity is now the measure of our times and misleadingly is used interchangeably with equality – just to confuse people. If women are 51 per cent of the population, then they ought to be 51 per cent of the executives at the BBC or 51 per cent of judges on the appeal court. Only that, argue the proponents of group parity, signals that true equality has been reached.

If an idea is a good idea, you do not need ministerial edicts to get a democratic society to accept it. But because ideas like group parity, or equal pay for work of equal value, or reverse discrimination would not survive in the arena of free discourse because of their intrinsic weakness, they have to be artificially entrenched by exclusion, by policies, by law. They must get the status of dogma or doctrine to be enforced by ministerial edict.

The dogmas are these: first, parity for the group. This statistical concept is not only wrong because it is illiberal, as I have mentioned. It is wrong because people do not exist in single interest groups. If you use gender as a basis for policy, favouring women, drawing up lists of women for jobs, you neglect the fact that women are wives as well with husbands; they have sons, they are the sisters of brothers, they live in families supported by fathers. This is a fundamental flaw in the entire notion of group rights. What are you doing to a society when you advance the cause of one group at the expense of others? How could a Conservative Government – as it does – embrace such a notion?

The second dogma is equal pay for work of equal value. This is entirely different from the notion of equal pay for the same or similar work, a decent principle with which few would argue. It may be a human right to be paid the same for the same job, but at best it is a human ambition to be paid the same for a different job. But if pay equity becomes the law – and every company has to draw up pay equity plans, grading their jobs and comparing them – as it has in a jurisdiction in which I lived for many years, Ontario, Canada, and which the EEC recommends as a model for the United Kingdom, the following happens: the cost to business skyrockets and investment falls. And in an arbitrary situation where committees rather than the market-place decide the value of a job there will be arbitrary winners and losers. In a practical sense, the equal value initiative could be as disruptive to jobs as once was unrestrained trade union power. Conflicts between men and women will spread to other groups as opposing racial, ethnic and professional interests surface. And underneath all this, of course, is the persistent drumbeat of radical feminism: low wages for women, women are victims, we are all victims, we are a society of the oppressed.

The third dogma is the notion that the two-parent, one-income family with a non-working mother is a structure based not on women's choice but solely on women's oppression. The suggestion that some mothers like to stay at home and bring up their children is anathema to feminism, including such bodies as the Government-supported Equal Opportunities Commission, whose research reports are filled with the contention that any social policy – such as a minimum income or transferable personal tax credit – which sustains the ability of a woman to remain at home without working is a bad idea and leads to – a favourite gloomy phrase of theirs – 'women's economic dependency'.

I am not optimistic that Mr Major will attack these problems, for the Conservative Government is guilty of furthering extreme views. One example of this is the Central Council for Education and Training in Social Work (CCETSW), the quango that sets the guidelines and monitors candidates for the Diploma in Social Work and effectively controls lecturers, students and practitioners in the social work field. It reports to Mrs Virginia Bottomley, the Secretary of State for Health. She appoints all its 25 council members and guarantees them £20 million of taxpayers' money.

On 16 June 1989, their council passed a series of equal opportunities and antiracist strategy statements – among other things these state:

> CCETSW believes that racism is endemic in the values, attitudes and structures of British society including that of social services and social work education. CCETSW recognises the effects of racism on black people are incompatible with the value of social work and therefore seeks to combat racist practices in all areas of its responsibilities.
> CCETSW will seek to ensure that in all dimensions of its activity – as an employer, validating body and in its development – individuals are not unfairly disadvantaged on the grounds of age, gender, disability, language (including sign language), race, ethnic origin, nationality, sexual orientation, social class or religion.

They then published a glossary of what was meant by these terms and it forms the basis of their so-called anti-oppressive policies to which any candidate for social-work diplomas or jobs must subscribe. What follows is a pure if not simple Marxist/feminist analysis. These are just some of the categories of discrimination as they see them:

> Gender: women are *not* a minority group (51 per cent of the UK population is female) but they are oppressed by systematic stereotyping and discrimination on the basis of gender and/or marital status. As a result they are seriously disadvantaged in employment, training and promotion and this remains the case in spite of legislation designed to ameliorate this state of affairs. It is also important to recognise that men are also oppressed by gender stereotyping, e.g., in terms of permissible roles and behaviour.
> Race: race is not a biological fact but a concept which has been socially constructed. The physical characteristics, skin colour, hair, facial features which distinguish various people from one another are invested with social meaning whch can prove advantageous to the group or not, depending on the ability of the group in question to assert its right of self definition and have it respected by others. Oppression of black people is acknowledged by CCETSW in its anti-discrimination statement of 4 November 1988.

My comment on this is straightforward. It is a lie: race is a fact and not a socially constructed concept.

What is evident is that no thinking person outside the extremist fringe could subscribe to these concepts. But if you want to study or get a job in social work you have no choice: you must. And that is why, for example, no member of the Conservative Party would be eligible for training or employment as a social worker.

This was brought to the attention of Mrs Bottomley by Gerald Hartup of the Freedom Association, who patiently photocopied the relevant passages and on 14 August sent them to Mrs Bottomley with the following questions:

1. Do CCETSW's equal opportunity statement, anti-racist strategy statement and its definitions of the necessary attributes for a social worker now represent your department's philosophy?

2. Were the above originally agreed with your department?

3. If your department approves of the philosophy outlined in question 1, does it approve also of restricting social work lecturers and students to those sharing that philosophy?

The letter was not answered until a month later on 19 September by the Health Minister, Dr Brian Mawhinney, on Mrs Bottomley's behalf. Here is what he said:

> The Department of Health fully shares CCETSW's commitment to equal opportunities for all. We have taken a number of initiatives to raise the profile of equality issues in the social service field and fund the Race Equality Unit at the National Institute for Social Work which advises social services departments on both staffing and service delivery issues. I would expect all social work students and lecturers – and indeed everyone working in social services – to show a real commitment to equal opportunities throughout their working lives. CCETW's Rules and Requirements for the Diploma in Social Work which were launched by Virginia Bottomley make this expectation quite clear.

Mrs Bottomley has effectively excluded any people from the field of social work but Marxist feminists or those who are prepared to lie about their adherence to the anti-oppressive creed. She has excluded all members of her own political party. (Incidentally, I understand similar policies exist in the field of youth work and I expect we can find equally disturbing creeds in the teaching polytechnics.) Why is Mrs Bottomley doing this? One could take refuge in the fact that the lady can't think her way out of a wet paper bag and that may be part of it, but I fear she genuinely believes in what she is doing.

Another example of this feminist infection in government is Opportunity 2000, officially launched by John Major on 28 October 1991. It is an initiative to get more women into business. Behind it is the Women's Economic Target Team, chaired by Lady Howe, a quango which spawned another quango, Business in the Community. The aim is to get the 'proper balance' of men and women in the workforce at all levels and in all areas. The CVs of the members of this quango are intriguing: Joanna Foster, 'chair' of the Equal Opportunities Commission; Brenda Dean, the former trade union leader; the campaign development manager has a 'strong equal opportunities background' and so on. By now, righting the perceived wrongs of women has become a career choice like dentistry. Here, Opportunity 2000 flogs the notion of group parity, extolled by Lady Howe and John Major as a primary aim of the Conservative Party.

Under Opportunity 2000, firms have pledged to up the percentage of women in senior management jobs. NatWest aims to increase women managers to 33 per cent. British Airways is upping its female workforce to 42 per cent, London Weekend Television to 43 per cent.

Mrs Bottomley is particularly keen on Opportunity 2000 and demands that every short list for NHS senior management must include women and, where there are none, she now has a regional short list of women on standby. Health authorities and trusts have been set eight goals in the field of breaking down barriers to women's careers – setting numerical targets of a 20 per cent increase in women representatives on health authorities and trusts. There are also targets for increasing the number of women consultants and accountants. Of course, as quotas are illegal, the state can only make known its 'preferential' policy. But persuasion is mighty: employers, particularly those getting funding or contracts from the Government, do not want to be accused of being sexist and socially retrogade. They put in place their own equal opportunities programmes, officers, counsellors and booklets. Preferring women may also have its attractions: it provides a cast-iron excuse for getting rid of a man, not least because of personal vendettas. And if he is replaced by a woman, women can shamelessly promote each other in ways that would be seen as favouritism if done by men.

At the BBC, the director general designate, John Birt, is in the lead in the running for the gold medal in progressivism. It was Birt who told a seminar I attended on women in television, 'Every time I am confronted at the BBC by a roomful of men, I am always struck by the thought that half of those men are standing in the way of more talented women.' The remark puzzled me. As in any bureaucracy, at least half of those men were probably standing in the way of more talented men. The BBC under eight numerical quotas (called 'targets', of course) intends to make women 30 per cent of senior executives, 40 per cent of senior management and 40 per cent of management by 1996. Just how this is possible without discriminating against talented men I do not know.

After the last election, Gillian Shephard, Employment Secretary, was given the cross-departmental portfolio for women's issues and became Minister of Women in all but name. She seems a talented, intelligent woman, as yet rather difficult to read. Aspects of her employment bill are very welcome indeed. The problem with a Minister of Women, however, is that they invariably become Minister of Women They Like. Thus, Gillian Shephard has set up the women's issues working group, which she describes as 'a small team to give her personal advice on practical measures to extend equal opportunities for women in the workplace and beyond'.

Who are its members? Lady Howe, Joanna Foster from the Equal Opportunities Commission, Sue Slipman from the Council for One-Parent Families, and so on.

I am reminded of a speech Mrs Thatcher made to the Conservative Women's Conference in May 1988. 'Conservative women are above all practical,' she declared. 'They do not attempt to advance women's rights by addressing you, Madam Chairman, as Madam Chairperson, or Madam Chair or worse [and the PM paused a beat before the lunacy] simply as Chair. With feminists like that, who needs male chauvinists?' That was shortly before Joanna Foster was appointed Madam Chairman of the Equal Opportunities Commission and on her first week let it be known that she wished to be referred to in office life simply as Joanna or Chair. Could Mrs Thatcher have foreseen, having defeated Ilea and the loony-left councils, that the spirit of Lambeth and Hackney would end up in the cosy niches of the Conservative Party, watered by its Prime Minister, nurtured by ministers and funded, as ever, by us?

Back to Mrs Shephard. She has appointed other members to her women's issues working group who appear to be practical people. But we all know the game: only the professional think-tankers and policy specialists can find the time to influence a minister. Business people are too busy actually running their businesses. But where are the Conservative thinkers? Where is the extremely crisp and knowledgeable work of Dr Patricia Morgan and her studies on the workplace, childcare and women's policies. Where is the name of Digby Anderson and all the associated thinkers he has assembled at the Social Affairs Unit? Where are those of us who do not cleave to the radical feminist line of the Equal Opportunities Commission and the muddled sentimentality of Lady Howe?

It is time that John Major, starting with the Government itself, put a stop to this march towards matriarchy (a government dancing like ours is to the pipes of the radical feminists); and that if his Government is to tolerate ministers who wish to intervene before breakfast, before lunch and before dinner, it should at least intervene to prevent the take-over of all our institutions by false, wicked and illiberal ideas.

Barbara Amiel is a columnist on the Sunday Times. This article is based on a talk to the Centre for Policy Studies.

17 October 1992

BOOKS

NOT MANY PEOPLE WANT TO KNOW THIS

Julie Burchill

WHAT'S IT ALL ABOUT
by Michael Caine
Century, £16.99, pp. 473

If Michael Caine did not exist, *The Spectator* would have to invent him. Or the *Telegraph*, or one of the Waughs. For he is the snob's dream of the self-made English oik; coarse, immodest, smarmily concupiscent – and, of course, a crashing snob himself. Which conveniently justifies the snobbery of those who might be tempted to mock him.

We've heard the story of the Caine mutiny from rags to Langan's so often that it has become almost a piece of family album apocrypha. Son of Billingsgate porter; made it big in the cocky Cockney Sixties; got leg over in the company of Terry Stamp; wondered what it was all about, Alfredo; saw Shakira Baksh shimmying across the television screen with her hands around a pair of maracas and wished they were his; married her; hired bolshy electrician who refused to work for such a flashy geezer (cf Politics of Envy); left poxy, envious, 'socialist' old Blighty for LA; made crap films; got homesick; came back to brilliant Thatcherite old Blighty. Swanked about, smirking irrepressibly; wrote book about it all.

Even in shorthand it's a fairly *ordinaire* success story, remarkable only for its gravity-defying level of self-congratulation; in close up, told over more than 400 pages, it is a banquet of banality. The interesting

'I don't want to go to their party and have a good
time. I don't enjoy having a good time.'

paradoxes of Caine's career – such as the fact that it took the moribund English film industry to give him his commercial and critical successes (*The Ipcress File, Alfie, Zulu, Educating Rita, Mona Lisa*) while in supposedly hot Hollywood he was landed with such turkeys as *The Swarm, Jaws 4* and *Beyond the Poseidon Adventure* – are related with bland self-regard and no analysis whatsoever. Yet pointless and even cretinous pieces of information – that in Somalia there is a type of camel which looks quite sexy or that Mr Caine regularly has to do battle with copious amounts of nostril hair – are given full rein.

The book is often quite unintentionally hilarious. On location in Africa, he begins to learn the true wisdom which 'we in the so-called civilised world have forgotten'. But then he goes on to relate the horrendous Masai superstition that every fly carries the spirit of a god and must never be swatted – even when crawling into the mouths and eyes of Masai babies and giving them God knows what germs. What's that all about, Mikey?

On a thankfully lighter note, one of the funniest bits of the book reads thus, with no apparent irony:

> I have new things to do and new places to go and I intend to keep dealing with the unknown and the unpredictable, two dangerous elements that have been the norm in my life . . . I am currently in the middle of making the *Muppets* movie version of Charles Dickens' *A Christmas Carol*.

So much for the comedy; the tragedy of this book is its appalling and vulgar obsession with royalty. We are asked to admire Prince Philip as a jolly old josher for calling Caine 'old Ipcress' whenever he meets him; in a member of the public, this would be used as proof of their moronic inability to distinguish between fact and fiction. We are pointed towards 'a picture of the Queen laughing at my joke'. Caine relates in shocked tones the story of Governor Brown's 'rudeness' to Princess Margaret (he had to leave a dinner before she did). Mr Caine obviously believes that running your state when you could be brown-nosing foreign princesses should be some sort of capital offence.

His other main squeeze is Mrs Thatcher. Politically he is a lethal blend of the sentimental and the cynical; there is a moving and genuine passage of writing about nurses, and how watching the care for his sick wife and baby made him ashamed to be an overpaid, underworked actor. But he proceeds to moan on ceaselessly about the 'socialist' taxation system in Britain; what else but taxes pay the wages of these wonderful women?

There is little sign of any intentional humour; what there is is bitchery of an archetypically actorish kind. Early in his career, Joe Levine told the young Caine he would never make it because he looked too faggy (it's the hair; it looks permed) and he did actually go on to play fruits in *California Suite, Deathtrap* and *Dressed to Kill*. Writing about making *The Romantic Englishwoman* with Glenda Jackson and Helmut Berger, he confides very queenily that Helmut obviously disliked Glenda because he wanted to play the title role.

It's a book in which even little things seem somehow off, but you can't be sure whether this is through dumbness or duplicity. Eliza Doolittle becomes Liza, several times (but he doesn't spell Liza

Minelli's name wrong); his role as Frank in *Educating Rita* he claims to have based on Emil Jannings in *The Blue Angel*, which is a bit like hearing that Leslie Caron based Gigi on Lola-Lola. He keeps complaining that films he was innocently involved in like *Dressed to Kill* and *Blame it on Rio* turned out 'vulgar' and 'gratuitous'. Surely he read the scripts?

And there are some weird, nasty little bits, like when he very elaborately forgets – 'Sorry, Sweetheart' – the name of the girl he took to the première of *Zulu*, when surely a quick call to his cuttings people could have supplied the answer. The girl in question was in fact Edina Ronay, who is not merely beautiful but beautiful in a quite singular, sinister way – not a forgettable identikit dolly by any stretch.

Or it just might be his wife's jealous temper, described in blood-curdling detail here. It must be this or a natural sense of chivalry which prevents Mr Caine from naming any of the women he 'dated'; instead, his voice suddenly becomes a stage whisper, and he says things like, 'Only you know who you are, and your secret is safe with me.' This is all very well and good, but the apocalyptic tone tends to make it sound as though Mrs X and Mr Caine share some absolutely appalling secret, not just a quick shtup.

The slight shadow of Shakira, the second Mrs Caine, falls full across these confidences, as indeed it does across the entire book. She is, as we must all know by now, a sleek Indian whippet of a woman, with a beauty that is almost sexless in its elegance. The pictures of them, scattered throughout the book, are strange; he, slack-jawed, goggle-eyed and gaping, his arm around her, looks like Joe Blow who has just won the pools and is posing for the press with the latest Asian supermodel.

Still, the chapter about Shakira is quite beautiful; when writing about his wife, Caine displays something suspiciously like talent. It is odd that the creator of the greatest slut in the British cinema can only come to life on the rather sticky wicket of monogamous sexual love.

31 October 1992

BE ABSOLUTE FOR DEATH

Hugh Massingberd

As I clambered out of a taxi outside the Royal Marsden in the Fulham Road I rather regretted that it was no longer called the 'Cancer Hospital'. I had come to hear the results of some tests and wanted to play the scene for all it was worth.

Besides sprouting tumours, my head – and more particularly my ears – was ringing with romantic notions of Peter Pan ('To die will be an awfully big adventure') and Charles Stringham in *A Dance to the Music of Time* ('Awfully chic to be killed'). An adolescent image of going down with the *Titanic* as I smoked a reflective cigarette, while the band played 'Nearer, My God, to Thee', gazing steadfastly into the middle distance, having given up my seat in the last lifeboat to a lady I had never met before, remained the perfect fantasy; but I reckoned I was ready to cope with the grittier reality of 'Tell it to me straight, Doc.'

He did. 'These little chaps,' the breezy young specialist told me as he manipulated my head, 'should be gouged out, but they're benign enough.' I felt distinctly deflated. *'But* I'm sorry to say' – my adrenalin started pumping – 'this fellow is malignant.'

Ah, so this was it. How long did I have: six months, a year? What would I do: try to finish, or rather start, that novel, or merely write my own obituary (on the theme of wasted promise), progress from one National Hunt race-course to another; or simply book into Ballymaloe in County Cork, where the breakfasts are ambrosial, for the duration?

My head swam with a glutinous mixture of self-pity and self-esteem. I felt partly inspired by a vision of Great War sacrificial chivalry and partly by the Warholesque notion that such an untimely demise might make me famous for 15 minutes. I am afraid the hideous whinge of *'Now* they'll miss me' came into the cassoulet. Death, I mused, is what you make of it.

To my disappointment, however, the specialist did not give me the death sentence or even tell me to brace myself, but merely made businesslike arrangements as to when the tumours in my head, both malignant and benign, could be cut out. Still, I could console myself with the fact that I *did* have cancer, in however immature a form. In relaying this information to my family and colleagues from the telephone in the hospital corridor, I was careful to underplay it to a degree – while, of course, secretly hoping it dramatically turned out to be much more serious.

The response was gratifying. Champagne, caviar and foie gras were sent round from Fortnum's by kind colleagues from the office. I duly scoffed the lot while planning my funeral (a coach to meet the London train to Lincolnshire and the family vault to be reopened one last time).

So far, so dandy. This was the life, or rather the death. One was the centre of attention, with the rare opportunity to appear to behave bravely and, moreover, one felt fine – which was hardly surprising as there was, in fact, nothing terminally wrong with me. It was only the trauma of the operation, which removed the tumours, that finally brought me to my senses.

I felt a fraud, a Walter Mitty, and thoroughly ashamed of myself. It was all very well hoping it might turn out to be terminal but how would I have coped if it really had been? Would I have turned 'yellow', as in that old James Cagney film where the anti-hero starts screaming on the way to the electric chair, 'I don't want to die, I don't want to die'? Or would I have faced up to it calmly and courageously?

For all my immature silliness, I genuinely wanted to find out, and the episode set me thinking about death and our attitudes towards it. In Victorian times, death, and all the rituals attending upon it, became something of a fetish, whereas sex was unmentionable. Today, the situation has been reversed and death has become the last taboo. (An indication of this is the way Remembrance Sunday, which falls at the weekend, has gradually been played down by Church and State. The rot set in when the traffic ceased to stop at 11.00 on Armistice Day, 11 November, whatever day of the week it fell. I remember one bearded vicar in the 1960s observing that the names on the village war memorial represented 'increasingly shadowy figures'; an irate parishioner muttered that Jesus must be getting pretty shadowy by now.)

Nowadays, instead of death, people invoke the dreary euphemism 'health'; hence the health fascism which dictates that we must not smoke, drink or eat fatty, fried foods, and that we must take exercise. Why? For the sake of our 'health', which is code for the bran-filled gauleiters' terror of death. The only light relief from this orthodoxy comes when one of their number collapses and dies out jogging – which happens with gratifying regularity.

Similarly, the obsession with appearing to be young, fostered by the marketing men, is another manifestation of this dread of dying. Not so long ago, it seemed that only in the materialistic, ultimately childish society of America did the urge to reverse the ageing process hold such desperate sway and that we could afford to snigger from this side of the Atlantic. Not any longer. Cosmetic surgery – why not a little tuck there, a 'saddle job' here? – has become big business in Britain and is taken (deadly) seriously. And not only by women. 'I'm getting my bags done,' I overheard one thrusting, not-so-young media figure confide in another. Presumably he referred to his eyes rather than his scrotum, but I wouldn't like to bet on it.

The battle against cellulite and sagging flesh is waged with passionate commitment; fat is hoovered away by liposuction; even old men with prostate trouble seek to prolong their sexual athleticism. 'He whose lust lasts, lasts longest,' as the lubricious doctor observes in Alan Bennett's farce *Habeas Corpus*. But it's no good, you silly boobies, we are all doomed (as Private Fraser used to warn in *Dad's Army*), we are all going to die. There is no escape.

The modern tendency, what psychologists call denial, is to avert our eyes, and thus our minds, from death.

For as the Matron observes in *Forty Years On*, another of Alan Bennett's masterpieces: 'Who now dies at home? Who sees death? We sicken and fade in a hospital ward, and dying is for doctors with a phone call to the family.' The medics have become all-powerful, often needlessly prolonging life with technology in an unthinking manner that has only served to fuel calls for official euthanasia (the old, unofficial practice exercised, without fuss, by decent family doctors had much to recommend it). But then the euthanasia movement itself could be said to be an anti-death crusade, born out of fear on the one hand and a desire to subvert God's will on the other.

Whereas the Victorians were surrounded by death – with high infant mortality rates and any amount of incurable diseases – we are becoming increasingly distanced from it. As a recent survey indicated, people are now living, on average, some 30 years longer than they did when Queen Victoria was on the throne. The Buckingham Palace flunkeys must be working overtime in sending out telegrams – sorry, 'telemessages' – to centenarians.

Death has become sanitised, brushed under the carpet. How many dead bodies do we see? As the photographer Rudolf Schafer has pointed out, 'Many people today don't know what a dead person looks like. In modern society we are separated from the event of death . . . We are constantly bombarded with newspaper and television pictures of catastrophes and wars – violent, extreme pictures – but we defuse one of the implications of those images – our own mortality – with the thought that nothing so extreme can happen to us.' It is something which happens to other people, an unpleasant and embarrassing thought which we try to banish from our minds. I remember being at a loss for words when an elderly aunt confided in me, 'I just long to die.' And a friend whose mother was killed in a motor accident told me she remembers noticing people crossing the street to avoid her.

The trouble is that we don't know how to behave around death any more. The bereaved are often longing to talk about the person they have lost but it is the one subject which their interlocutors shy away from mentioning. We seek to justify our reticence on the shaky ground that it might prove too upsetting to the bereaved, though in reality it is our own selfish cowardice.

And while we pride ourselves on having grown away from stuffy old customs in other respects, we fall back on the most strait-laced behaviour when confronted with the rituals of death. Our letters of sympathy are couched in formulaic pious platitudes ('He will be greatly missed') and our facial expressions at funerals are set in a ghastly genteel simper – what one cynical clergyman describes as 'that caring Communion look'. Death is natural enough, so why can't we conduct ourselves naturally in its presence?

In what struck me as a touching, natural gesture, an American friend popped a personal letter to her father into his coffin, but her pompous brother was outraged. Such things, apparently, are just not done. So, with our compassionate features carefully arranged, we sit on the pews while a parson who probably hardly knew 'the loved one' stumbles over an excruciatingly dull *curriculum vitae* which reminds one of nothing so much as a leaving speech at school – 'He was in the Torpid rugger XV'.

Once in a blue moon, a genuine friend of the deceased will ascend the pulpit and dare to recall the dead man as a human being with foibles which evoke a glow of affection, even exasperated affection. I went to such a requiem the other day and found myself laughing uproariously during the address. But when I looked around I saw frowning faces in the congregation: evidently laughter, in their eyes, is out of place in the Valley of Death.

Those who have made the final journey would, I suspect, surely prefer to be remembered with warmth and smiles than cold, monumental panegyrics. Yet the view persists that it is out of place in obituaries to include jolly anecdotes or jokes that, so to speak, bring the subject to life.

I have earned my living as an obituarist for nearly seven years now and it has been a much needed education in dealing with death. Friends and colleagues treat one warily as if one was a ghoul, vampire or a necrophiliac. Their fear of death is expressed in the fact that they never use the d-word itself, but instead a wearisome range of maty slang – 'snuffed it', 'kicked the bucket', 'popped his clogs', 'bought the farm', 'handed in his dinner pail', *et cetera ad nauseam.*

At the outset of my career as an obituarist, I felt uneasy about dealing with undertakers on a daily basis but I soon found them to be a cheery, practical and down-to-earth bunch. 'Would you say that, er, Colonel So-and-So was a, um, tall man?' 'Well now, let me take a peep, sir . . .'

Most of all, I dreaded intruding on the grief of widows. To affect a bogus sympathetic tone *à la* Godfrey ('he shakes hands with your heart') Winn seemed to be the most contemptible trick of all in the odious trade of journalism. Experience has shown me, though, that a simple matter-of-fact approach with a view to giving the subject of the obituary a decent 'send-off' could be not only unintrusive but perhaps beneficial and even therapeutic – part of the process of grieving which makes some sense of death.

Widows and widowers have told me what a relief it is to talk about the person they have lost in a straightforward manner. The hypocritical attitude of *'de mortuis nihil nisi bonum'* (how I would like to get my hands on the blasted Roman who coined that one) merely enshrines the deceased in a haze of sanctity.

Yet to allude to the dead in a conversational way is a much more trustful tribute to their memory. The words of Canon Henry Scott Holland ('Call me by my familiar name. Speak to me in the easy way which you always used. Put no difference into your tone. Wear no forced air of solemnity or sorrow. Laugh as we always laughed at the little jokes we enjoyed together') are deservedly popular at funerals precisely because they strike a genuine chord with the bereaved.

Much of my daily life is spent perusing death notices ('obituaries' as some pretentious undertakers wrongly insist on calling them) and I often wish the ones in the national papers, with their litany of 'suddenly' or 'peacefully', would let themselves go as they do in the provincial press. 'God blinked his eye,' one Ulster announcement went, 'at where you sat.' My favourite, though, remains the late 'Cockie' Hoogterp's correction of a false report that she had died: 'Mrs Hoogterp wishes it to be known that she has not yet been screwed in her coffin.'

'Hasn't your job,' people sometimes ask, 'made you terribly morbid?'

I usually reply that obituaries are not about death but rather a celebration of life, and leave it at that. If I went on to say that, in any event, death is an essential part – indeed the object – of life they would doubtless make their excuses and leave.

Fear of death is, of course, the best means of *not* enjoying life. As the Duke says in *Measure for Measure*, 'Be absolute for death; either death or life shall thereby be the sweeter . . .'

So don't bore me by telling me that I might die if I eat this egg, bacon, sausage, kidneys and black pudding on my plate. Naturally, I am going to die, but I will damn well enjoy myself while I am alive.

In the meantime, however, I might just pop round to see the specialist again. New growths seem to be popping up on my head. Maybe, as the song goes in *Cabaret*, this time I'll win.'

Hugh Massingberd is obituaries editor of the Daily Telegraph.

7 November 1992

THE ANATOMY OF PUBLICITY

Anthony Sampson

I have been revisiting the British power structure for a new version of my *Anatomy of Britain*, which was first published 30 years ago. At the outset, I wondered which single factor has most transformed the British scene, and now I have little doubt: it is publicity.

Thirty years ago the landscape of British power looked like a dark forest with a few narrow, well trodden paths and some shafts of daylight which lit up familiar clearings – like parliament, the TUC or the Institute of Directors. Most of the important denizens, including bankers, company chairmen and all civil servants, were almost invisible.

The City was only revealed by impersonal columnists on the city pages or a few raffish tipsters. The Governor of the Bank of England, Cameron Cobbold, informed me that he never gave interviews. Big companies replied to enquiries with anonymous letters warning that 'all communications should be addressed to the secretary'.

A few exhibitionist bosses, like Sir Bernard Docker of BSA, Sir Miles Thomas of Morris Motors or Jack Cotton, the property tycoon, were much publicised and photographed; but serious investors assumed – usually rightly – that publicity was the prelude to disaster.

The dark forest was much more fun for a journalist or anatomist to explore: you could evade the PR men, who were still thin on the ground, simply by writing direct to the bosses, who were often glad that anyone wanted to talk to them. When I tracked down the master-financier Harley Drayton, who controlled the biggest television company and a chain of newspapers, I found a rugged man in country boots who quoted the Bible and was delighted to have a chat. He was so little known that when he died a few years later a reporter from one of his newspapers had to rely on me for his obituary.

Politicians of course were public property, but they were much more unwary and unrehearsed before the coming of the tape-recorder. I still have my bulky old Grundig, and when I tried it out recently I heard the voice of Hugh Gaitskell, who was leader of the Labour Party in 1962, crackling out of an old tape: 'What a remarkable machine: I've never seen one of these.'

Today it's all so different: floodlights everywhere, manned by skilled

PR men who can lure journalists into well prepared encounters or train company chairmen to appear on television to push up the share price. Businessmen feel they don't really exist until they appear on television. Everyone from the Queen to the Governor of the Bank of England has their PR offices.

Even the civil servants have crept out from the undergrowth. Last month, a new book called *The Whitehall Companion* was published giving photographs, telephone numbers and details of senior officials in every department. It's introduced by the prince of secrecy, the Cabinet Secretary Sir Robin Butler, who praises its contribution to open government, 'to help you to find your way round the bureaucratic jungle'.

The police are determined to compete with their fictional counterparts on television, dramatising themselves with programmes like *Crimewatch* and alerting the press to the arrest of a celebrity like Kevin Maxwell. I had an early warning of the police media-mania 20 years ago, after I had written to the Commissioner, Sir Robert Mark, for an interview. He rang back to ask, 'Will you come to me, or shall I come to you?' He became so addicted to publicity that after he retired he began appearing on television commercials.

The machinery of publicity makes the pursuit less fun. Thirty years ago even Number 10 was pleasantly informal: when I wrote to Harold Macmillan for an interview his press chief, Harold Evans, rang up the next day and suggested a drink in three days' time. When I wrote to John Mayor, I eventually received a reply to say that the interview had been approved by the diary conference, I must submit a list of questions and a date would be negotiated.

Television has changed everything. The late Peter Jenkins used to say, 'Politics is television'; and some politicians seem hardly to exist off the screen. All are ready with the careful soundbites designed to be broadcast over and over without causing embarrassment.

So if there's so much publicity, why do we still know so little about what's going on? The first answer is obvious: that's not what publicity is for. It doesn't produce daylight but arc-lights which show up the good bits and leave the rest still darker. The more the forest is cleared, the more the PR men can provide their own scenery.

But there's another answer: the journalists have themselves joined the show. No profession has been more changed by publicity than the publiciser's. Three decades ago all the *Times*'s reports were anonymous, no serious journalist had his photograph in his paper, and very few appeared on television. Journalists hardly ever wrote about other journalists until they were dead.

Now the reader can't escape from them, whether they're praising, attacking, interviewing or suing each other; and they generate each other's stories. Celebrity journalism, as the Americans call it, has no need for news outside the magic circle. BBC reporters are always happiest interviewing other BBC reporters, preferably about the BBC. And by the time the broadsheets with their endless 'media pages' have finished writing about Rupert Murdoch, Andrew Neil, Selina Scott or Tina Brown there's not much space left for other news.

The politicians have become more fascinated by the media than the media are fascinated by politics, and the Palace of Westminster begins to look like a waiting-room or rehearsal-room for the television programmes. When one minister was asked how Major's Cabinet meetings compared with Mrs Thatcher's, he replied it was like being interviewed by David Frost after Jeremy Paxman. That just about sums it all up.

As for books, the original medium, their success now depends on all the other media, as Madonna realises. When the first *Anatomy of Britain* was published, I fled to South Africa the week before and never said a word about it on radio or television – which did not stop it selling 150,000 copies in hardback. In the Sixties, an author could still bid his work goodbye to make its own way in the world, like Chaucer's *Troilus*: 'Go, litil book . . .'

Now any litil book which wants to be famous has to be accompanied by the author through every kind of talk-show, interview, scandal and confession, together with outrageous views about everything except the subject of the book, and if possible revelations of the author's sex-life. And now I must go out and publicise my litil book . . .

7 November 1992

POP MUSIC

THE RAPPERS RAPPED

Marcus Berkmann

Pop music reflects its time, and no current genre seems more of its time than rap music. The brutal rhythms, the strutting arrogance of its performers, the baseball caps turned backward – it's hard to know what's worse. As a result, anyone over the age of 25 who says he likes rap music is either a) lying; b) a record company executive, and so probably lying anyway; c) a rock critic, but that is the rock critic's particular and terrifying fate, to be borne alone and in silence; or d) a professional rapper. You may like mainstream music, may tolerate heavy metal in short bursts, you may even quite like disco versions of theme tunes from computer games – but if you can shave, rap will almost certainly remain beyond you. It's youth rebellion, class rebellion and race rebellion all whipped up into one indigestible whole.

But at least you and I can hate rap with honesty and gusto, and without the remotest vestige of shame. For others it's much harder. The white liberal rock establishment, for whom rebellion is an ingrained part of pop's appeal, feel that they must find it within themselves to like rap music, or at least to approve of it. The conditions in those inner city ghettoes are, well, disgraceful. The only problem is that many young rap-persons tend to espouse opinions that, if one were to be charitable, don't entirely tally with those of white rap fans. Many rappers are, after all, young American black males with large baseball bats, prone to profoundly illiberal sentiments. For a while the fashion was to speak of women as mere chattels and vessels, and only last year the 2 Live Crew released an album which included tracks called 'Pop That Pussy' and 'Up A Girl's Ass', amongst others that are too repellent even to think about. More recently, racial hatred has appeared on the menu, as Public Enemy and others have freely associated with antisemites. Listening to a white middle-class rap fan trying to defend all this has come to provide matchless dinner party entertainment for rap-haters.

Suddenly, though, the stakes have now been raised. Encouraged by the rock establishment's prevaricating, rappers have now started talking in serious and heartfelt terms of the benefits of killing policemen.

Indeed, virtually every rapper worthy of the name now feels obliged to include at least one song on each album advocating the wholesale slaughter of plods, and if it can be shown that he's actually 'dusted off' a few at some point in the past, so much the better. Ice-T's wittily titled 'Cop Killer' sparked off an enormous row earlier this year, which naturally sold vast quantities of records, and now it is the turn of someone called 2pac Amaru Shakar, a Californian rapper of unequivocal opinions. 2pac's mother was a Black Panther militant and his father was shot dead shortly after leaving jail, but now he's in real trouble. A young fan of his was caught speeding along Highway 59 in a stolen car and promptly shot the arresting officer. Unfortunately, it turned out that he was listening to one of 2pac's most recent efforts on his tape machine. 'Cops on my tail,' rapped 2pac, 'So I bail till I dodge them/Remember Rodney King/And I bust his punk ass/Now I got a murder case . . . /What the fuck would you do?/Drop them or let them drop you?/I choose droppin' the cop.'

Oh dear. For this tiny indiscretion has led, as most things in America seem to lead, to a multi-million dollar court case. The policeman's widow is suing the record company and the distribution company, Time Warner, for $100 million, while the young murderer is planning to plead for leniency, claiming he was unduly influenced by the music.

Of course, other acts have been sued in the past for similar 'offences', but most of them were dim heavy metal bands who had inadvertently said something nice about Beelzebub. This is different. Suddenly, all those fine sentiments about freedom of speech are looking mildly redundant. The widow is said to have a good case, and if that's not bad enough, police pension funds have threatened to sell huge quantities of Time Warner stock unless matters improve. The rap world is reportedly aghast. For the dedicated rap hater, though, it's as though Christmas has come early: the sound of bucks being passed and petards being hoisted is music to our ears. And it's not rap music to our ears, either.

7 November 1992

HOW TO BE A REBEL

Nigel Nicolson

Not many people can isolate a single moment which they call central to their lives, but I can. It was at 10 p.m. on 8 November 1956, when I sat silent in the library of the House of Commons while all but seven of my Conservative colleagues filed into the lobby in support of Anthony Eden's handling of the Suez crisis. I knew that my abstention could lead to the loss of my seat, as it did, but nothing that I have ever done gives me greater pleasure now. Let that console any young Members who have defied the Whips this week on an issue of equal importance, and now face the consequences in Parliament and in their constituencies. I would not have joined them on this occasion, but I know how they feel.

Although the parliamentary pressures to conform were much the same in 1956, the outside pressures were different. Then it was a vote of confidence in the Government, not a craftily constructed motion, so our rebellion was seen to be all the more disgraceful. There are no emotions aroused by Maastricht comparable to those involved in the Suez operation, when our troops were heavily engaged and our national honour was challenged. There is no mystery about the Maastricht Treaty except its complexity, but in the Suez crisis those of us in Parliament who had had a hint of the Government's collusion with France and Israel, as I had had from William Clark, Eden's press secretary, were pledged to secrecy and could not use in our defence a suspicion, soon to be confirmed as a fact, that would have justified our rebellion and if revealed at the time would undoubtedly have led to the fall of the Government.

Then there was, and is, the loyalty factor. In a constituency like mine, Bournemouth East, many of the stalwarts were men whose careers had been in the armed or colonial services and to whom disloyalty to the leader was the ultimate crime. In calmer times they would probably have agreed that they send a Member to Parliament to use his best judgment in their interests, but in a moment of great crisis Burke's famous distinction between a representative and a delegate is forgotten or turned on its head. One constituent wrote to me,

'You know what the great majority of us think about Suez, yet you spoke and acted against us. In what possible sense, then, can you be called our representative?' It was a reasonable argument which I found difficult to counter among those whose minds were made up. It was undeniable, as Harold Macmillan replied when asked for his opinion, that if an Association loses confidence in its Member, they have every right to change him for another candidate at the next election. Of the eight Suez rebels only two, Robert Boothby and Edward Boyle, survived politically.

It seems unlikely that the Maastricht rebels will suffer the same fate. There are more of them and they have massive support outside. But if they are seriously challenged in their constituencies, let them call a primary election, such as we held in Bournemouth in 1959 with the support of Lord Hailsham, then Chairman of the Party. Every member of my Association was invited to take part in a postal ballot to decide whether they wished me to remain their MP; 7,433 votes were returned, and I lost by 91. I reflected (but that was some time afterwards) that if I had won by 91 it would have been much worse.

One final tip to rebels: always have a second profession in reserve.

7 November 1992

CITY AND SUBURBAN

TIP FROM HONG KONG

Christopher Fildes

Safely returned, I can now disclose the secret purpose of my flight to the Far East. I was not, as you might think, simply swanning around the Temple of Heaven or getting some shirts made. These activities were mere cover. I noted the significant sequence of deals in which Hong Kong's leading companies have bought British – Hutchison Whampoa going for Felixstowe Dock, Dickson Concepts for Harvey Nichols, Hongkong Land for Trafalgar House, the Hongkong Bank group for the Midland. It was time, I thought, to bring this trend to its logical conclusion. I therefore arrived with proposals for Hong Kong to take over the United Kingdom. For Hong Kong, itself confronted with a takeover bid from China, this riposte would come straight out of the textbooks, where it is called the Poison Pill Defence. In this, the target company swallows something to make itself indigestible. For the UK, the attractions are of another order. How happily the Treasury would merge its overstretched finances with Hong Kong's, knowing that Hong Kong has no national debt, only a national honeypot! How we might all hope that Hong Kong's growth rate and tax rates and interest rates would rub off on us! How we must wish that we had followed Hong Kong's example and tied our currency, not to the mark but to the dollar! Better still not to put that shirt on any one horse, but since that horse is improving, we might stay with it for a while. Reorganisation would be kept to a minimum. Christopher Patten would remain Governor, but, like the top brass of the Hongkong Bank, would relocate to London, probably to Downing Street. The post of lieutenant-governor (or *taipan*) would rotate among the Keswick family. Signing accounts at the Ritz would be honoured at the Mandarin. UK plc would find itself part of a free trade area next door to the world's fastest growing economy. Await the offer for UK and do not dispose of your shares.

14 November 1992

ANOTHER VOICE

WE HAVE LOOKED IN AMAZEMENT ON THE UNEARTHLY AND FOUND IT COMMONPLACE

Charles Moore

'The case of the Church of England at this moment is a very dismal one, and almost leaves men to choose between a broken heart and no heart at all.' So wrote Gladstone to Lord Lyttelton in 1850. The occasion was the Gorham judgment. The Revd G. C. Gorham had been presented to the living of Brampford Speke, but his Bishop, Phillpotts of Exeter, had refused to institute him, on the grounds that he was unsound on the doctrine of baptismal regeneration. Gorham took the case to law, and eventually the judicial committee of the Privy Council decided in his

*'I distinctly remember the brochure saying this is
where the gods chose to live.'*

favour. There was outrage among High Churchmen that doctrine should
be settled by the civil authorities. Several, including the future Cardinal
Manning, went over to Rome. Gladstone agonised, but stayed.

I thought of this long-dead dispute when I heard last Wednesday
evening that the General Synod of the Church of England had decided
by two votes to pass legislation allowing women to be ordained priests.
Strictly speaking, the comparison does not work, for the argument
here is not about temporal power in spiritual matters. The Synod's
members were exercising what the parson in the Somerset church I
attended on Sunday called their 'democratic rights', and Parliament's
opinion will only be invited afterwards and will not be invited on the
principle at all. But there is an emotional similarity between the cases.

First, there is the sheer absurdity of all ecclesiastical controversies.
What on earth (or, more to the point, in heaven) did it matter what
the vicar of Brampford Speke thought about baptismal regeneration?
What does it matter that a Church body meeting in Westminster has
said that a thousand or two Englishwomen can call themselves priests?
Surely the great truths that Jesus taught and the love He bestowed
upon the human race rise above all such stuff?

One shares such exasperation, until one follows its logic through. If no Church dispute matters, then no Church matters, and if no Church matters then religion becomes no more than what any individual chooses to make it. Many believe exactly that. But to me it seems a recipe for solipsism and madness. A Church is the greatest of all human institutions, and for the reason that it is not merely a human institution; so its fate matters to humanity.

In this particular case, it matters most to that part of humanity which is English, and to the millions in other parts of the world whose churches have grown from the English root. And because I am English, and for more personal reasons as well, it matters to me. Like many others, I have about 18 months (the time before the legislation comes into force) to decide what to do.

In assessing the consequences of women's ordination, one can be reasonably confident that the *appearance* of the national Church will not change very much. Large, though steadily declining numbers of people will marry in its buildings and be buried or burned according to its rites. The Queen, though she is said to oppose women priests, will bear the indignity as she has borne so many others, and continue as Supreme Governor. Bishops will still sit in the House of Lords (for as long as there is a House of Lords), and the Archbishop of Canterbury, even if he is a she, will crown the new monarch (assuming we have one). People who do not know what their religion is will still put 'Church of England' on forms which demand an answer.

It is also possible, obviously, that everyone will come to accept women priests. It may become clear that something which the universal Church has not countenanced throughout its entire existence is indeed a natural development of what it has always believed. The chief arguments that one hears for women's ordination – that women can 'do the job' just as well as men, that many women feel 'deep hurt' that they cannot be priests, that the Church should fit in with public opinion and the spirit of the age – only serve to make me more bigoted in my opposition. But it surely is odd to assert that women *cannot* be priests. If Rome and the Orthodox and the Anglican Communion all agreed that they could be, I should be surprised, but I should hardly feel that I had any right to hold out against it.

So there is a chance that, after a painful period, the Church of England, invigorated by a new spirituality, will show the way for the whole of Catholic Christianity and Dr George Carey will be up there in the big league with St Paul and St Augustine.

But I do rather doubt it. For the historic achievement of the Church of England has been to develop an institution which is part of the universal in its understanding of divine truth, but national and particular in its political and cultural manifestations. It has been as if, when Christ gave the keys of the kingdom to Peter, He allowed a special version to be cut which would loose the complicated mortice which locks in the English heart. Thanks to this infinitely subtle adaptation to time and place, Archdeacon Grantly was able to step into the shoes of the fisherman. It is a comic idea almost, but it is also a very touching one, and I have believed it.

Now I wonder whether I can any more. For the vote by the Synod declares that the universal understanding of all Christian history can be overturned by a majority of those worthy middle-class, middle-aged persons who have the time to play the politics of deanery and diocese, and it therefore suggests that that majority is happy to cut itself off from that history and that universality in favour of its own beliefs and preoccupations. Such people have the power, foolishly ceded to them by Parliament in 1974, to decide what the Church of England is. They appear to have decided that it will be a sect. If that is the case, the person who wants to be a member of the whole Church must leave.

But an even more melancholy prospect confronts the Catholic Anglican. It is that the edifice which he thought he knew and loved was always built on sand. Newman came to that view, and he expressed it thus, in lectures delivered in response to the Gorham judgment:

> If, indeed, we dress it [the Church of England] up in an ideal form, as if it were something real . . . as if it were in deed and not only in name a Church, then indeed we may feel interest in it, and reverence towards it, and affection for it, as men have fallen in love with pictures, or knights in romance do battle for high dames whom they have never seen . . . But at length, either the force of circumstances or some unexpected accident dissipates it; and, as in fairy tales, the magic castle vanishes when the spell is broken, and nothing is seen but the wild heath, the barren rock, and the forlorn sheep-walk, so it is with regards to the Church of England, when we look in amazement on that we thought so unearthly and find so commonplace or worthless.

I hope that is not what I am about to discover. It is particularly sad to think that, if I do, I shall not be able to bring up my children in what I had thought was their chief privilege in being English. Anyway, we all have 18 months. Is there a Roman Catholic priest who can help me make up my mind?

21 November 1992

TELEVISION

HOUSE OF FRAUDS

Martyn Harris

It is the purpose of ritual to dignify the expedient, and nowhere more so than in the House of Lords, whose only function these days is to stand in the way of something more sensible. The Lords is all about ritual, most of it risible, but it is almost impossible to take the piss out of, as Denis Healey found in his first day as a new boy (*Cutting Edge*, Channel 4, Monday, 9 p.m.). 'Wotcher mate,' he boomed to a flunkey, before switching accents from Hackney to Leeds. 'Ah've coom to see Black Rod.' But in minutes he had become a solemn student of flummery, rehearsing his initiation under Garter King of Arms.

'Now the bow is a head bow, not from the waist. And you must be six paces back from the supporting peer.'

'And I do the first bow where? Here?' said Healey.

'No, no, no,' said Garter, with the weary tolerance of a kindergarten teacher coaching the school Nativity play. 'In the middle here. Facing the throne.'

What better metaphor could you have for social assimilation than this? one wonders. An ex-communist, and ex-Labour Chancellor, bobbing and bowing to the bidding of a scarlet-nosed old fraud in a frogged coat. And what better proof could you ever have of Ezra Pound's taunt at the corruption of the professional politician: 'We are six hundred beefy men (but mostly gas and suet)'?

The governing image of this fine documentary was the public school where, indeed, most of the 1,200 peers had begun their careers (400 of them at Eton). There were the shared coat-pegs in the lobbies, the solid Victorian ugliness of the building, the petty humiliations of a hundred inscrutable customs. And just as a school is ruled by its janitors and stokers, so the real power in the Lords lay in the hands of lackeys like Black Rod, whose main function was control of car-park passes and of the tea-room waitress, courted by the noble peers for her cream-filled éclairs.

'They do the most marvellous tea,' Lord Teviot enthused. 'Tea-cakes and crumpets in winter, muffins, toast and sandwiches . . . and the *naughtiest* cakes.' With his floppy grey fringe and sellotaped spectacles, Lord Teviot was the star of the show: a perfect specimen of that cultivated idiocy which is the armour of the upper class.

'How did you get to be in the House of Lords?' an interviewer asked him.

'Well, um, because my father died,' said Lord Teviot, after some thought.

'And what did you do before the Lords?'

'Oh, um, various things. Nothing terribly special. I went to Eton. Then I went to Spain for three months . . . worked on the Brighton buses for six months. Then the bacon counter at Sainsbury's.' For visiting the Lords he gets £29 a day attendance allowance, £29 secretarial allowance plus travel and overnight stay expenses. 'I can't say how much it comes to. I'm not good at sums, but it's usually a nice surprise at the end of the month.'

As he submitted his expenses another formidable lackey cross-questioned him: 'I see you have claimed for today, my Lord. You *have* been in the chamber, haven't you?'

'Ooh yes. Though I can't think what I listened to at the moment. It will come to me in two seconds.'

Of course the Lords has a serious constitutional function, as Lord St John of Fawsley would remind us – namely to delay and to advise. The Lib Dem peer Lord Russell was conscientiously engaged in just such an activity, which would have provided extra money for people in bed and breakfast hostels. To everyone's astonishment he won his vote against the Government. To nobody's astonishment the Government ignored it completely.

21 November 1992

YOUR PROBLEMS SOLVED

DEAR MARY . . .

Mary Killen

Q. I wonder if you can solve a predicament which occurred during a recent interlude abroad? A lady hotel guest asked if I was on holiday. I replied that I was, but that it was a business trip for my boyfriend who was with me. As his and my combined ages reach over a century, he found this embarrassing and said I could have used a different way to describe him. Neither of us could think of anything suitable. Lover might have implied I frequently went abroad with sundry men; partner could have referred to a business relationship, and our sharing a room might have indicated the business was doing badly; and husband was out of the question because we talked to each other throughout dinner. Can you give him a suitable title? I would be grateful.

F. B., London

A. I recently looked into this subject in some depth, examining all the descriptive possibilities for 'boy-friends'. I concluded that almost all the options were unacceptable, particularly the word 'partner'. One can joke to friends that one is now 'romantically linked, as they say in the tabloids', but in the scenario you mention you might have described your elderly boyfriend to the lady hotel guest as 'my unofficial fiance'. A conspiratorial wink enacted as you said these words would have ensured that she did not ask him any embarrassing questions about wedding dates.

Q. May I pass on a solution to you readers? I was recently pressed to make a decision about a certain social invitation by a certain time of day and agreed that I would do so, but when that time came round I was not ready to give my answer. Basically I was bet-hedging and trying to decide which of two invitations I had for the night in question would be the better one. Meanwhile the call was about to come through and I knew I had to say yes or no. So what did I do? Speaking in a high-pitched and unnatural voice, I recorded the following message into my answerphone: 'Sorry. All lines to the Carmarthen exchange are temporarily out of service. Please try later.' With the aid of a tape-recorder, I was able to make this message come continuously out of the outgoing message tape. It worked a treat. Neither hostess suspected a thing and I was able to make the (correct) decision at leisure.

Anon

A. Thank you very much for taking the trouble to pass this tip on to other *Spectator* readers.

21 November 1992

ANOTHER VOICE

AN EXPOSITION OF THE BENEFITS OF CULTURALLY INSENSITIVE CATHOLICISM

Auberon Waugh

Whether one liked her or not, Andrea Dworkin cut a strangely moving figure when she defended the American notion of Political Correctness – nowadays called Cultural Sensitivity – a few weeks ago at the Oxford Union. Sincere to the point of tearfulness, she ignored all the repressive aspects of political correctness – its denial of free speech, civil rights, logic, linguistic clarity, common sense or any of the other instruments of male oppression which it has singled out. Instead she identified 'political correctness' as an avoidance of such 'hate-words' as 'nigger', when applied to an Afro-American schoolgirl, an avoidance of genocide (she believed 200 million 'native Americans' had been massacred by the white settlers) and vague opposition to a system whereby the non-white, poor majority was endlessly exploited and gagged by the rich, white minority. It was the sort of stuff that brings the roof down in almost any campus theatre the length and breadth of the Union, but at Oxford the undergraduates contented themselves with looking more impenetrable and goofier than usual, before voting Dworkin politely back to America.

Obese to the point of freakishness, unattractively dressed in ill-fitting workman's trousers, stupid, ignorant, self-pitying and (as the

Americans say) full of shit, she cut an undeniably heroic figure in the Oxford Union, enumerating what to her and her friends were self-evident truths: even if they could be disproved by the costlier information bases and crude logic of rich, white males, they must yet surely have carried some sort of prayer to heaven by virtue of her obvious sincerity.

If I say I detected the same sort of heroism, the same sort of sincerity last week in Charles Moore's cry of pain against the ordination of women in the Church of England, I hope nobody will misunderstand me. Charles is not obese, I have never seen him in workman's clothes, he is not stupid, ignorant or self-pitying. Of all the Dworkin properties, as I say, heroism and sincerity are the two that shine out. The sincerity is quite worrying enough.

After the Synod vote on the ordination of women, Charles concludes: 'They appear to have decided that it will be a sect. If that is the case, the person who wants to be a member of the whole Church must leave . . . Is there a Roman Catholic priest who can help me make up my mind?'

There are a few misunderstandings here which need to be cleared up. In the first place, it is only the Anglicans who see themselves as members of the Catholic church. They may believe that 'when Christ gave the keys of the kingdom to Peter, He allowed a special version to be cut which would loose the complicated mortice which locks in the English heart'. Charles finds this idea touching, I find it smug, twee and rather nauseating. Outside High Church rectories and seminaries, everybody else sees the High Anglican phenomenon as a sect within a sect. Nothing wrong with that, of course. Perhaps Charles supposes that when Dr Carey starts laying his hands on women (I wonder if Dworkin would let him get away with it) in order to make 'priests' of them, the Apostolic Succession will be broken. But does he seriously imagine that by the same mistaken gestures Carey will be making the Pope infallible, the wine and bread at Roman Catholic masses transubstantiate? Both these propositions are involved in joining the Roman Catholics as Charles tantalisingly suggests he might.

He intimates that if the Catholic and Orthodox churches agree to ordain women he, Charles Moore, will not hold out against them on behalf of the High Anglican faction. But what if he joins the RCs, only to find them going one way, the Orthodox churches the other? I would be surprised if the Roman Catholics could hold out against the tide for more than 20 years. A poll of 300 RC priests conducted by the *Tablet* last week revealed 31 per cent in favour of female ordinations, 15 per cent 'don't know'. In America, the figures are much worse. If ever – heaven forbid – we have an American Pope, they will be canonising pet animals within a month.

A little study of Church history should discourage too much pomposity about this or any other subject. In Addis and Arnold's splendid *A Catholic Dictionary* (1884) the matter is stated clearly enough:

> Women are incapable of being validly ordained, in as much as both the healthy natural instincts of mankind and positive Apostolic injunction (1 Cor. xiv 34; 1 Tim. ii 11) require that women should be 'silent in the churches'.

The entry goes on to explain that ordained deaconesses, although entitled to make any amount of noise in church when reading homilies or gospels before the congregation, are not properly ordained – any more than female choir members are. 1 Cor. xiv 34 reveals the familiar passage, forbidding women to speak in church – 'And if they will learn anything, let them ask their husbands at home.' 1 Tim. ii 11 is even more specific: 'Let the women sit in silence with all subjection. But I suffer not a woman to teach, nor to usurp authority over men, but to be in silence.'

The moment Christianity abandoned these precepts might have been a good moment to join the Muslims. Then, just across the page from 1 Tim. ii 11, the eye falls on 1 Tim. iii 2–4, Paul on bishops:

> A bishop then must be blameless, the husband of one wife, vigilant, sober, of good behaviour, given to hospitality, apt to teach; not given to wine, no striker, not greedy of filthy lucre; but patient; not a brawler, not covetous. One that ruleth well his own house, having his children in subjection with all gravity.

As we all know, both the Catholic and Orthodox churches forbid bishops to marry at all. In this they both defy St Paul's injunction, and have done so for about 1,500 years. It is all very well to say that the clerical celibacy is a matter of Church discipline, while the injunction for women to be silent in church is a matter of unalterable truth, but there is nothing in the text to support such a view, and one may doubt whether it is capable of such an interpretation.

Whatever pompous faces we choose to make at each other, the issue of Anglican ordination of women is a storm in a teacup. I think Charles Moore would be wasting a Roman Catholic priest's time, if he insisted on seeking advice from that quarter. All religion with him, I suspect, is a celebration of his Englishness, possibly connected to certain frissons he experienced in Eton College chapel, and an overwhelming feeling that foreigners have nothing to teach us. If he really wishes to open his mind to the attractions of western Catholicism, I suggest he spends an hour or so with Dr Carey, or with the Revd Tony Higton, an Essex vicar and member of the C of E Synod, who has taken over the J. C. Flannel Godspot on the *Sun*. The new English are pretty dreadful people, for the most part, when all is said and done.

28 November 1992

DIARY

Dominic Lawson

How very unwise of Mr Norman Lamont to have taken on the banks. No sooner had our incautious Chancellor announced that he would investigate the way the banks have failed to pass on the full benefit of his interest-rate cuts to borrowers than details of his National Westminster Access account debts became mysteriously and embarrassingly public. And those details meshed neatly with the revelations that the tax-payer had unwittingly contributed £4,700 to Mr Lamont's costs in evicting a 'sex therapist' (delightful euphemism) from his London flat. It is a tribute to the way in which the tabloid press is now dictating public debate in this country – on the monarchy downwards – that such trivia should decide whether or not Mr Lamont is deemed fit for his job. We should rather take our cue – as does Mr Samuel Brittan of the *Financial Times* – from the respected periodical *Central Banking*. In its autumn issue, *Central Banking* has attempted to discover exactly how much the Treasury blew permanently and irrecoverably on its hopelessly ignorant defence of the pound's parity with the deutschmark on Wednesday 16 September. The figure is close to £3 billion, which loss, says the magazine, is 'just as if Norman Lamont had personally thrown entire hospitals and schools into the sea all afternoon'. Or, put another way, it is a sum which would not only

'Let's play soldiers!'

comfortably have covered Mr Lamont's legal fees, but also his Access overdraft and, for that matter, the overdraft on every Access account in Britain.

Mr Lamont is not the only notable suffering harassment by National Westminster Bank's credit card bloodhounds. Another is Sir Stephen Spender. The great poet has sent me a letter he received from National Westminster's card service department. It begins 'Dear Sir Spender . . .' (If you say that quickly, you get Nat West's little joke). 'Sir Spender', claims the bank, is in arrears on his credit card to the tune of £23, and thus is to be served with 'a default notice under Section 87 (1) of the Consumer Credit Act 1974'. Among the dire legal threats heaped upon the head of 'Sir Spender' by the bank if he does not cough up, is that 'any points awarded to you under our air miles scheme will be withdrawn'. So there. 'Sir Spender' tells me he has replied as follows:

> Dear Sir. For utterly ridiculous letters this is hard to beat. To save yourself and myself all this trouble, all you need do is arrange that monies in one account of mine which is in credit are paid into the other one to which they are owing.

What an elegant solution. I am passing on a copy of 'Sir Spender's' letter to Mr Lamont, in case the same idea has not yet crossed the Chancellor's fertile financial mind.

There are interests other than the banks which it is unwise to take on. The Metropolitan Police for a start. But I am sorely tempted. One morning in mid-October I parked my car in Clarendon Street, SW1. Like most parts of central London this is a road liberally sprinkled with yellow lines and residents' parking spaces. I have a resident's parking permit for that area, but on this occasion it would not have been necessary: I spied a four-yards-long length of kerb which was undefiled by any prohibitive or exclusive marking. There I neatly parked my car. On my return I found it had been clamped. It was necessary to pay £60 to the police in order to free the vehicle. Naturally I complained, pointing out that the car was parked legally. After over a month's deliberation the Met has finally replied. Policewoman Mrs D. Farley has written to me, politely saying, 'Although there is a gap in the yellow line approximately four yards . . . where the local authority originally intended the line to exist, the parking restrictions still apply.' We Londoners are in deep waters now. Not only do we have to avoid parking on yellow lines, we must also avoid parking on imaginary yellow lines. Doubtless we shall soon be suffering on-the-spot means-tested fines for going through imaginary red lights, for failing to stop for pedestrians at imaginary zebra crossings, for driving the wrong way down imaginary one-way streets. But I must take my hat off to the girls from the Met: I had never imagined that they were so imaginative.

5 December 1992

LIFE & LETTERS

NEWS FROM NOVEMBER

P. J. Kavanagh

Irregular bangs are going up not very far away, and near the place where I am writing the beaters have just passed, going, 'Prrr, Prrr' and bashing the hedge with their sticks which have bits of white rag attached to them; they are like an army advancing to surrender. It is all slightly disturbing. Most of the bangs, presumably, signal a death. Not that I have much against shooting, and nothing at all against eating pheasant, but those bangs make me restless. The side-roads have been crowded for weeks now with convocations of pheasants standing about in the middle of the road; mostly cocks, for some reason. Have they found a way of ensuring the embryo inside the egg is male? Or is it the way of pheasants, 'forming buggery clubs and sodomite circles', which the late Viscount Montgomery thought would be the case if homosexuality was made legal in the Services. I have always remembered that phrase because it struck me as, um, queer that the Field Marshal should so underestimate the heterosexuality of soldiers.

Anyway, these smartly dressed pheasants stand in the middle of the road, in conversational groups, daring you to run them over, and when you slow down and nose the car among them they are in sudden great alarm but appear to have difficulty taking off. Mostly, they scuttle. But maybe they've learnt a thing or two. 'A thousand pounds a gun' is the mutter in the Green Dragon, the price people pay to join in the fun.

I tried it myself once. At least, I borrowed my father-in-law's 12-bore and went out to shoot pigeons. That seemed reasonable, there were so many of them, they seemed about to take over. But the crafty pigeons always took care to be on the wrong side of the tree, and in desperation I took a pot at a pheasant (a hen, I remember.) It fell out of the air and lay flapping on the ground. For a bad moment I thought I was going to be required to deliver the *coup de grâce*, but then it lay still. I felt that it had been minding its own business, perhaps enjoying itself in a pheasant-like way, and now it was just a lump. I did not give myself credit for my sensitivity, I just thought that changing the status of anything, from alive to dead, was to be avoided if possible. So perhaps that is why those bangs – which have now stopped, not many thousand pounds being paid today – make me uneasy.

Otherwise, I have been thinking that I rather enjoy November, which is now coming to an end. (The thought of December horrifies me. Yesterday, at least four weeks in advance, the sad woman in the tobacconist was wearing a red Father Christmas stocking-cap, trimmed with cotton-wool. This, for some reason – for every reason – reminded me of the other bad sight of the month. The Government documents in the Iraq armaments case appeared on television, and instead of having some sort of reassuring official heading, the letters DTI danced across the top of the page in a mincing logo, like the ridiculous thing on the side of British Telecom vans. And this morning I passed a cardboard box put out for burning, from my publishers, which has printed on it 'PLEASE TURN ME THE OTHER WAY ROUND. "I'M UPSIDE DOWN"'', thus punctuated, which would be funny except that when grown-ups pretend they are in playschool they are either trying to cheat you or are terrified to death.)

However, I enjoy November for several reasons. Some poet, I think it was Thomas Hood, I can't find the poem, made a list of negatives: No-warmth, No-light . . . November. But November is enjoyable for its late dawns, pink and gentle, at least to begin with. Emerson, that steely optimist, said, 'Listen to what the morning says, and believe it', and that first light is usually encouraging, the slate wiped clean by the night. Of course, what follows may be mucky, and there are days when there is no dawn at all, night just thins, without conviction. Well, that's life, and if it makes you particularly lugubrious you can always depress others by pulling on a red Father Christmas cap.

Also, throughout the month the hedges are strewn with necklaces of briony, the berries of which vary, on the same string, from the bright yellow of unripe tomatoes to jade-green, to darkest cherry. It takes time to notice these in the bleakness, you have to get your eye in, but when you do they are a wonder. An American friend once gasped at them, when they were pointed out, and asked why we didn't use them for Christmas decorations. I wondered, too, which was unobservant, because by that time they are wrinkled and their colours dead. Otherwise, in the tobacconist's, they would be tied in bows round the tins of Panatellas.

Fieldfares come in November, erect, soldier-like birds; similar to thrushes, but more richly coloured. They come from Greenland and northern places; this is their Mediterranean, which is also encouraging.

Less so, for me, were two November poetry readings. They usually ask you a year in advance, so it is easy to say yes because the day may never dawn. But it does, even if not noticeably so.

At the first one, in Gloucestershire, there was an audience of two. I told a friend about this – Jaspistos, to drop a distinguished name – and I doubt if he has stopped laughing yet. I dare say it is salutary to be reminded how little one's carefully coded messages are heeded or needed by the outside world. Embarrassment made them all buy the book and I was able to say, 'Page 200', like a schoolmaster. The audience swelled to six in the end and we all huddled in a corner. I asked them why they had come and a girl said, 'When you're grown-up nobody reads to you any more. It's nice to be read to.' I'd never thought of that.

The other reading was at Lincoln, worth it for the sight of the cathedral; it soars, inside and out. More people came to that reading, and at the end a smiling woman asked why I so often mentioned birds. Did I? Didn't everyone? I answered that it was because I thought birds magical, and she carried on nodding and smiling, because poets are expected to say loopy-sounding things like that. But I find it horrible to imagine a world without birds. Try it.

In fact, today began with a dead kestrel in the larder. How in heaven's name did it get there? Did the cat bring it in? There was no sign of a struggle. Could a cat catch and kill a kestrel? Kestrel it indubitably was, and as certainly dead. No use putting this one the other way round ('I'm upside down'). Perhaps the cat found it dead, shot yesterday by a short-sighted pheasant-culler.

The bangs have started up again.

5 December 1992

LONG LIFE

ALDERNEY COWED

Nigel Nicolson

The disclosure of 27 files on the occupation of the Channel Islands has added little to our knowledge of what went on there in 1940–45, and whetted curiosity about the contents of the files still kept secret and the identity of the many names blacked out. The islanders deserve the benefit of the doubt. The islands had, after all, been abandoned by the army without a fight and declared 'open islands', which must be the only time that phrase has been used in war. It was not for the inhabitants to do or die. The great majority neither went underground nor collaborated. They just looked disagreeable whenever a German soldier passed.

There was one exception: Alderney. The entire population of 1,500 chose to leave the island before the Germans landed, and on Hitler's direct order it was converted into an impregnable fortress by thousands of slave labourers imported from the mainland. They started with the advantage that the British had done exactly the same a century earlier.

Alderney was ringed with massive Victorian fortifications, to which the Todt workers added concrete casemates, pill-boxes, bunkers and gun emplacements. When they had finished it was more like a grounded battleship than an island. It was this outpost of the Atlantic Wall, infinitely stronger than any other part of it, which my brigade was ordered to capture in May 1942. If the operation had come off, this column would have had to be renamed 'Short life'.

It was Mountbatten's idea, and by his enthusiasm, plausibility and charm he convinced Churchill. There had been commando raids before, but they were mere pricks of a pin on the Continental hide, and we needed to demonstrate our mounting strength and bellicosity by something more dramatic, a dress rehearsal for Dieppe. What better than an assault on Alderney? What better way to blood the Guards Brigade? So we were moved down from Perth to the Isle of Wight to practise and prepare.

My chief memory of those weeks is the extraordinary method by which we hoped to cross the wide moat that surrounded the strongest of the Victorian forts. We were to fire on to the battlements a grappling iron attached to a long rope, swing ourselves across and climb the far wall to overwhelm the garrison. At this point I could do with a diagram or set-square, but words must suffice. You must imagine yourself the weight at the end of a pendulum, with the difference that you would not swing free in an unimpeded arc, but smash against the fortress wall, crippling yourself, while a torrent of fire descended on your head from the parapet 40 feet above.

We were not even to hold the island once we had captured it. Our sole purpose was to give the Germans a fright and the British people a treat. We were to withdraw within 12 hours after doing as much damage as we could, leaving the enemy to exult in our 'defeat' and the slave workers to be sacrificed as tokens of it. Only in retrospect do I question the absurdity – in fact the suicidal wickedness – of the scheme.

There were no second thoughts by the High Command. The operation was cancelled at the last moment only because the Air Force insisted on bombing in darkness, fearing the proximity of the Messerschmitts at Cherbourg, and the Navy on landing in daylight owing to the dangerous shoals offshore. Their plans were irreconcilable. I would like to boast that we were greatly disappointed, but when I announced the cancellation to my doomed platoon, there were loud cheers, in which I joined.

12 December 1992

NICE WORK IF YOU CAN GET IT

Martin Vander Weyer

When I talk about my office in the City, I no longer mean to imply that I have a job there. Like many professionals and business people, I have not had one of those for some time.

What I mean is that I enjoy a co-operative office arrangement which is a model of survival for middle-class victims of the recession. An elegant building within a stone's throw of the Bank of England, much of it has been 'To Let' for as long as I can remember. On the floors which are occupied, only one small company is still fully operational.

Perhaps half a dozen people in the building actually draw salaries. The rest of us are 'between jobs', 'looking at new ventures', 'doing a bit of consultancy work' or just passing the time of day. I gather that one or two have not got around to telling their wives that their employment circumstances have changed. It is sociable, convenient and discreetly impressive if you bump into former colleagues in the street outside.

Such set-ups are increasingly common as the rate of executive job losses rises. In the financial sector, that rate has reached 30,000 per year – with the greatest concentration among the overpaid young bucks of the City. Even lawyers and accountants are feeling the chill breeze up their striped trouser-legs.

Worst hit of all are professions caught by the property slump. According to Riba, more than a third of all salaried architects have been axed; many scratch along doing loft conversions, some run sandwich bars or draw cartoons. For surveyors, so little activity is in prospect, so many young people are still seeking to qualify, that middle-aged job-losers may never find work in the profession again.

Computer programmers, advertising executives, fine art specialists, all feature on the casualty lists. Overall, the carnage is more severe than at any time since the early 1930s, when the number of 'black-coated' unemployed passed 300,000.

The social consequences – unpaid school fees, respectable wives driven to pyramid selling – have been discussed extensively in *The Spectator*. I am not about to mock the distress of redundancy. It is traumatic, whoever you are. But it is surely much worse for a miner than a merchant banker, who may be more susceptible to a dent in the ego but is almost certainly better cushioned financially. What it does present to him is a test of personality – a rare opportunity to show true grit, to rise to the difficult occasion.

Perhaps, in the spirit of 'Dear Mary', I can offer some useful tips, starting with how to conduct yourself when the chopper falls. The time allowed to you may be a matter of weeks or it may be no longer than it takes to fill a bin-liner with personal belongings and depart under the eyes of a security guard. They may even bar you from the building while you've gone out to lunch.

Conventional minor-pub-school advice, to retreat in silent dignity, is best ignored. This is a rare opportunity for a short burst of cathartic rage of the sort which you might otherwise pay £10,000 to an exclusive Arizona clinic to induce. The perpetrators of your redundancy should be made to feel absolutely rotten, to provoke them to pay maximum compensation.

Social embarrassment, however, is no longer something you have to feel, now that so many of your confrères are occupationally challenged. The P45 form is this year's fashion accessory, a lifetime office career is as 'Eighties as a Filofax'; or so you can tell your friends. Nonchalance on your part will make it easier for them to look you in the eye, and will make you feel better: the dice have rolled, so many other things to be done, so much demand for your kind of wisdom; the world is your oyster.

The best display of this I saw came from a senior banker in New York, whose departure 'by mutual agreement' had just been announced. Still entitled to the privileges of rank, he entertained me in a panelled Wall Street dining-room. 'I may go and do political work in Washington, on foreign policy issues,' he drawled, casually ringing for the butler, 'or get together with some friends and make another fortune.'

But, however you behave, getting fired is irrevocable. You cannot get unfired, and you have to work out what to do next.

My own response was, as it happens, a good example of what sensible career advisers urge people not to do. I gathered suggestions as varied as joining the Foreign Office and buying a motor-cycle repair business in Clapham, and took a series of holidays. Then I listed the choices which appealed: find some consultancy work until something more exciting comes along; write; dabble in politics; or look for a serious job. I decided to do all of them, except the last.

As a stopgap, 'consultancy' is nice work if you can get it. Several of my friends have successfully resorted to it. One of them even invented the title 'Leisure Consultant' for his business card. Daily fees are attuned

to the rates charged by big firms with all the usual office overheads, so if you operate from a briefcase, the money looks quite good.

Other areas of keeping busy are equally crowded with involuntary non-executives. Local politics is a haven for slightly downtrodden men in their fifties who used to be 'big in knitwear' or 'something at ICI'. In the literary world, itself hard hit by falling sales, new manuscripts arrive by every post. 'My dear,' an agent told me breezily, 'all the unemployed are writing novels.'

For some sufferers from executive joblessness, treatment is available in the form of 'outplacement'. This sounds nasty, like colonic irrigation, and I was curious to find out what it actually is: counselling paid for by the ex-employer (or 'sponsor', as he now becomes) to assist the ex-employee (the 'prospect') to 'cross the employment gap'. It is, you may guess, an American invention. I visited Coutts Career Consultants, the first British firm to offer the service.

The first thing that happened, as I waited for a lift, was that a man from a different company sprang out of his office and said that if I was going to see Coutts I should come to see him as well, as he was in 'executive search' and had lots of opportunities to offer. It seemed possible that this is staged as part of the therapy, to cheer the new prospect as he arrives.

Colin Walkinshaw, a reassuringly ex-naval Coutts director, told me that new prospects often need 'picking up off the floor', especially those who have been dismissed with particular abruptness. Counselling aims not to restore self-respect, but to combat complacency in those who expect a new job just to turn up; or in others, the irrational urge to 'go self-employed' or drop out of the rat race forever. The key to the treatment is momentum and focus, making people work at finding a viable new future, rather than sloping off to the bookies after a quick browse through the Sits Vac.

But outplacement, which costs the 'sponsor' several thousand pounds a time, is not offered to everyone. For many others, the last resort is the Jobcentre, and with it the dole. The middle-class unjobbed don't usually admit to claiming – a notable exception being Kevin Maxwell, whose weekly hand-out was detailed to the penny in the national press. Proud ignorance of the various entitlements is probably a more typical attitude.

One friend of mine said, 'I went into one of these benefits offices but I came straight out again, it just wasn't for me. It seemed somehow, you know, unethical to claim.' 'But you've paid plenty of tax in the past,' I suggested. 'Why shouldn't you claim something back when you need it?' 'Oh sure,' he agreed, rather spoiling the effect. 'But the thing is I've got this consultancy contract . . .'

Hunched into a raincoat for fear of meeting anyone I knew, I set off to sample the experience at my local small-town Jobcentre. The ground floor shop-front had been abandoned, its display stands forlornly empty on the day that the number of vacancies across the country slumped to an 11-year low. An arrow directed me up linoleum stairs. I anticipated a long wait, passively smoking amongst hostile ex-cons, punks and new-age travellers. I could not have been more wrong.

It looked exactly like a travel agency, and a good deal smarter than my last real office in the City; just like Coutts Career Consultants, in fact. The only other 'client' – which is what Jobcentres now call their prospects – was a respectable middle-aged man in a suit. On the wall was the Jobseeker's Charter ('If you have an appointment, we aim to start on time. If you do not, we aim to see you within ten minutes . . .').

I had no appointment, but a matronly woman labelled 'Reception' saw me immediately. She showed me a copy of *New Executive Post*, a mixture of vacancy ads and features on 'opportunities in franchising', 'coping with stress' and '"It'll never happen to me!" Why you need financial planning'. I learned about Executive Job Clubs, now to be found in most big cities, providing office facilities and 'networking opportunities' for managerial job-hunters.

And how much dole would I get, if it came to the crunch? The answer was £43.10p per week, plus up to £30 of Income Support. In the tradition of this sort of journalism, I made an excuse and left. But (for job-seeking rather than benefit-claiming) the experience was not an unpleasant one. Whoever has redesigned the Employment Service is to be congratulated. If you have, as it were, nothing better to do, it may be worth a visit.

There is, however, an alternative last resort (some would place it higher up the order) and that is the 'on yer bike' solution, going abroad to find new fortune. Hong Kong, always a mobile job market, is still a good bet for the last boom before the Union Jack comes down; and an all-in expatriate package will solve most financial problems. For the really bold, eastern Europe offers long odds for all kinds of otherwise redundant skills and enterprise.

In Poland last year, for example, I came across Alan Bond's ex-finance director, shaking off his former boss's business crash and trying to relaunch a local brewery. Prague was full of young chancers, 'bored with the City', looking at 'leisure opportunities'. Albanian contacts report that the irrepressible Peter Earl, a 1980s City take-over merchant fallen on tough times, has been spotted in Tirana.

Earl is also, I hear, planning to climb Everest, and I take my hat off to him. If your job or your business has gone, there's no point in repining. It may be a ghastly shock, but it is also a moment of what Clinton-speakers now call empowerment – of taking responsibility for your own destiny, of making things happen. If that means trying to achieve your wildest fantasy, why not?

Those who need an inspirational role model should remember how Jelal ud Din, youthful ruler of Bokhara and Samarkand, faced his employment gap. Having lost the day against the Mongol hordes, he galloped his horse over a cliff, swam the Kabul river and went on to conquer another splendid kingdom. Go for it, is the moral of the story; you cannot go back.

19/26 December 1992

A NATION OF SCROOGES

Nicholas Shakespeare

On a visit which has so far escaped the scrutiny of his biographers, John Major once spent several days at the British Residence in Lima. It was 1984 and he was a Junior Whip embarked on 'a fact-finding tour'. If I have a single abiding memory, it is of our future Prime Minister at breakfast describing to me the present he intended for an important Peruvian functionary. Initially tempted to give a Commons ballpoint, Mr Major had opted instead for a parliamentary mug.

Christmas apart, we are not naturally a nation of present-givers. The British male especially puts little joy or imagination into the act, relying on a formula of Bittermints, champagne and flowers. He is also tremendously embarrassed at the receiving of gifts. I cannot recall what the PM accepted in return for his mug, but I well remember a visit to Rabat by a British Home Secretary and his wife four years later. With all the solemnity at his command, the Home Secretary presented to Mr Driss Basri, the Moroccan minister of the interior, a House of Commons blotter. After admiring the said artefact – made of Moroccan leather – Mr Basri heaped on his guest a chestful of hand-woven carpets and silver teapots, all of which the recipient would be later obliged to hand over to his Department 'for disposal'. Meanwhile at a separate venue, the Home Secretary's wife was doing her little bit for Britain. 'Very nice,' said Mrs Basri, respectfully gazing at a small replica of the House of Commons fashioned into an ashtray. 'Now I have a little something for you.' And, clapping her hands, she proceeded to deck her opposite number in an amazing array of embroidered kaftans.

Today's ministers are not permitted to accept gifts over the value of £125, but how rarely does their own generosity even approach this sum. The souvenir kiosk at Westminster bears witness to many a parsimonious, last-minute dash. Along with insignia'd ballpoints, this offers Wedgwood boxes (with nothing inside) for £21, ashtrays for £8 and selected cutlery at £4 a piece. The notion that it might be less embarrassing to give nothing at all than any of the above has been seized upon by the House of Commons Foreign Affairs Committee, who recently made it a policy decision when travelling abroad to dispense altogether with bangles for natives. No doubt there are members of the committee still mindful of Prime Minister Heath's visit to the Pope in 1971, when, in return for a handsomely bound facsimile of Palestrina's music, the Vicar of God was rewarded with a signed photograph of the Grocer and a gramophone record of himself conducting an orchestra.

Such meanness is not only a prime ministerial prerogative, but it extends into the highest reaches of state. I will never forget the presents to King Maswati III of Swaziland at the time of his coronation in 1986. Splendid among them was President Kaunda's large copper gong suspended between elephant tusks. ('Feel free to hit that gong,' Kaunda urged, 'and Zambia will respond to your call.') P. W. Botha's gift was a Swazi battle-axe and the promise of a hunting gun once measurements were taken, while the King of Lesotho had presented a horse. As for our own royal family, one might say they had borrowed a leaf from Edward Heath's book. Representing the Queen, Prince and Princess Michael of Kent offered a silvertopped cane and a framed photograph of themselves. More significantly, they also bore Her Majesty's coronation gift: a cut-crystal goblet decorated with an engraving of Sherborne, where Maswati III was shortly to return to complete his O levels.

I hesitate to jump aboard a bandwagon, but there is compelling evidence to suggest that our stinginess as a nation – if this is what it is – begins at the top. The occasion is well documented of the Queen berating Prince Charles when a teenager at Sandringham. He had taken a dog for a walk and lost the lead. He was promptly despatched to look for it: dog-leads, said his mother, cost money. But so too does hospitality. The royal family have a less than gracious tradition of enjoying this, a tradition of *sponging* did not die with Edward VII. Certain current members in particular are notorious for exploiting friends' hospitality until the moment sometimes arrives when the host cannot any longer afford them, at which point they invite themselves elsewhere. Somehow it never occurs to some royal highnesses that their loyal subjects are not prepared to bankrupt themselves in their honour.

This attitude – that everyone you meet has nothing better to do than to entertain you – permeates downwards, hallmarking many a Briton's behaviour abroad where, generally speaking, the poorer the country the better hospitality you get. Those who knock unexpectedly at a foreign door betray the royal habit of expecting to be fed, accommodated and fêted. It is emphatically not intended to be a two-way trade. If a foreigner lands on your doorstep, the chances are he or she will remain there while you look intently at your diary and find you can't do anything for a fortnight. 'You're only here for two weeks? How sad. If only I'd known. We might be able to make a drink next Tuesday. Where are you staying? I wonder if I can recommend a good hotel.' You can't, and the conversation peters out with a suggestion that they might try ringing the British Tourist Authority. This attitude is summed up perfectly by the experience of Mary Wesley when staying as a young woman with a banking family in Brussels. 'They took me to operas, theatres and restaurants all over the place,' remembers the novelist. 'I arrived home full of verve and when I said to my mother we must do something for them she quite agreed: "Oh, do ask them to tea, darling."'

Not knowing how to indulge ourselves, we don't know how to indulge others. When I was in Italy this summer, the local grocer insisted on vacating his premises for half an hour in order to treat me to an *aperitivo*. It was my last day; he wished to bid me farewell and to thank me for having patronised his shop. I could not imagine an Italian visitor receiving reciprocal treatment in England. Should we be so surprised that the Holy Family settled on Bethlehem rather than, say, Basingstoke?

If there is any consolation, it is that we do not behave better amongst ourselves. The late Lord Faringdon was famous for being able to carve a grouse for six, and many are the hostesses who have been heard softly to murmur into their husband's ear, 'DCSC' – aristocratic shorthand for Don't Cut Second Chicken. More chilling is the memory of James Lees-Milne when visiting Lord Leconfield at Petworth. After an exhausting day, Lees-Milne was led down a long ungainly passageway to a door that opened on to the street. 'I'm told you can get very good snacks there,' said Lord Leconfield, pointing to Priscilla's Pantry. 'Put yours down to me.' Quite visible to both men was an enormous sign saying 'Closed'.

What can be the reason for this social reticence, this apparent ungenerosity of spirit, this desire not to let anyone inside our homes if we can possibly help it? In part it derives from a frosty suspicion of all outsiders, not just guide dogs and Bosnians; in part from an inbuilt puritanism which exalts the Christian virtues of living off very little. If you say to an English woman, 'What a lovely dress,' the chances are she'll blush and say, 'Oh, but it's very old,' rather than reply, as an Italian might, 'It cost a bomb, and isn't it a dream?' In fact, we consider it wrong to spend money on anything other than bricks and mortar, private education and charity (in which field we are immensely generous). At its most warped, this thriftiness can lead to the ridiculous spectacle of extremely rich families convincing themselves in audible mutters that they are poorer than church-mice. Hence the antediluvian understanding of money affected by Lady Walpole-Wilson, the wife of the unstuck diplomat in Anthony Powell's *A Buyer's Market*, who makes a fantastic show of paying for her share of the taxi-ride with Archie Gilbert. When asked by Nicholas Jenkins if he took the money, Gilbert replies, 'Oh, I took it. Why not? It wasn't enough. It never is.'

This is one of our main faults as a race. We never really give enough or we tend to give cast-offs: I do not know what goodies Mr Major is planning to wrap this Christmas, but there is a story that when Mrs Thatcher first met Gorbachev he gave her a ball-point and she offered him Labour-voting Scotland.

19/26 December 1992

JOTTINGS FROM MY NOTEBOOK

Alec Guinness

Almost within sound of the chimes of St Fortnum and St Mason stood, east and west, two hospitals; recently both have been converted to hotels, each of them, I suspect, rather too expensive for the average Londoner or provincial family to put a foot through the door. And now we hear of plans to close another ten London hospitals. Unreal city. Of course it isn't only hospitals which are made into hotels; *vide* the *Miami Herald* for 25 October this year, which informs us that in 1993 rooms 'with good quality robust antiques' can be rented at Hampton Court Palace. Prices from £240 for a four-day winter break. No promise of breakfast with the Queen.

Venice, we are told, is literally sinking under the weight of its daily visitors – 12 million a year, mostly crammed into the summer months. The city doesn't even benefit commercially (except from the sale of souvenirs) as most of the visitors bring their own packaged meals and leave their rubbish to be collected by the civic refuse cleaners.

The Sistine Chapel is nowadays a horrific experience. You can boast you squeezed in and managed to squeeze out, bruised, breathless and deafened; but you can no longer boast that you have actually *seen* the Sistine Chapel.

Early in 1939, when I first visited it, there was only one other occupant – an elderly lady in tweeds, unmistakably English, lying on her back on a bench studying the ceiling through opera-glasses. She was a genuine sightseer – appreciative, respectful and silent.

The Taj Mahal, in spite of clearly visible pleas for silence written in half a dozen languages, shudders under the impact of human voices and slippered feet. It sounds, even from outside, like a demented bee-hive. Needless to say, the whole structure is now in danger.

Stonehenge – magical, inviting and almost deserted when I was a boy, with neither fencing, carparks nor kiosks – is now an eyesore in its necessary fight against vandalism.

Next week my wife and I will put on our boots to add our tourist weight to Vienna and probably ease some Austrian bums out of their opera seats. So we are all victims and oppressors alike, caught up in some incomprehensible market force (May The Force Never Be With You), throwing ourselves like lemmings into some overcrowded, over-publicised cultural sea. (Oh, the weight of travel brochures which thump weekly through the letter-box like logs from felled trees.)

Thirty years or so ago, the West End theatre was self-sufficient; the audiences were almost entirely home-grown (as they still are in the provinces). The block-busting bookings, made so often from overseas as part of package deals, were unheard of. Now, it seems, the London theatre has to cater to 30 to 40 per cent tourists to pay its way. The tourists, of course, are welcome for their cash – and for keeping the old, successful, perennial shows *in situ* for almost decades – *if* that is seen as lively and desirable.

Recently, in answer to a sudden question about all this while being interviewed about something else, I replied tactlessly (not for the first time in my life) and this was treated as if it was some *ex cathedra* pronouncement from the Vatican. The flippant tone in which I spoke was entirely misjudged by those who heard me, as a casual glance at their over-serious faces should have warned me. The point I laboured was that it is hell for actors to play light comedy to an audience if there exists an acute language barrier. It is nothing new. There was an old theatrical joke, current before the Second World War, about a comedian playing to a dead, unresponsive house. Exasperated, he advanced on the footlights to address the audience. 'Anyone here speak English?' he asked. 'Yes, I do,' came a voice. 'Well, f – you for a start!'

I witnessed a cheering Christmassy sight in Bond Street: a vast metal angel – either the Angel Gabriel or one of the heavenly host who hovered over Bethlehem – was being manhandled by eight stalwart workmen. They were carrying Gabriel, if it was he, face down. They were very inconvenienced by his huge wings as well as his weight and could only manage a step or two at a time towards the waiting lorry. Breathless and sweating, they stopped for a moment and then, with renewed vigour, they burst into song and heaved the statue aboard.

They didn't sing 'I'm Dreaming of a White Christmas' or the nauseating 'Jingle Bells' but a deep bass version of 'The Volga Boat-

man'. The biggest, toughest and jolliest of the heave-hoers wore a
tangle of gilded tinsel in his grizzled hair. He was no fairy at the
top of a Christmas tree but he scattered charm and goodwill on all
passers-by.

A week ago at my bank I watched a tall, fine-boned elderly gentleman
cash a cheque. 'I'd like two fives and a ten, if you would be so kind,'
he said. He wore a light tweed overcoat with a velvet collar and a large,
expensive-looking black hat with a brim which had been steamed into
various extravagant curlings. 'Oh, thank you *so* much,' he said when
given the money. He waved the notes at the smiling cashier and
slightly raised his hat. 'Too kind, too kind!' he said; then he tripped
and slid to the floor. 'Of no consequence,' he re-assured us all as he
picked himself up. Someone retrieved his banknotes for him. 'Mine?'
he asked, and seemed astonished. Somehow it could only happen in
London, I thought.

In the men's trouser department at Simpson's in Piccadilly I heard a
foreign-sounding salesman of about 50 say into a telephone, 'Phyllis,
can you give me the words for *Auld Lang Syne*? I know the *tune.*' He
hummed it unrecognisably. 'You can't? What am I to do?' I said, over
my shoulder, 'We'll take a cup o' kindness yet, etc.' Another salesman,
whom I hadn't noticed, spoke in my ear: 'I *beg* your pardon, sir?' No
use explaining.

Recently I returned from filming in Normandy, where work and interest took me to some of the war cemeteries. The weather was foul. It
was a moving experience, not only because of the vast visible evidence
of tragic loss but also because of the loving care with which the graves
are tended. All honour to the War Graves Commission: they have
found beautiful resting places, with the greenest grass, for our dead in
France from 1914 onwards. American, British, French, Commonwealth
and German soldiers lie, for the most part, within sight and sound of
the sea they can no longer hear or scent. I saw a few of all sorts and
conditions of men and women – some old, others quite young – step-
ping between the lines of crosses like gentle visiting ghosts, smiling
with remembrances of father, brother, friend or grandfather. There was
perhaps a sweet sadness in the damp air, but no deep melancholy.

Normandy's most famous icon is the Bayeux Tapestry. When I first
saw it, nearly 40 years ago, it was poorly presented in harsh light and
looked almost drab, like some endless (well, 70 yards long) crude strip
cartoon. Now it has been handsomely rehoused and beautifully lit. It

is a dramatic knock-out. The five-year-old son of the film producer of *A Foreign Field* was taken to see it by his grandfather, who had landed on one of the Normandy beaches in 1944. The boy gazed with fascination at various characters decapitating each other. 'Grandpa,' he said, 'did you have a long sword like that?' From 1066 and all that to 1992; perhaps there is not as much difference as we sometimes think. I hadn't known until this visit that Napoleon had removed the tapestry to Paris, where it was put on display to whip up interest in the idea of invading England.

London continues to surprise me. One day in the summer I turned away from the souks of Oxford Street towards Soho Square. There was a screech of brakes behind me. I twisted round and just glimpsed a man fall – hit by a van. He struck his head on the kerb with a sickening thud. It was probably instant death. Oxford Street was, as always, an ebbing and flowing mass of people and several must have seen the accident. What surprised me was the curious sound people made: no shrieks, shouts or cries but a sort of twittering, like a flock of frightened small birds. Very eerie. We were all thinking, I imagine, of sudden accidental death. Images of death stayed with me for the remainder of the day. When I got home I casually picked up, while shifting some books, the *Apocrypha Old Testament* and flicked it open. My eye fell on the passage about Death being sent by God to Abraham which ends: 'Abraham said, "I understand what you are saying; but I will not follow you." And Death was silent and answered him not a word.'

Well done, Abraham.

19/26 December 1992

IN SEARCH OF A NOVEL PLOT

P. D. James

A novelist who is visited by what he or she thinks is an original idea experiences a surge of excitement which is invariably ill-founded; experience shows that there are no new ideas, only fresh treatments of the old. This, of course, particularly applies to plot. The adage states that there are only five and I have been amusing myself trying to identify them.

The Cinderella story and its sub-plot of love triumphant over difficulties is a theme which covers virtually all the novels of Jane Austen and such very different writers as Charlotte Brontë and Barbara Cartland. Then there is the mystery and its solution, plots ranging from the conventions of the classical detective story to the subtle investigation of hidden motives and unfolding psychological discoveries, including novels which manage, like Wilkie Collins's *The Moonstone*, to combine both. Another category is the hunt and the hunted, which covers novels of espionage ranging from the patriotic simplicities of Buchan's *The Thirty-Nine Steps* to John le Carré's fascinating exploration of personal and international treachery. Then there is the confrontation of opposites, whether of ideas or across boundaries of age, sex, nationality, religion and social class, a box which can conveniently accommodate a wide variety of novels old and new. I'm uncertain about my fifth category. Exploration of the human condition is an easy opt-out which covers all categories. Perhaps I should choose revenge, always a powerful plot-maker.

Another categorisation could be by the seven deadly sins. It is difficult to think of a novel which doesn't deal with at least one of that reprehensible list: gluttony, sloth, envy, lust, avarice, wrath and pride. The popular Victorian novelist, Hall Caine, claimed that he found the plots for all his sensational books in the Bible, and I can see that the Old Testament, in particular, is a fertile field for literary harvesting. An example is the story, told in the Second Book of Samuel, of King David walking on his roof and beholding the wife of Uriah the Hittite washing herself. The King, immediately in love, sends for her and, learning subsequently that she is pregnant with his child, writes that fatal letter to Joab: 'Send ye Uriah in the forefront of the hottest battle, and retire ye from him, that he may be smitten and die.' This treachery and its dramatic sequel could, and probably has, inspired a large number of novelists, all of whom could write happily in the knowledge that they would face no accusation of plagiarism.

Detective stories and clue-making abound in the Old Testament. One of the earliest examples is to be found in Genesis, when the smooth-skinned Jacob, wearing the skin of goat kids on his hands, steals from his father the blessing meant for Esau, the first-born: 'The voice is Jacob's, but the hands are the hands of Esau.' The Apocrypha, of course, gives us the well-known story of Susanna and the Elders, surely one of the earliest examples in literature of successful cross-examination.

It seems to some of us novelists that a good idea for a novel, whether related to plot or theme, is like a benign infection borne on the air, waiting to be caught and used by others if one doesn't get the book written quickly. I particularly sympathised with Susan Hill who, in the issue of *The Spectator* of 18 January this year, described an astonishing series of coincidences of plot, detail, theme and setting between her books and the books of others, although neither author had the slightest knowledge of what the other was writing. She must be beginning to think that she has only to plan a book to discover that an equally highly regarded novelist is already working on the same theme.

This kind of coincidence seems not to happen with crime fiction, somewhat surprisingly in a genre which, after all, depends heavily on plot and in which original ideas are not easily come by. As a *Blackwood's* reviewer wrote in the late 1800s of the latest Sherlock Holmes: 'In view of the difficulty of hitting on any fancies which are decently fresh, surely this sensational business must shortly come to a close.' We know that 'death hath ten thousand doors to let out life', and most of them have been used with varying degrees of ingenuity over the centuries. A number of clues, too, in this sensational business are fairly well-worn – the torn letter, the trail of blood, the dropped handkerchief – and there is inevitably a limited number of credible motives for murder. In one of my novels, a detective sergeant tells the young Dalgliesh that the four Ls cover them all – love, lust, loathing, lucre. Even so, I don't recall two crime books published close together which bear any real resemblance.

I did, however, have an interesting experience a few years ago when I was talking to a group of would-be writers at Cambridge. I was talking about possible ideas for a plot and said that some writers occasionally found them in newspaper reports. There had that day been the story of a pathetic, maternally deprived woman who had stolen a baby from outside a supermarket, and we explored how that could be used in a crime novel. I suggested that the woman could be given a husband or boyfriend who was both violent and criminal. Finding she had taken the baby without detection, he could have the idea of blackmailing the parents for the child's return. We developed this theme together. That night I picked up the Ruth Rendell paperback I had brought with me, previously unread, and discovered that Ruth had indeed dealt, with her usual admirable skill, with just that plot, and had developed it in much the same way I had been elaborating. I suppose I should be grateful that the whole group, including me, didn't decide to do the same.

My present interest in the extraordinary coincidences of fiction and in the way an idea is taken up by different people arises from two coincidences in connection with my new novel, *The Children of Men*. Unusually for me, this began when I read a review of a scientific book which mentioned the extraordinary and unexplained fall in the last 30 years in the sperm count of western man. I began to ponder on what the world would be like if, suddenly and without warning, the human race ceased to be able to breed. I had read a number of apocalyptic novels in which *homo sapiens* was wiped out by a rapidly spreading, fatal pandemic. One I remember from childhood was called *The Red Death*, although I can't recall the writer. Another, of course, is *On the Beach* by Nevil Shute, where the cause of the calamity is radiation. But I thought I was the first to imagine a world in which suddenly the human race was unable to reproduce itself. I should of course, have known better. After my book appeared, Brian W. Aldiss wrote to me pointing out that it is almost 30 years since he published *Greybeard*, a novel also set in Oxford and in the not-too-distant future, envisaging a world in which the human race has become universally infertile through radiation. Mr Aldiss's powerful novel is suffused with grief at the loss of children and, like others, he uses the genre novel to explore themes of importance to him. I should have known of this book, since we share the same publisher. *Greybeard* has never been out of print and will reappear in hardback next year, and in paperback from Penguin Books.

A more recent and more remarkable coincidence has been brought to my notice by the editor of *The Spectator*, a short story by Walter Voght, published in 1984 and translated from the German. I can't even have subconsciously recorded it, since I have never read nor previously heard of it. It is short and starkly told and reads more like a synopsis for a novel than a short story. But the resemblance to *The Children of Men* is uncanny. Voght describes a world in which the entire human race and the animal kingdom are all struck by sudden infertility. He calls the year in which the last children were born Year Zero and the children the Last Ones. I called them Omegas and, like my Omegas, the Last Ones are pampered and spoilt. They carry the weight of the hopes of mankind, hopes which are finally disappointed. Walter Voght describes how in some countries the Last Ones are sacrificed to the gods; I state that they are ritually sacrificed in fertility rites. Voght postulates that, as the population ages, laws are passed to guarantee the maximum concentration of population in approved areas. In my book, the Council of England makes plans for people to move into towns so that facilities and services can be guaranteed to the last possible moment. The conclusions of the Voght short story and my novel are radically different and they are totally dissimilar in style, setting and characterisation. But the central idea is identical. Brian Aldiss, however, undoubtedly thought of it first, since *Greybeard* was published in 1964. But perhaps I am unwise even to write these words; it is inviting an aggrieved letter from someone pointing out that his grandfather published a book remarkably similar both to *Greybeard* and *The Children of Men* many years before.

19/26 December 1992

HANDS OFF MY BABY!

Vicki Woods

I went to visit an American baby in New York: his mother is a friend of mine and lives in the meat-packing district, which is a lot smarter than it sounds. The baby's father, a banker, is called Jeffrey; so the baby is called Jeffrey Junior and is known to his family as J. J. He is their first child, long-awaited and much-loved, and his entry into the world, at a fashionable New York hospital, was very expensive. I visited him, with my children, when he was three months old, and was delighted to find him tactfully wearing my gift of a little apple-green, Italian outfit printed with big red ladybirds. My daughter chose it at Harrods; it took all morning. He looked a treat, little J. J. His mother woke him up for us. I put my arms out and started tuning up the lengthy raga with which women welcome boy-babies to the world (girl-babies are just as welcome, obviously, but with different adjectives). Thus: 'O Jeffrey Junior, you *handsome* boy, just *look* at you, so big and *strong*, how *intelligent*-looking, how *alert*, come here, you angelic thing, you; give him to me *at once* –' but his mother held him tight. 'One second!' she said, speaking very fast. 'I *know* you're British, I *know* you're going to get me for this, but I *have* to say it! I *have* to ask!' Ask what? 'It isn't me – it's the *doctor*, believe me. My paediatrician *insisted*; he said I have to tell everybody to – everybody that holds the baby to – picks up the baby to –' To what, in heaven's name? 'To wash their hands first.'

I looked at my hands and blushed with embarrassment and so did she, but she ploughed on gamely, righteously. 'Ohmigod, look at your face, you think I'm nuts!' 'Erm, you are nuts,' I said. 'Please! Bear with me! I know you're from England and you think I'm crazy! It's to cut down the risk of cross-infection! My paed insists! Even my mother! The bathroom is right here – soap and towels are ready. Please! Don't look at me like that!'

Well, I tidied away the look on my face and went into the little cloakroom to scrub up. I felt completely ridiculous and oddly filthy. 'Mine are clean,' said my daughter, reaching out a finger to poke the baby, but I hauled her towards the wash-basin, too, before there was another cross-cultural outburst. My 14-year-old son folded his grimy hands over his chest. Not touching it, OK?

J. J. was worth the wash, wrinkling his pretty nose and sneezing an alert sneeze, and I forgave his mother her battiness; she came to motherhood late, after all, and perhaps she had an over-zealous paediatrician. But next morning I cast an eye over the Ann Landers column in the *New York Post* as I ate my breakfast bagel. Ann Landers is the famously long-running agony aunt. She had a letter from a woman with a baby. Her baby was beautiful, healthy, happy, the apple of her eye and so forth, but every time she took her out in her stroller 'strangers' made life hell and torment. Strangers not only admired her beautiful daughter, but continually attempted to pat her, prod her, stroke her or tickle her. How could she prevent this? They leaned right into the stroller. It was unhygienic and posed risks of cross-infection, according to her paediatrician. She had tried saying, 'Please don't touch my baby,' but felt it sounded rude. Did Ann have any advice?

You would imagine that Ann Landers might advise Tormented that she had more to worry about in late 20th-century America than people chucking her baby daughter under the chin, but you would be wrong. Miss Landers was deeply sympathetic. She urged the mother to remember that her first duty was to the child, not to a bunch of unhygienic strangers. The risks of cross-infection, Miss Landers allowed, were very real; therefore, the mother shouldn't worry about appearing 'rude'. She should be robust in fending off *tout le monde*. She should say, 'Whilst I am happy for you to admire my beautiful daughter, I do not want her touched at all. Please respect my wishes in this.'

I was even more depressed by Ann Landers' snooty protocols on hygiene than I had been by J. J.'s mamma. I thought about my own babies, brought up in an England teeming with unhygienic strangers. Here, the spirit of Ann Landers is at work in the baby clinics, as it were, and issues new mothers with fierce leaflets that define their duties. New mothers read them with care, and start off with very clear intentions about hygiene, Stranger Danger and the deadliness of sugar. We rinse, scald, sterilise and bleach as though Typhoid Mary was running the playgroup. I raised a son to the age of 14 months without his ever tasting chocolate or sweets (an incredible feat, considering there were two Christmases inside that short lifespan). I remained holier-than-thou against all grandparental sweet-lobbying: no, no, the boy must have unblemished teeth and grow up on muesli and organically grown vegetables. One day I left his pram outside an ironmongers in Turnham Green for four and a half minutes, while I ran in for a pair of hairdressing scissors; when I ran out again he looked like a Black and White Minstrel. Chocolate to the eye-brows. Half a bar of Cadbury's Dairy Milk lay melted over his blankets, the biggest grin of his life split his fat little face and an *extremely* unhygienic old drunk was rocking the pram wildly, crooning 'Your Spanish Eyes' and leaning over to poke squares of chocolate into his mouth with a grubby finger. Ann Landers would have had a dicky fit. The poor old jongleur got a flea in his ear and no mistake, but I realised I had to stop being mueslier-than-thou.

Ann Landers speaks for great swathes of middle America and her measured responses to its problems have the ring of truths universally acknowledged. Clearly, most Americans wouldn't agree with me that J. J.'s mother was temporarily bats and Tormented over-protective to the point of neurosis. Nor would they agree that a delicious baby, like

Windsor Castle or views of Shap Fell at sundown, is the property of the nation, and must therefore submit to having its chin chucked and its curls twirled by the community at large. And so must its mother. (Whereas a fractious baby, as everyone knows, belongs only to its feckless parent.)

Most depressing is this hysteria about 'risks of cross-infection'. American medical bills are famously large, of course, and the paramedical establishment so legendarily rapacious that they will refuse to put any oxygen into the oxygen mask until the patient has located and handed over his Amex card, but there must be more to it than that. What unbelievably lethal and immediately contagious infection could it be that they don't want their remarkably sturdy bairns to risk crossing in the slightest degree, even by a pat on the head? Something hellish, obviously. Something death-dealing, inescapable. Leprosy. Meningitis. Cholera. Smallpox. Tuberculosis. Something like that. Legionnaires' Disease. The Evil Eye. Aids.

Oh – Aids. Right. There we are. I think 'risks of cross-infection' for middle America translates very simply as 'fear of Aids' and I think that for middle Americans – most of whom will never come across an Aids case outside their television screens – 'Aids' is a metaphor for 'death'. Americans are much possessed by death. Germs, lack of hygiene, cross-infection, smoking, Aids, eating butter . . . all lead to death, especially in babies. Please wash your hands. Please do not touch my beautiful daughter.

After I'd had a beautiful daughter, we took them both to Italy: the daughter in arms and the son kicking about in his new Start-Rites and a Paddington Bear sun-hat. My daughter was a green-eyed blonde, and at six months old a fat cartoon of a baby. I couldn't keep hold of her. It wasn't just a question of being poked, stroked or tickled – she was lifted bodily out of my arms every single time we went out. Italian mammas took her. They shrieked with delight and passed her from hand to hand among their families. 'O che bella bionda bimba! Che bellissimi occhi!' they said, while they kissed her fat little feet and poked her hamster cheeks with unwashed fingers and curled her wispy ringlets over their brilliant manicures. I waited rather helplessly to get her back each time: there was no hurrying this adoration. My daughter simpered and cooed at the worshippers. 'Grazie tanto,' they said politely, handing her over. I began to like Italy a lot. We stood outside the Duomo in Siena, realising that we were hampered in our desire to see inside it by having two children under two with us. I said, 'Oh, well, next time.'

-PILBROW-

Sitting in a slice of shade to one side of the entrance was a line of old women dressed in black: they watched us turn away from the cathedral door, carrying the children. '*Signora!*' shouted one of them, patting her knee and holding out her arms. My husband said, 'We can't just leave the children with them.' And I said, 'Of course we can.' I had the hang of a nation that liked children by now. The senior crone took the *bellissima bionda bimba* and three others swooped down on the boy, who opened his mouth to yell with fear until one of them popped into it something unhygienic and sugary that she just happened to have on her. The senior crone took me by the wrist, drew a half circle on my watch face to show me how long they'd baby-sit and waved us into the cathedral. When we came out after half an hour, they handed the children back, *Grazie tanto.*

19/26 December 1992

COMEDY

'SEE YA, VIC'

Emma Forrest

Young girls screamed and threw underwear when Rik Mayall appeared at the National Theatre. They were similarly moved by Hugh Laurie in *Gasping* and now Tony Slattery in *Radio Times*. The anarchic surrealist Vic Reeves packed the Hammersmith Odeon (previously only a music venue) for nine nights. Rob Newman and David Baddiel of *The Mary Whitehouse Experience* were doing the same this week.

As a 15-year-old comedy enthusiast, I find myself wondering what it is about these new superstars that evokes the kind of passion formerly reserved for the likes of the Beatles, Marc Bolan and Bros. Although my heroes have always been comics, ranging from Lenny Bruce to Peter Cook, via W. C. Fields and Sid Caesar, I doubt I would queue for three hours in the rain on a Saturday to get a book signed by them. So why did I do just that for an ex-pig farmer who calls himself Vic Reeves? Why have Rob and David claimed the *Smash Hits* and *Just Seventeen* centrefolds that used to be Jason Donovan territory?

Teenagers like energy, surprise and something to share, and it's easier to share the jokes than the songs. With television being part of every teenager's after-school ritual, you meet the next morning shouting the latest catch-phrase. If you've got it, you're in the group. If not, you're out of a 20-minute conversation. As for the unexpected, today's music technology has put paid to that. There is no such thing as a 'live' pop performance: what pretends to be spontaneous looks rigged. Where is the danger in miming to a tape? Comedy is our real home – the only place where subversion lives. We love the shocks that Kylie Minogue, packaged Madonna or even Axl Rose, with his scripted violence, have failed to provide. We are weary of inane lyrics – we want issues and words. And language is the basis of comedy. Vic Reeves, whilst not as obviously cerebral as, say, Stephen Fry, still makes his living by playing with words. He may well be the first person to use 'petri dish' and 'Caramac' in the same sentence. What the pop moguls have failed to pick up is that teenagers are not monosyllabic mutants from someplace else: we are intelligent life and deserve to be addressed as such. And there is no good comedian who is not highly intelligent.

In pursuit of this theory, I went to see the current favourites, David Baddiel and Rob Newman. They are both achingly brilliant: 'I'm actually still theoretically doing a PhD in English Victorian Sexuality and Literature,' mumbles Dave sheepishly, 'but I haven't touched it in a few years.' Rob looking like a psychotic Daniel Day-Lewis has such a sharp and original mind that I was torn between asking him to start a religion and calling the Samaritans before he did himself damage. His heroes include R. D. Laing, Bertrand Russell, Aldous Huxley and, intriguingly, Julie Burchill. I asked him if he thinks the hero-worship is entirely healthy. 'At times, I think not . . . Whatever I'm doing, if you do something else it's probably correct. What I'm doing is wrong.' Yes, we know. That's what makes him so attractive.

Whether they like it or not, Newman, Baddiel and contemporaries like Sean Hughes and Bob Mortimer are sex symbols. Unlike the days of Marty Feldman and Spike Milligan, when looking odd was a career move, it is now entirely beneficial to be young and attractive. The glamour and mystique of being on TV is enough to enhance your appeal overnight. I asked Sean Hughes, at the launch of his first TV show, what he thought about comedians as pop stars. His response? 'I know it happens to David Baddiel and Rob Newman, but I have a much more mature audience.' A year later, his live shows are often inaudible over the shouts of 'We love you, Sean!' from the girls in the front row.

I'm troubled that my generation plays it so safe. I am a child of the Eighties and it seems that there is too much about us that our parents understand. Every younger generation should have a secret language that the Establishment cannot learn. Where is our version of the cultural revolution that found its voice with *Oz*, the Rolling Stones and Punk? The closest we've come to a code is the comic's catchphrase: 'See ya, Vic.' 'Fluffy.' 'That's you, that is.' If today's pop musicians were doing their jobs, I wouldn't have to carry out midnight raids on my parents' record collection to feed my Janis Joplin addiction (I'd like to see Kylie down a bottle of Southern Comfort in one gulp). You, the adults, had the Doors and the Who to tear up the place on your behalf; that's why you could afford to be more reserved about the Goons. Today, the goons are all we've got.

19/26 December 1992

CELEBRITY PROBLEMS SOLVED

DEAR MARY . . .

Mary Killen

Q. Earlier this year I led a group of three EEC foreign ministers and a European commissioner on a visit to South Africa. We flew overnight in a plane in which the RAF had kindly put four beds. As we finished a nightcap, I wondered whether I should wait for my guests to realise they should start to make the most of the few hours' flight, and move off to their bunks, as they would if house guests. Or should I lead the way and risk accusations of the host breaking up the party?
   D. Hurd, Foreign and Commonwealth Office, London SWI

A. Despite initial resentment, most people are usually grateful to find themselves tucked up in bed, when they might otherwise have been staying up and undermining their health. A tactful way of bossing your fellow ministers into their bunks would have been for you discreetly to ask the pilot to dim the lights in the cabin – or even to flash them on and off as on commercial premises. You could have then stood up, with a sign of reluctance, and said, 'Oh dear, I'm afraid this happens. We have to go to our beds now.'

Q. In the National Trust shop attached to my house they sell, among many others, copies of my own books. One of the shopladies asked me to sign a copy for her. I crossed out my name on the title-page and rewrote it underneath. 'Oh please put my name too,' she said. I should have known it, because she has been there several years. I thought it was Sally. To make sure, I asked, 'I forget – is it Sally with a "y" or an "ie"?' 'Who's

Sally?' she said. What should I have replied?

N. Nicolson, Sissinghurst Castle, Kent.

A. You should have whispered, 'I'm sorry. It's just that you remind me so much of a girl I was in love with as a young man. Her name was Sally.' Then, suddenly coming to your senses, you could have said more formally, 'Of course I know what yours is but can you spell it for me?'

Q. Last June, in the depths of the Brazilian jungle, the local shaman had prepared an unpleasant-smelling, hallucinogenic brew for his village, and a beaker of the stuff was ladled out and handed to me. But I had heard that strange and nasty things happened to those who drank it; so I indicated that I would take just a single sip. As I put it to my mouth, I became aware that everyone was making signs to me that I should drink the entire cup: a very large one. Various things happened in the hours after that: a six-foot goldfish in a straw hat put its fin round my shoulder and asked me how I was, for instance. I didn't know how to answer him and I didn't know how to decline the full drink. How should I have replied to the shaman?

John Simpson, BBC, London, W12

A. I consider my solution to be something of a breakthrough. It will benefit intrepid newsmen and even teenagers being urged to swallow dangerous toxins by their peers. Purchase a 'Femidom', the new female prophylactic. This has a diameter of roughly three inches at its 'entrance' point. Pop the prophylactic into your mouth – having first removed the detachable plastic ring at its farthest end. Allow the balloon-shaped slack to sit comfortably on your tongue. 'Fit' the opening ring so that it sits between your teeth and lips. The device, which is opaque-coloured, is now invisible and can be left in situ to collect unwanted drinks, pills, even a limited amount of foodstuffs, which you can then expel discreetly once the focus of attention has moved from you.

19/26 December 1992

DIARY

Nigel Dempster

The head of the Guinness family, the 3rd Earl of Iveagh, died last June, aged 55, from cancer of the throat, while living at the Kensington home of his former wife Miranda. As chairman of Guinness from 1962 to 1986, he was responsible for appointing Ernest Saunders chief executive in 1981. The brief to Saunders, formerly with Beechams, Nestlé and Great Universal Stores, was 'make the family rich'. This Saunders set about doing with a series of divestments and takeovers, culminating in the victorious battle for Distillers. As a measure of Saunders' success the share price at the time of Iveagh's death had increased by 1,000 per cent since 1981, with the Guinness family profiting by £180 million. Benjamin Iveagh, who had long fought a battle with drink as well as cancer, made promises to Saunders, following the arrival of DTI inspectors at the company's headquarters in December 1986, that the Guinness family would never renege on undertakings to safeguard Saunders' financial interest. He reiterated them on 10 January 1987, four days before he was party to the board decision to kick Saunders out without a penny. These promises he signally failed to keep even though, when I pressed him about his intentions while Saunders was standing trial, he said that the matter would be honourably dealt with on the completion of the case, whatever happened. If Saunders had not won Distillers, Guinness would be a so-so company with a capitalisation of around £1 billion, not the current £10 billion. In November, Saunders, who had to sell his Buckinghamshire home to pay lawyers and has been living with his son in Putney, received a tax-free lump sum of just under £150,000 from Guinness in respect of his pension rights. He also receives an annual pension of £65,000. (Sir Ralph Halpern left Burton with £2 million and a pension of £10,000 a week.) Iveagh's will has not been published yet.

But his own (not family trust) shares in the company are worth £60 million, he had a 23,000-acre estate in Suffolk, valued at £50 million, property in Ireland, where he was domiciled, worth in excess of £10 million and holdings in Guinness trusts in North America, primarily Canada, estimated in excess of £250 million. It would be charitable to believe that Saunders receives a mention in Iveagh's will. But I suspect he does not.

2 January 1993

A LESS THAN HAPPY EVENT

Harriet Sergeant

Tokyo

Japan's birth-rate is one of the lowest in the world. The government has just published a report blaming this on cramped housing and the cost of education. The real reason became clear to me when I had a baby in Tokyo last month. Only a fool would do it twice.

Pregnancy had already demoted me to somewhere near the bottom of Japanese society. I first noticed this on the underground. Each compartment reserves six seats for the aged and the infirm; these were always occupied by middle-aged businessmen. They never moved and no one asked them to. The frailest old lady, the woman clutching a child and I were all left to sway at our peril. My complaints shocked a Japanese friend. 'Our businessmen are so tired!' she exclaimed, then went on, 'They are not being unkind, they are just ignoring you.' I said that was worse. She remonstrated, 'Oh no! They are too embarrassed to give you a seat and are waiting for the right moment.' I wondered when that might be. She said, 'Ask them just as they are about to get off. That is always a good time.'

Japanese doctors think as little of women as do Japanese businessmen. Startling statistics reveal a certain carelessness about a woman's life once the baby is born. The Japanese infant mortality rate is the lowest in the world, but the maternal mortality rate is another matter. In 1986 it was the second highest amongst the developed countries: 13.5 Japanese women died in childbirth per 100,000 live births compared to 7.2 in America and 6.8 in England and Wales.

Ignorant of all this, I rang a private hospital consultant for an appointment. The nurse said, 'Japanese doctors don't make appointments. You just have to wait.' I asked for how long. 'Three or four hours,' she replied cheerfully. I explained that I worked. She told me to try coming along first thing next morning. I duly arrived at 8.30 the following day. The hospital fees had led me to expect the Japanese equivalent of Harley Street. It could not have been more different: instead of a settling into an easy chair and a back copy of *Vogue*, I joined 50 pregnant women slumped on benches in a corridor. Some had produced picnics and were feeding their children. Others sat knitting and gossiping with their mothers. There were no husbands to be seen. I waited for an hour, then walked to the top of the queue.

The consulting-room was as crowded as the corridor. Nurses rushed me, with assembly-line efficiency, from a changing room to a row of curtained cubicles and onto an examining table. The doctor made his way from patient to patient, his every comment audible to the entire room. One woman had a husband with a dismal sperm count; another appeared to be suffering from genital warts. This proved amusing until I remembered my own problem. Hastily I sat up. The nurse entered, pushed me down and drew a curtain firmly across my stomach. I stared at it in astonishment. On the other side of the curtain, hidden from my view, the doctor and his students gathered around my legs. I felt the examination begin. Just as I began to wonder how long I could bear this, the nurse returned, 'Why are you so upset?' she asked. I pointed out that an unknown number of men were examining my body. She looked puzzled. 'They can't see your face,' she assured me.

The nurse then explained that the doctor would spend five minutes talking to me. 'He spends five minutes with all his patients, so please do not ask questions.' She frowned at me, 'You foreigners always want to question doctor. That is not the Japanese way.' Nevertheless, I asked doctor a question. 'What about pain relief?' I asked. This seemed not the Japanese way either. Epidural injections, routine in the West, are known about, but not given, in Japan. 'I tell my mothers to get on and bear it,' said the doctor. 'Pain makes you love the baby more.' I said if I hit him on the nose would he like me more. He sighed, shook his head and advised me to improve my attitude 'for the baby's sake. We Japanese believe an angry mother makes for a difficult delivery,' he added.

The following week we received a letter from the consultant. I had forgotten to send him a present. 'Everybody does,' said our Japanese neighbour when we asked her advice. Would a bottle of whisky do, I wondered? We had already paid the consultant's fee. She explained the consultant expected at least 100,000 yen (about £500). The year before she had given her surgeon 300,000 yen in order to ensure good treatment. 'So it's a bribe,' said my husband. She shook her head vehemently, 'There's no bribery in Japan,' she insisted. We sent a box of shortbread instead.

It was perhaps fortunate that the consultant and I did not see each other again. He failed to reach the hospital in time for the birth and so, nearly, did I. Japanese traffic almost forced me to have my son on a Tokyo expressway. 'We have stopped outside an animal hospital,' my husband remarked helpfully at one point. When we finally arrived, half a dozen midwives took charge of me with kind efficiency. They gave me a shiatsu massage to relieve the pain and hurried me to the delivery room. Just as we entered, one gasped, 'You have not changed your slippers.' The delivery room, it appeared, required different footwear. Everything stopped while I shuffled out of one pair of slippers and into another. After that I never managed to climb onto the delivery table. So it was that I gave birth standing up over a red, plastic bucket but shod, at least, correctly.

Two days later I found myself once again sitting in line with some 40 Japanese mothers. This time we wore nightgowns, a compulsory, hospital-issue bath-cap and a pair of compulsory, hospital-issue, sterilised plastic slippers. New-born infants sucked away at us. The hospital permitted mothers to hold their new-born children only in this one corridor at feeding time. Otherwise babies were confined to a nursery with a glass wall in front of which friends and relatives gathered during visiting hours. The mother would ask for her child, a nurse would wheel up the cot and everybody would exclaim and video-tape through the glass. The western theory of bonding has not, it seems, arrived in Japan. Before we could touch our baby at feeding times, we had to change our footwear, cover our hair, remove any watches and scrub our hands and arms.

The other mothers wore flannel night-dresses and their hair in plaits. They started disapprovingly at my lace negligée. It was indeed hard to imagine any of us as sex objects, however briefly, nine months before. Nurses walked up and down massaging engorged and naked breasts. Women closed their eyes and submitted with only the occasional grimace of pain. At my turn I screamed, begged for aspirin and burst into tears. 'Is it so different in the West then?' demanded the exasperated nurse. I stared at the line of mothers, and recalled all the treatment we had received with its lack of sympathy, pain relief or privacy. I

imagined their future with a child in a tiny apartment, an absent husband and no system of health visitors or even baby-sitters. Many, to
the despair of the Japanese government, would refuse to go through
the process again. 'Very different,' I replied, without hesitation.

2 January 1993

DIARY

Dominic Lawson

Mr Alan Clark, who is drawn to controversy as a housefly is to rotting
fruit, has done it again by writing an article in the *Times* accusing
Churchill of being 'obsessed' with fighting Hitler, and denouncing our
great war leader for failing to sue for peace with the Nazis in 1941. Mr
Clark somehow left out from his article the fact that Hitler broke

every one of the six treaties he signed between 1933 and 1939. But I am surprised that anyone is surprised by the ravings of the former defence minister. It is widely known that Mr Clark is a man who keeps a Rottweiler called Eva, named after Eva Braun, and is a keen collector of Nazi memorabilia. There are times when I think that Mr Clark is the only good argument against inherited wealth, as it is that which gives this particular unemployed ex-MP the time to devote to his historical researches and his subsequent verbal venting of them through his least useful orifice. Without his inherited millions Mr Clark might have to spend his time more usefully, working as a chauffeur perhaps, or as a commissionaire. I must therefore take issue with our diarist of last week, Mr Nigel Dempster, who stated here that Mr Major's failure to ennoble Mr Clark was 'the most glaring omission' in the New Year's Honours List, since 'his innate honesty in the witness-box led to the collapse of the Matrix Churchill trial in November and the acquittal of three directors who otherwise would probably have been found guilty and jailed'. The fact is that Mr Clark had earlier made statements to the police which were instrumental in the decision to prosecute the three innocent men. It was only in court, when confronted by a defence counsel in possession of hitherto suppressed Government documents detailing Mr Clark's role in the affair, that the former defence minister blurted out the words which led to the acquittal of the Matrix directors. Mr Clark, as one minister regularly put it to him face to face, is 'a bad man'.

9 January 1993

THE STATE STOLE
THEIR CHILDREN

Alasdair Palmer

Because of restrictions imposed by the Administration of Justice Act 1960, as amended by the Children Act 1989, all names in this article have been changed.

If you walk into Sheila and David Maggs's home in one of the less privileged parts of the Home Counties, the first thing that strikes you is what looks like an altar. It is in fact a small dressing table covered in photographs of children aged between nine months and seven years. Sheila and David spend most of their spare time staring at those photographs. They are all that they have left of their children. The State has taken their two sons away from them. Despite their desperate attempts to get them back, Sheila and David's children are now in the process of being adopted. They have been told they will never see them again. The most they can do is send presents to them. But – as the official correspondence calmly states – 'it cannot be guaranteed that they will receive them.'

What had the Maggses done to merit losing all contact with their own offspring? What hideous crime had they perpetrated against their children? Sexual abuse? Physical battery? Criminal neglect? Whatever it was, it must have been monstrous. The smiling faces of the growing boys in the photographs – and the infinite sadness of their parents when they look at them – must disguise a family history of unspeakable horror.

But inspect the files, read the case notes, and talk to the family doctor, and you will find nothing which suggests anything of the kind. Sheila and David were not guilty of abusing their children. There has never been any suspicion of abuse of any kind. On the contrary, even hostile reports on their behaviour say that 'Mr and Mrs Maggs genuinely love, and care for, their children' and that the children 'are well-nourished and physically healthy'.

So why did the State feel the need to take them away from their parents, and to ensure that they never again have contact with them? Sheila and David do not understand. They can only blame it on the vindictiveness of their social worker who 'always wanted to swipe my children. They told me when I was pregnant with Gary that they would take him away when he was born. Later, I told the social worker he had no reason. He said, "Don't worry, we'll find one." And now my babies are gone . . .'

But the implications of what happened go far beyond the actions of one individual or one department. Nothing in the documentation suggests there was anything out of the ordinary in the way the Maggses' children were taken from their parents. No special powers were invoked, no extraordinary conference convened. Everything was not merely legal, it was routine. The implications for the power of social services to break up families, even in cases where there is not the remotest suspicion of physical or sexual abuse, are terrifying.

David and Sheila stood accused of many things – poverty, stupidity, obstreperousness, and of living in a dirty, run-down council house. But the crucial charge which led to the abduction of their children was of 'failing to stimulate' their eldest child, Darren, as much as a better parent would. That lack of stimulation was blamed for Darren's failure to develop intellectually and emotionally at the normal rate, for his low concentration span, and his bouts of hyperactivity. Since the Social Services were convinced that the cause of Darren's problems was his parents' inadequacies, the social workers determined that Darren's younger brother, Gary, would suffer the same fate. So – with impeccable logic – they decided that if Darren should be taken away from his parents, so should Gary. And that is what happened. Both children were first made wards of court, then taken into care and placed in foster homes.

Sheila and David opposed the decision. So did their general practitioner. 'It was obviously not a family where the children were at risk,' he says. 'The problem was with the "carers", not the family. Social workers can be very inexperienced. They can be in their early twenties and without children themselves. Yet the only thing which enables you to see the difference between a loving but difficult family and a dangerous one is a lot of experience. But all they have are the latest theories from social work training.'

Their GP made his objections to any planned break-up of the family loud and clear. The Social Services disposed of them with Prussian efficiency. First they fixed the court hearing for a date when they knew he could not be present. Then, when he attempted to procure an assessment of the children from an independent paediatrician, they had their solicitors reprimand him for daring to take such a step. They used the same method to persuade the paediatrician that he was not allowed to submit his report to their GP.

With no one present to give a professional opinion in their favour, the outcome of the court hearing was inevitable. The judge ruled that David and Sheila's children should remain in the care of the Social Services, who would have discretion over whether their parents had access to them. The judge also ruled that there should be an independent psychiatric assessment to check that the cause of Darren's problems was indeed poor parenting.

The court-ordered assessment took nearly a year. Sheila and David were promised access every two weeks. In fact it occurred once every six months. When the assessment finally arrived, the Social Services did everything they could to keep it from the parents and their lawyer (officially, neither have been allowed to see it).

For the assessment did not, in fact, support the contention that Darren's problems were due to his parents' incompetence. On the contrary, the medical report suggested that Darren's difficulties were genetic. They had nothing to do with 'lack of stimulation' by his parents at all. It followed that if Darren was not being damaged by his parents, then neither was Gary.

Admit the mistake, apologise for it, and return the children to their natural parents: that is the conclusion most would hope to be drawn from what had happened. But it was not the conclusion which the Social Services drew. They still proposed compulsory adoption for Darren and Gary. Why? Because the children had now been away so long from their parents it would only harm them to be returned. The 'health professionals' concerned could see 'only further distress to both boys and parents coming from any form of continued access from Mr and Mrs Maggs'.

Was there any evidence that Darren and Gary were happier away from their parents? No. There was only the say-so of the 'health professionals'. The facts did not suggest that Darren was doing well after being taken from his mother. A number of different foster parents had found him impossible to cope with. Even the affidavit from the Social Services sworn in support of his compulsory adoption notes that after being taken away from his mother he was 'very destructive'; he 'threw massive temper tantrums'; he had 'begun to constantly throw things' at one of his foster mothers; he was 'very unsettled at school . . . his attention span deteriorated . . . he had reverted to crawling round on his hands and knees.' Unable to find a permanent home, Darren was placed in an institution. The only people who wanted to look after him were the only people who the State would not let do so – his natural parents, Sheila and David Maggs.

Gary, less troublesome, more 'normal', had been luckier. The official documents note with evident pleasure that the father in the proposed adoptive family is a 'sensitive man'. He is also 'employed by the social services department as a residential social worker within a children's home, and it was considered that the expertise he had would enable him to deal with any problems Gary may have'.

There is not much doubt that David and Sheila's circumstances, and even their attitudes, are unfortunate and undesirable. They are poor, inarticulate and uneducated. Their housing is inadequate. They are not social workers. And they did not respond well to being told that other people knew better than they did how to bring up their children – which was taken as further proof that they did not know how to bring up their children. They lost their tempers with the social worker assigned to them, and told him to 'fuck off' – perhaps a not wholly surprising response to being told that, unless they did as they were told, they would lose their children.

It is also probably true that Sheila and David's children would fare better brought up in nicer, more comfortable circumstances by smarter, richer, parents more receptive to social worker's advice. But if that were enough to mean that children should be moved to the nearest 'better home', few children would ever grow up with their natural parents. Give the State the power to remove children, not merely when they are being physically abused or neglected by their parents, but whenever the State's representatives think children might do better elsewhere, and it is hard to see what rights parents – or even children – have left. Yet that appears to be the power which the State has acquired, and still has, in Britain, in 1993. And David and Sheila are powerless to stop it.

That power would be utterly tyrannical even if social workers' convictions about children's welfare were infallible. But, of course, they are not. 'It is rating our conjectures highly to roast people for them,' wrote Montaigne at the height of the witch craze. It is also rating them highly to split up families for them. Child psychology, still more social work, are not exact sciences. They both consist in little more than a set of conjectures – however passionately social workers or child psychologists may hold them. No one can honestly claim to know with any degree of certainty what the final outcome of following one way bringing up a child rather than another will be. No one knows what turns a child into a stable, happy, responsible individual. Apart from stable, loving parents – and they are no guarantee, only (generally) a prerequisite – what child psychologists and social workers consider to be 'essential' to the process of development changes as often any other fashion. And their conjectures on the subject often turn out to be horribly wrong.

Yet families continue to be broken up for the sake of those conjectures. According to the Department of Health, around 10,000 children under four are taken into care every year. Many of those children are not the children of abusing, neglecting monsters. They are often the children of parents like Sheila and David – poor in every respect, inadequate perhaps, and needing help, but not needing to be deprived of their children.

David and Sheila's children were first taken from them before the new Children's Act came into force in October 1991. Its provisions cannot help them, or others like them, to get their children back. Yet, despite that Act, which was specifically designed to curb the powers

of social workers to take children compulsorily into care, the conjectures of child psychologists and social workers continue to go unchallenged in the courts. The essential problem is that there is no
'professional' alternative to their views. Almost all the medical
opinions are based on evidence collected by social workers: they are
the only ones who keep notes on the 'emotional development' of the
children; they are the only ones who can supply details on how that
development is being harmed. In many cases, child psychologists and
psychiatrists write authoritative reports recommending the break-up
of families without seeing the family whose fate they are deciding.
Their opinions are based only on the notes supplied to them by social
workers. For the courts to accept those reports as independent confirmation of the social workers' view – as they do – is like buying two
copies of *The Spectator* in order to convince yourself that what it said
was true.

Family lawyers who deal with cases like the Maggses' stress how
difficult it is to get a second opinion which might favour the family
on to the record. This is not necessarily because alternative views
cannot be found – child psychologists and social workers seem to agree
amongst themselves about as much as economists. It is rather because
judges in such cases do not like to hear contradictory views from the
professionals whose advice they have to rely on in making a ruling.
When two health professionals give opposite opinions on what the
consequences of leaving children with their natural parents will be,
how is a judge – who is not a health professional – to make a rational
decision? Seeking more opinions from each side serves only to duplicate the impasse. So judges discourage it.

No one would deny that children sometimes need protection from
their parents. But sometimes parents and children in poor families
need protection from officials who act as if their arguments about the
unfitness of the underprivileged to bring up children represent not a
fallacy of the most morally obnoxious kind, but a blindingly obvious
truth. Sadly, the fallacy seems to be built into the law governing most
of these cases. In 1980, for example, the European Court of Human
Rights ruled that Essex County Council had wrongly taken Linda
Hyatt's child and placed the infant in adoption. But the British courts
upheld the original compulsory adoption order, on the grounds that
the child was now better off with the new family.

Whilst it remains unchallenged, that reasoning threatens every
mother and father, rich or poor, with the irreversible loss of their
children. It also continues to carve an enormous swathe of avoidable
suffering. Sheila and David are not the only parents who now find

themselves in the position of pleading with a court to give them leave to appeal against a decision which, as well as denying them custody, has deprived them of access to their children. Reading the austere legal and medical pronouncements of the case, it is sometimes hard to remember that they are not criminals requesting parole, but parents trying to touch their own flesh and blood.

Few have any chance of success. Sheila and David hope to appeal against Gary's adoption, but too much time has now elapsed; whether or not the original decision to remove him was correct, time has rendered it irreversible. The 'professional' consensus is now solidly behind the view that he is better off with his new family, with its social worker accreditation.

All that is left for Sheila and David is their altar of photographs, and the blithe reassurances from officials that their children are 'really much better off without them'.

Alasdair Palmer works for Granada Television.

9 January 1993

DOWN SOME DARK DEFILE

John Simpson

Sarajevo

The glass door of the shattered building swung laxly behind me, and I headed into a world of utter dark, loneliness and cold. It became instantly clear to me that the decision to walk back to my hotel was an act of foolishness and bravado, rather than the amusing adventure I had expected. It was 11 at night: the only people at large in Sarajevo were snipers. Artillery grumbled on Mount Igman and Zuc Hill, and occasional distant magnesium flares gave a blueish tinge to the skyline, like the fingernails of a dead man. The city was dead, too, and sprawled around me abandoned. Not a window glowed in the huge blocks of flats down the main avenue. No street-lamp was left standing. The snow itself barely showed in the darkness.

Under Tito it had been named the Boulevard of something empty and pompous, but now the journalists called it Sniper Alley. Every intersection was dangerous, and in the daytime those who couldn't avoid crossing did the nervous stuttering dash which the journalists also had a name for: the Sarajevo shuffle. The snipers were in buildings which lay 100 yards or so back from the southern side of Sniper Alley – the right-hand side, as I did the two-mile walk from the television station to the Holiday Inn.

Within 30 seconds, the cold had worked its way through my protective clothing. Protective in a double sense: I had put on the whole armour of Messrs Tetranike, complete with the latest in ceramic plates. It bound my ribs and stomach like a Victorian corset. Usually I disliked it with great intensity. Not now: it gave me warmth, and the feeling that, if something struck me, I might live. I especially didn't want to die in this loneliness and dark. 'A scrimmage in a border station,' I quoted to myself uncomfortably from Kipling:

> A canter down some dark defile:
> Two thousand pounds of education
> Falls to a ten-rupee jezail.

A Kalashnikov rifle costs more than that in Sarajevo, but the principle is the same.

A car passed at speed. It raced across the intersection which I would soon have to cross. I couldn't tell if anyone had fired at the car. There was the crack of a bullet, certainly, but the echo from the vast, smashed, empty buildings of Tito's dream deflected the sound confusingly. Yet they were not entirely empty: as I ground on, avoiding the polyhedrons of glass that lay everywhere, I saw a window just above my head which was lit by a candle, dark gold in the darkness. Inside there was a repeated quiet, dry coughing, like an animal rustling in fallen leaves: the sound of the last inhabitant of a dead city.

Who killed Sarajevo? I asked myself as I left the little flicker of life behind me. The predominantly Muslim government, which insisted on a referendum on independence and so provoked the Serbs? The Serbs themselves, with their push for *Lebensraum*? Tito, who bottled up the passions of a century and insisted there was nothing other than Yugoslavism? The Germans, who recognised the independence of their friends, the Croats? The United Nations, which ought to have imposed its moral authority on a city from which every other form of authority was in flight, and failed humiliatingly?

It doesn't really matter, I thought, as I headed towards the first sniper

*'We've been here a week. I've yet to see the
Romans do anything.'*

intersection; but people in a state of advanced despair need someone
to blame, and most of the candidates were too vague or distant to
qualify. Only the United Nations, driving round in its large white
vehicles, was on hand for everyone to see and revile. And indeed it is
hard sometimes to fight down one's anger at the crassness, the slow-
ness, the lack of imagination and drive which characterise some of the
UN's activity here. On Christmas Day I visited a bakery, the only one
still operating in the city, which had to close down because the UN
failed to deliver its fuel oil on time; and even when the oil arrived,
there wasn't enough of it. Three days later I went to the old people's
home on the front line between Serbs and Muslims, only a few hundred
yards from the UNHCR headquarters, where the inhabitants were
dying of cold even though a couple of hundred blankets and some
insulation might have saved them. And meanwhile there was a foolish
little episode wherein UN headquarters in Zagreb seems to have tried
to teach General Morillon, the French commander of the UN forces
in the city, a lesson by leaking information that he was thinking of

pulling out of the city after a few mortar shells had landed near his headquarters.

The UN has not helped Sarajevo with its doctrine that the soldiers of one UN member country are the equal of those of any other. Why should Ukrainian soldiers remain in Sarajevo, for instance, when they have to be prevented from selling so much of their fuel ration on the black market that they could not always carry out their missions? Only the Canadians, the French and the British have shown the firmness and efficiency which are required here; and the Canadians have left the city, while the British carry out their duties with great skill and polish, but for the most part operate in the countryside.

There are other bureaucratic curiosities here. While the soldiers of every other country in the UN force are paid more – sometimes very much more – than they would get for their normal duties, the Ministry of Defence pays the men and women of the British UN contingent less than they would usually get. There is logic of a kind to it: things cost less here than they do in Germany, Britain or Northern Ireland. But when everyone from Bosnian government ministers to Chetnik soldiers in the mountains overlooking the city acknowledge that the British are the most efficient of the UN forces here, it is extraordinary that they should serve alongside units which are far better paid.

I came, eventually, to the crossroads. It was hard to work out in the darkness whether the darker patches on the faint glimmer of snow underfoot were pieces of fallen metal or holes in the ground. I launched out into the roadway; no point in hanging around. My armour hung heavy on my back, and the extra clothes that fought the cold slowed me down. I began to run, but found my feet entangled with a thick metal cable: the tramwires had been felled by a mortar. I tried to imagine a sniper following my Sarajevo shuffle across the open intersection: would he pause to speculate about the reasons which brought someone out this late, as I swam through the greenish haze of his night-sight? Or would he squeeze the trigger automatically as soon as he saw me?

I waited for the terrible, shattering blow on my right side, and then I reached the pavement. It seemed like safety. Yet as I reached a line of burned and looted shops, the tatters of their curtains stirring in the wind, and remembered from the daytime the charred frames of chairs and desks lying inside, there came the vindictive crack of a high-velocity rifle close by: perhaps from the vast block of empty flats opposite. Something slammed into the concrete above my head, and I ran along, bent double, until there was another crack and another hammer-blow even closer. Two thousand pounds of education sprawled on the ground, defenceless before the jezail. Someone in the cold and darkness knew I was there.

Time passed. Another car drove fast down the boulevard and no one fired at it. Had the sniper gone off duty or grown bored, or was he just playing with me? I moved a little; no response. I got to my knees, stood up, and began walking again; nothing except distant artillery and the upward rush of rockets a mile away. In a minute or so I was alongside the white wall outside the museum of Tito's largely fictitious revolution.

The building was burned and empty, and someone had written 'Bad Boys' and 'Devil Rapers' on the wall with spray-paint: I could just make out the words even in the dark. The Holiday Inn was very close now, a mere boulevard-width away, and I was safe.

Tens of thousands of people run these risks here every day, and dozens are killed or wounded each week by snipers. The gun confers enormous power; and ever since the siege began at the start of last summer education and decency and determination have been impotent against it. Any solution to the problem — and in particular the Owen-Vance proposals — will be based on an acceptance of the Serbs' act of banditry. There is no encouraging moral to be drawn in Sarajevo.

9 January 1993

THE VARSITY ENTRANCE TORTURE

Hester McIntyre

'What is reality?' The question, along with smoke from what was probably a cigarette, ascended languidly from beneath a table. The response, in the real world, would have been the kick that Dr Johnson gave the stone to refute Bishop Berkeley's idealism. But this was not the real world. This was Oxford, and it was the season of candidates' — one should call us supplicants — interviews for admission.

Reality at Oxford during the Supplicant Season is three days of psychological torture. A professor jumps from behind a sofa crying, 'I disagree with that statement!' to a bewildered interviewee who had merely asked where he was. One tutor, from behind the safety of the morning newspaper, orders a candidate to 'entertain' him. This brave respondent reputedly sets fire to the paper. Most of the timid souls who came to Oxford this winter are neither as courageous nor as resourceful.

For reasons best known to the selectors, the hopefuls are starved (guessing the contents of college meals is a pointless pastime) and deprived of sleep (the college duvet is, in the words of one survivor, 'thinner than an Access card'). Hungry, tired and tense, the hapless 18-year-old is demoralised before the interview room is in sight. In two or three days at Oxford, the interview does not last more than an hour. One girl waited two days for 13 minutes with a tutor. The 'interview experience' is usually an hour confined in a book-lined room with a professor or two. Part of the ordeal is the hours spent chain-smoking and swapping anecdotes with the competition in the JCR.

Are the interviewers as vindictive as they appear or do they premeditate schemes to weed out those lacking in fluency and intelligence? If the latter, the dons demonstrate little, if any, willingness to succeed. It has also crossed my mind that they do not actually know how to interview and are almost as nervous as the candidates.

My interview did not constitute reality. The first session was relatively relaxed, although the two dons had cunningly placed me opposite a window so that the sun shone directly into my eyes. What is more surprising is that they admitted having done so knowingly, making it impossible for me to move. The two men then sat at opposite ends of the room so that answering each of them in turn was like watching a game of tennis. This was the gentle introduction to the Second Session. That came later, when it was dark.

My eyes no longer needed protection from the sun, but the tennis-match continued. The interrogators, as they all do in films, dropped the pretence of relaxed informality. 'So, Miss McIntyre,' one of them started, 'can you identify the economic trend that affects the curve on the graph in front of you?' I stared at the graph I had been given earlier. It was of wages in terms of consumables of building craftsmen from 1264 AD to 1954 AD. I had applied to read history, and I doubt that Sir Steven Runciman would have made much of the graph. I responded with, well, silence. I stared at the notes I had made and which were now useless. Eventually, I stammered out the ostensible causes of change for a couple of periods. That was not enough. 'Well, yes, Miss McIntyre, but we were thinking of something more general.' Why had I not chosen economics for A-level? Why was there no sound in that room, not even the ticking of a clock? I was occasionally silent, but not incoherent, until one of them said smugly that the answer was so obvious I would kick myself when I knew.

The interrogators moved on. They showed me a map of the distribution of lunatics in Great Britain in 1902. Could I tell them why, in my opinion, there were so many lunatics in Surrey and so few in the rest of the south of England? Not really, no. I began to guess. I suggested there were perhaps more lunatic asylums in Surrey than elsewhere. I thought this was probably a stupid thing to say, but it seemed to be right. What I wanted to ask was how, in the 90 years since, so many lunatics had made their way to Oxford.

Worse was to come. They asked if there was anything I wanted them to ask me. I wanted them to ask me to return next autumn, but they had something else in mind. In order to move on from what they called history (wage charts and lunacy), I answered that I was surprised not to have been asked about my other interests. At this, they laughed. These were grown men. The only time they showed any interest at all was when I mentioned that my father, who had been tutored by one of them (although I had not mentioned this), was a publisher; and I feared for a moment they might ask me to give him their manuscripts on the wage development of lunatic craftsmen through the ages. After a brief discussion of nothing in particular, I was released from interrogation to eat my unidentifiable supper and contemplate a move to Surrey, where I would in due course commit suicide.

I was not alone in suppressing my inclination to speak more frankly. Aspiring lawyers were asked perverse, and perverted, questions about sado-masochism and the law, and their embarrassment was greater even than mine. Some may have spoken too frankly, particularly when several music candidates fell for one interviewer's ploy of getting them drunk at a party he organised in an undergraduate's room. One attractive young woman was wholly disconcerted to be required to answer her interviewers while seated in a rocking-chair, exposing more of her legs than her intellect.

An un-British camaraderie developed among us, despite the fact we were competing with one another. We were all in the same rudderless boat. Thus, when I saw the person sitting next to me in the Haagen-Dazs shop staring into his coffee with his head in his hands, we had a common, bitter experience to talk about, as though we had been through the Blitz together.

Only Oxford could get away with the maddening and unsatisfactory selection process that so often fails to find the best in its applicants. It plays with people who have worked hard, and it tries to demoralise them. The most soul-destroying aspect of the whole process, however, was that for a few days we were in that fairy-tale world of beauty, culture and erudition, where time stands still and alcohol is cheap; but we knew only a few would return. For most of us, nowhere else would do.

A few days later, my letter of rejection arrived. Obviously, I hate Oxford. Just as obviously, I shall apply again.

9 January 1993

BOOKS

AN UNLIKELY FRIENDSHIP WITH GOD

Hilary Mantel

MAKE BELIEVE
by Diana Athill
Sinclair-Stevenson, £13.99, pp. 136

'What have I lived for?' her grandmother said as she lay dying. It was the question Diana Athill had in mind when she wrote *Instead of a Letter*, an essay in autobiography which one reviewer described as among the 'few totally honest accounts of human life'. Candour is the hallmark of her work. Her new book *Make Believe* finds her older and not much wiser, as she would be ready to admit. It is a record of friendship against the odds, of an attempt to bridge a gap between a woman and a man. She is an Englishwoman in middle age, a publisher and author, well-travelled and well-informed and serene; he is a young black American, a radical, his background dirt-poor, his temperament excitable, his ignorance profound. The story ends badly, and ends off the page, but the enterprise, the effort, is recorded here in a memoir with the immediacy and grip of a good novel.

To understand why she thought the enterprise worthwhile it helps to know something of her earlier life. Born in 1917, she came from a landed family, and her childhood was happy and secure. Until she was 14 she stayed at home with a governess, wondering only a little about the smug insularity of her family's values. At school, her eyes began to open; she went up to Oxford 'an imperfectly informed but convinced socialist, pacifist and agnostic'.

Adherance to these demanding creeds had to fit in with the pursuit of undergraduate pleasure. She habitually thought of herself as frivolous and lazy, and so she was; her political commitment extended to cutting sandwiches for hunger marchers. She was following a conventional path for an educated person growing up in the Thirties; skirting communism, flirting with it, and at the same time trying to work out where she fitted in the adult world, and how to cope with sex and love. Yet her vision of the precarious nature of life was far from conventional. Since the age of ten she had been beset by visions of herself as a huddled voyager whirled across the seas in a bowl: thrown sometimes against the rim of the bowl so that she glimpsed the ocean of chaos on all sides. It is true that her experience of life's dangers came secondhand, from pictures and books, but this vision was her own property, part of her essence, and it drives her in her quest to find meaning in her life. Her autobiography may remind some readers of a similar quest by Joanna Field, who in the 1930s published *A Life of One's Own* and *An Experiment in Leisure*. Athill shares something of Field's willed passivity, and of her anxiety about the nature of feminity, but she is less earnest, better company for the reader.

Despite her occasional foreboding, the young Diana was 'well-disposed to life' and inclined to believe that hers would be contented and satisfactory. Then, during the war, came the desolating experience of a broken engagement; her fiancé was in the RAF, was posted abroad, broke off contact, married someone else, and was killed shortly afterwards. She could not recover from this. She acted on a belief that casual affairs in sufficient number protect one from the depredations of romantic love, and she accepted that she had failed to get the ordinary things in life: a husband, children, a home. For 20 years of her life 'failure was its essence' she says, and her book bears out Orwell's contention that autobiography can only be trusted when it is about failure: 'A man who gives a good account of himself is probably lying, since any life when viewed from the inside is simply a series of defeats.' Yet she became absorbed in her work – she started in publishing with André Deutsch, working from two dingy rooms and watching every penny. She began to write herself, and found it an activity as natural and necessary as breathing. The reader sees the transformation of the storm-battered soul into a buoyant woman, open-handed and open-hearted, able to offer friendship but able to draw back and preserve herself. A faculty for self-preservation is necessary when you have friends like hers.

Hakim Jamal, the subject of her new book, came into her life in 1969. He was born Alan Donaldson, in a poor district of Boston; he was much darker than his brothers and sisters, and they used to tell him that the family had found him one day in the garbage pail. Aged ten, he began to sneak drinks from his stepfather's liquor bottles; he was a serious drinker at 12 and using heroin at 14. He went to prison, had a spell in a mental hospital, seemed to be sucked into a downward spiral that could only end in an early and perhaps violent death. But then, aged 27, he met Malcolm X. He embraced the Black Muslim creed, gave up drink and drugs, involved himself in an educational project in a Los Angeles ghetto. When Athill met him he had been invited to London by people who were interested in his work and thought he ought to write a book about his life.

Athill worked with him on this book, inviting him to stay at her flat. She was sexually attracted to him, and he sometimes demonstrated great tenderness towards her; he became her close friend, occasional lover. But he was a proud, touchy, oversensitive man, something of a fantasist; he was a womaniser, never had money, and was ready 'to feed my weakness for having my heart wrung'.

Have we been here before? Athill's 1986 book *After a Funeral* chronicled her relationship with an author she called 'Didi'. He was a Communist, an exile from Nasser's Egypt; he was a charmer and a gambler, a drunk and a depressive; she met him in 1963, endured much from him, and watched by his bedside as he died of a deliberate overdose. The reader can see that a pattern is being repeated; these very different men have a common core and a common facility. They are destructive and self-destructive, and they touch her heart.

She says of Hakim,

> In a sweet mood he could establish a feeling of harmony and peacefulness . . . In an evil mood he could harass and exhaust one . . . I have never known anyone so impossible to disregard.

It was difficult to know when Hakim was telling the truth. Had he really murdered people, turned a gun on the white oppressor? Possibly. Had he, as he claimed, had an affair with Jean Seberg? It turned out he had; and the actress makes a fleeting, intriguing appearance in Athill's story.

Hakim brought to Diana's flat a young Englishwoman, Gail Benson. She was the daughter of a former Tory MP, her childhood was unhappy and, as Athill describes her she was a neurotic mess, though not without a resourcefulness and charm of her own. Gail was besotted with Hakim and travelled with him in North Africa and America, sharing his life of sponging and semi-starvation. With painful clarity Athill describes nightmare interludes with this pair: hours of mind-games, of emotional confusion and dwindling sanity. At first Hakim seemed unstable; then he seemed frankly mad. He claimed he was God. Gail Benson accepted his claim, recording in her diary:

> Diana is unable to believe that Hakim is God. It is strange how people refuse the light when it is offered to them.

Hakim's book *From The Dead Level* was finally published, but his other writing was degenerating into nonsense and his schemes were becoming ever more grandiose. He heard that in Guyana the government was giving grants of land to settlers, so he and Gail flew off there to found a commune. Diana Athill did not see him again. But a man she had been careful to keep out of his life now entered it. The malign presence of 'Michael X' broods over this story. Athill knew Michael de Freitas because her firm had published a book of his. Her first opinion of him was that he was 'either a nut or a conman' and he had proved to be a difficult man to work with. She knew that, while he aspired to be a black saviour, most people thought him a joke. Hakim had asked to meet him and she had steered him away. But as Hakim's paranoia worsened he began to insist that there was a plot to keep him and Michael apart. The Guyana venture failed, Hakim and Gail travelled to Trinidad, and Hakim decided he was not God after all: Michael X was God. The story takes its ugliest turn: Hakim connived at the murder of Gail, who was butchered and buried alive by Michael X's followers. Hakim returned to Boston, to the slum where he had been born, and was murdered there in 1973 by a black vigilante group who called themselves De Mau Mau.

In Diana Athill's hands this story is sad rather than sordid, thought-provoking rather than depressing. As an author she has a knack of seeming to speak directly to the reader, so that you feel you are living her life with her. She is good at pinpointing a moral dilemma, at describing life's double-binds; you feel she would not be mistaken about the nature of an event, or misperceive a person's value. She is a soft touch though, and she knows it. Her fiancé who so nearly ruined her life, once recommended her to read a poem by Emerson:

*'Isn't that typical? Just as we were
getting comfortable!'*

Give all to love;
Obey thy heart;
Friends, kindred, days,
Estate, good fame,
Plans, credit and the Muse –
Nothing refuse.

She thought at the time, 'What a terrible poem to choose and what
a splendid message to send.' No doubt she thinks it still.

9 January 1993

DIARY

Keith Waterhouse

A cartoon in the current *Private Eye* has a beggar sporting a placard with the words 'Massive January Reduction. Was asking 10p – now 5p.' Art imitates life. In New York there is a panhandler who works Central Park South with the cry, 'Twenty dollars minimum, folks!' He does a brisk trade, too. On a brief visit over Christmas I found that he had changed his spiel to 'Holiday sale, folks. Ten dollars only.' And he was still getting customers. But the best New York beggars are a witty breed who put our own whingeing, cardboard-clutching tube platform squatters to shame. There is said to be a beggar on the Upper East Side who shakes not one cup but two. When asked why the duplication, he explains, 'Business was so good I opened another branch.' My own favourite mendicant has always been the chap who stopped me on Fifth Avenue with the request, 'Sir, will you give me a dollar if I undertake to put it to no good use whatsoever?' He got five. But he was upstaged on this trip by the cheerful black who buttonholed me with, 'Could you spare a little change to help me through college? I have to take a refresher course on how to hold a fork.' He got five too. This was outside the Algonquin, an establishment which I am happy to see is being patronised by the Brits again (and with a cat back in residence) after a period of ostracism in favour of the Royalton opposite in protest at the new owners turning the old Blue Bar into an office. For myself, I regret-fully no longer stay at the Algonquin, having found of late that the rooms are getting smaller as I get older. But they did show you to your broom closet with panache. The last time I stayed there I arranged a room for my son, who was joining me. The desk clerk apologised for its smallness even by Algonquin standards. When I retorted that the boy was a student and lucky not to be sleeping on a bench in Central Park, he beamed. 'That's the spirit, Mr Waterhouse. In future years your son will be able to say, "I may be rich and famous now, but I can remember the day when I had to rough it at the Algonquin."'

16 January 1992

BOOKS

WOMEN ARE WIMPS

Julie Burchill

SEX, ART AND AMERICAN CULTURE
by Camille Paglia
Viking, £16.99, pp.337

Like her heroine, Madonna, Camille Paglia (the 'g' is silent – the only thing about her that is) is a blue-collar Italian-American broad with a striking name and a striking gift for *la publicité*. Unlike her, she has swelegant cheekbones and brilliant legs. But, like her when it comes to sex, she couldn't think her way out of a wet paper bag with a machete in one hand, a Bowie knife in the other and Friedrich Nietzsche leading the way with a flaming torch. Is it entirely suitable for one feminist to talk about another feminist in this way? You bet; when that feminist is CP, a woman whose feminism expresses itself mostly in high-handed contempt for other women, especially feminists. Steinem, Dworkin, Millet; all have come under Camille's vicious toffee hammer in their time, their entire bodies of work dismissed because their bodies were out of shape, or because they were 'nuts' or because they'd been 'dumped' so many times by men that they were now unreliable witnesses.

Not surprisingly, Paglia – Professor of Humanities at the University of the Arts in Philadelphia (no, I'd never heard of it either) – has made big waves in the world of American academe, especially with the publication of *Sexual Personae* last year. It was impressive, but for the wrong reasons; it made you feel guilty and shallow and shirking because of the sheer volume of research that had gone into it – a cool 700-pages worth. But after a bit, it strikes you that the weight of the guilt is probably not the best way to judge a work.

Nothing daunted, Professor Paglia proceeded to attend color co-ordination school, hired a brace of burly bodyguards and posed for *Vanity Fair* with a couple of black men done up as Nubian slaves; Richard Hoggart she is not. Yes, girls just want to have fun! – and like Madonna before her, Professor Paglia found that in the bland lo-cal cultural wasteland of the contemporary USA it is quite easy to become famous by saying a little very loudly and a lot. Here, in a collection of her essays, book reviews and lectures, she says it again.

Had she followed a more conventional career route for one of her caste and ethnic origins, Paglia would have made a brilliant cab driver. Whatever happens between men and women – including rape – she can boil down to one basic dictum: 'It's human nature, isn't it?' Victims of date rape, for example, are tale-tellers out of school, 'neurotic, middle-class girls'. Does she have the statistics on this? And since when were middle-class and/or neurotic people not protected by the same laws as the rest of us? As a well-paid woman who is obviously crazy as a loon, she'd better not complain to the good British bobby if she gets her handbag snatched in Leicester Square. Some of Paglia's pronouncements are so weird that they make you giggle in sheer molten awe at the nerve of the woman. Rape, for instance, is 'a mode of natural aggression'. 'Well, you have to admire her for saying the unsayable,' pout my sophisticat English feminist friends, not as easily shocked as their Puritan sisters across the water.

In admiring those who stand up strongest against the silliness of political correctness, one often ends up endorsing another sort of silliness altogether. Paglia's silliness is sex. She is basically – as she has boasted – a male homosexual in a woman's body, with all the prejudice and contempt that many male homosexuals feel for women. Experiencing first-hand discrimination from them – amusingly, being kept out of an orgy she had tried to gatecrash dressed as a man – has not made her admire them less but more. This can make her seem almost lovable, like the tough tomboy in *West Side Story* who had to prove she could talk dirtier and fight harder than the boys so they'd let her in the gang (how well I know the feeling!). But it can also make her numb and dumb.

Because women tend not to dress up in leather aprons and nail each other to coffee tables in their spare time, Paglia thinks they're wimps. It is one step from this conclusion to a view of women balanced somewhere between the Victorians, the Iranians and the King of Siam as played by Yul Brynner; women are passive and nurturing, except when they're sluts, when they should either be stoned to death outside Stringfellows or date raped. Despite her ceaseless listing of her modernist credentials ('I'm in favour of drugs, abortion, pornography' – that's fine as part of a broader picture, but it seems to be *all* she's in favour of, which is a bit tragic) her view of sex is rabidly conservative, green feminism meeting red-in-tooth-and-claw masculinism: all men are rapists/you're asking for it dressed like that.

Like Madonna, who calls herself a feminist and poses for photographs as a rape victim who quite enjoys it, and who can write that any woman who stays in a violent relationship must be 'digging it', Paglia – despite her blue-collar beginnings – does not seem able to comprehend that many working-class women are abused by men not because they're smart manipulators who want it that way but because they're unlucky. Both Madonna and Paglia can imagine what it feels like to be a man, jailbait or a rape victim who digs it; they can't, for some reason, imagine what it's like to be a working-class Italian-American woman with four children, no job and a violent husband. And I really do not believe that anyone who lacks such simple comprehension can be called a creative artist.

Steinem, Dworkin, Hite, Paglia: those Am-fems just keep on coming. They loathe each other, and they're easy to mock. But I admire them all, in a way; for their very stroppiness, their scrappiness, their lack of ladylikeness and their engagement with their issue, after all these years. It is very hard to imagine any of them writing a gardening column, as the risible Germaine Greer does, and good for them.

But what is unattractive and essentially untenable about all of them is their obsession with sex; not sex as sex, but sex as symbol, mixing fundamentalist fervour with profound pomposity. Every time an act of sex is engaged in, according to these broads, we're staring into the abyss, spitting into the eye of the hurricane and legwrestling with God. Well, maybe that's true in America (and Norman Mailer was right all along), but in the rest of the world sex is quite often about nothing more than bagging a cheap thrill; profundity simply doesn't come into it.

A bit of English understatement wouldn't exactly kill Professor Paglia, who seems to believe that irony is something anaemics are prescribed in pill form. Great seriousness can lead to great mistakes; date rape is *not* the norm, and every night thousands of drunken young women go home with equally drunken young men, tussle on sofas and make promises they won't keep before straightening their clothing and going home with no tears before bedtime. Neither is rape always about sex and never about power, as Paglia outrageously claims here; the briefest acquaintance with police work on rapists shows that most of them would choose to rape an ugly or elderly woman who looks weak rather than a sex bomb who looks stroppy. What is creepy about Paglia is that at times she seems to be *willing* such horrors to be the standard practice, just so they'll fit in with her crazy theories.

Despite all this, there is a part of me that has a severe crush on this mad professor – but it is the stupid, gum-popping Poindexter in me which also loves Keith Richards and staying up all night stupefied. I'm 33, and desperate to kick the habit; Paglia's 44, and I really don't see how much longer she can continue her solitary cheerleading for rough sex, recreational drugs and rock and roll – like Mick Jagger still singing 'Satisfaction' at 60.

Ironically, it is when writing about subjects which are not 'sexy' that she is at her most brilliant; her essays on junk bonds and academe are the best things you'll read this year, no doubt about it. The truism about all of us using only five per cent of our brains is one I've never believed, but it does seem true of Paglia. There is a great writer in there fighting to free herself from the media monster trapped in her hamster wheel of sex, lies and Madonna videotapes. If she doesn't get out soon, it's going to be both a flimsy career and a lonely one. Get a life, Camille. Or a wife.

16 January 1992

TELEVISION

HAVE I GOT NUDES FOR YOU

Ian Hislop

This week I was asked to appear on a chat show. Naked. Channel 4 is planning a Love Weekend to coincide with Valentine's Day and the culmination of the events is, naturally, to be a *Naked Chat Show*. The researcher described the format in the letter as one in which 'our couch guests, undressed, share their thoughts on beauty, body-image and desire'.

I appeared on television last week in *Biteback* (BBC 1, Sunday, 4.20 p.m.), where I sat on the couch, dressed, and shared my thoughts on the ethics of laughing at the royal family. Sue Lawley was also dressed, as were an audience of angry BBC viewers who did not laugh much and shared their thoughts on the subject of myself: 'Your generation has no concept of duty', 'You have no sense of morality', 'You are a terrible role model for children'. As the programme continued I kept wondering why on earth I was sitting there. Then I remembered that it was something to do with access, accountability, public service broadcasting and various other things I want to believe in. So there was no option but to grin and bear it.

I do not, however, have to grin and bare it for Channel 4. I have the option of saying, 'Absolutely no way, you must be off your head'. So does everyone else. But the confidence of the invitation suggests that someone is going to accept it. Someone is going to take their clothes off and discuss the nature of body image. This prompts the same disbelief in me as so much other television. I keep asking the screen, 'Why on earth has anyone agreed to do this?'

I found myself doing it again during *Anna Lee* (ITV, Sunday, 9 p.m.), in which Imogen Stubbs played yet another detective. But this one was different from Inspector Morse in the sense that she was female. And Morse does not wear knickerexposing short skirts with black stockings. Amazingly, this was what Imogen Stubbs wore, and only a couple of minutes after the title sequence she bent over to reveal her bum. A few minutes later she ran up some steps and the camera stayed below in order to look up her skirt. More bum. Before I get into an actress-suing-over-remarks-about-bum situation, I should make it clear that it is a very nice bum. Much more appealing than my own would be sitting on a Channel 4 sofa. It is just that I don't understand why an actress as good as Imogen Stubbs is providing what cruder cameramen call 'butt-shots' to spice up such a dull programme. The plot explained the skirt and stockings as Anna Lee choosing a suitable outfit for undercover surveillance in a record shop. Or something like that. I may have missed the detail but it does not begin to answer the question. Why would someone who is that good in so much theatre (*Two Noble Kinsmen* I remember in particular) take on something as bad as *Anna Lee*?

And why did those women in *The Good Sex Guide* (ITV, Monday, 10.40 p.m.) agree to sit in the tub in their swimming costumes and tell the camera about whether they fake orgasm? There they all were, solemnly talking to Margi Clarke about penetrative sex in between clips of synchronised swimmers opening and closing their legs. Why did a girl called Isabel agree to appear in a cowboy hat and discuss her sexual 'cut-off point' with the aid of a fork? Why did those other women agree to be filmed giggling and blowing up condoms and passing round vibrators? Margi Clarke, sounding like Cilla Black taking a biology class, told the camera, 'The clitoris is a bit of a mystery'. Not as much as television sometimes.

16 January 1993

LONG LIFE

ACCOUNTS OF WAR

Nigel Nicolson

The controversy over John Charmley's mischievous book and Alan Clark's even more mischievous gloss on it is salutary because the wrongness of their judgments has made Churchill's wartime perform-ance seem even more admirable than it seemed at the time. It is as if their motive was to set up the skittles for the fun of seeing other people knock them down. What could be more demonstrably false than the argument that if we had made peace in 1940 and '41, the Empire would have remained intact and Britain would have preserved an honourable independence while Hitler and Stalin battered each other to pieces? The Empire was already breaking up under the surge of history, and far from emerging from the war exhausted by her efforts, Britain was more highly respected than at any other period of our history. We were offered the leadership of Europe on a plate, and turned it down.

All the same, Charmley's exercise was valuable because war is the activity of man about which more lies are told than about any other, and even irreverence helps to unravel truth. The Tolstoy-Aldington trial, in which I had a walk-on role, brought to light contemporary documents astounding in their perfidious attempts to cover up a griev-ous betrayal, and it has taken 50 years to admit that even Australian soldiers were sometimes guilty of cowardice. When I tried my own hand at military history, I found myself tempted, or under pressure, to plaster over unsavoury facts. Let me give two examples.

We were attacking a hill somewhere in central Italy, and it was going badly. I was sent to find out what was happening and discovered that the commanding officer of a battalion attached to our Brigade had been drinking heavily. I returned to the Brigadier. 'The Colonel's drunk, sir,' I said. 'Is he capable of command?' 'Well, just.' 'Then let him carry on. A little drink never did a man much harm.' When I came to describe the battle for posterity, I omitted this incident, but a percipient reader might have noticed in the Appendix that a new commanding officer was appointed next day.

The second instance was more serious. Dunkirk, May–June 1940. The War Office files told a different story from the official version.

There were reports of British soldiers looting the town's drink-shops and of unseemly rushes to the embarkation moles. In my biography of General Alexander I only hinted at this: 'He was shocked by acts of indiscipline that he witnessed'.

More awkward was the false legend that we had played fair with our French allies and evacuated them in equal numbers with our own men in accordance with Churchill's promise to Reynaud: 'The three British divisions will form the rearguard'. In fact the French army held the line for two days until every English soldier had escaped. Forty thousand Frenchmen were taken prisoner in the end. French historians were well aware of this. Never, they wrote, has there been a more outrageous example of British perfidy. But when I discussed the episode with General Sir William Morgan, who had been Alexander's Chief of Staff at Dunkirk, he denied it hotly. We were sitting in the Garrick Club, and he could not raise his voice to the pitch that he would have liked. 'But I was there and you were not!' he cried. Yes, but the eye-witness sees less of an event than the historian. The French, German and some British documents proved beyond doubt that we owed the survival of the BEF to French resistance. I said so in my book. But when I saw Sir William at a later function, he cut me dead. Mine was the ultimate betrayal. I was no longer an officer, and clearly had never been a gentleman.

16 January 1993

AND ANOTHER THING

WHEN THE KISSING HAD
TO START

Paul Johnson

One of the ways in which the Western style of life is being imposed on the entire world is in the far from minor matter of kissing. The outstanding example is Japan, the ultra-modern-archaic society *par excellence*. Some peoples, of course, do not kiss at all, preferring to rub noses or make other points of intimate contact. The Japanese do kiss, but until comparatively recently it was always in private. Looking through the magnificent three-volume *Japanese Prints and Drawings from the Vever Collection* by Jack Hillier and distributed by Sotheby's, I can find only one example of lovers actually kissing, though occasionally they are doing what are to us rather more indelicate things.

The failure of the Japanese to kiss in public angered the Americans when they took over in 1945. Hollywood had made an art form out of the kiss, since in those days the Hays Office permitted little else, and all over the world GIs were imitating Clark Gable's prolonged close-up osculations. So kissing was democratic, almost by definition, and the Japanese, by refusing to do it, were demonstrating their obstinate attachment to authoritarianism. This could not be tolerated. Word went down, not perhaps from General MacArthur himself, who was not a great one for kissing, but certainly from senior aides, that the kissing had to start. Kyoko Hirano, who has made a study of one aspect of the American cultural impact, *Japanese Cinema under the American Occupation 1945–52*, published by the Smithsonian in Washington, says that Japanese film-makers were positively ordered to include kissing scenes in their movies. As their subject matter tended to be ferocious hand-to-hand combat, kissing looked a bit incongruous; and some of the cast declined to be filmed doing it, rather as a few actresses in the West still hold out against nude scenes. But in general the *diktat* was observed.

It is not clear what is the present line on kissing in the White House. Bill Clinton appears to be a great kisser, not always in public either. But it may be, now he has actually won, he will renege on this, as on other election promises or hints, on the grounds that compulsory kissing is politically incorrect. All the same, the march of democracy and kissing continues relentlessly. Certainly, there is much more of what used to be called bussing. When I was a young man, in the second half of the Forties, very few men and women greeted each other by kissing cheeks. That was a custom practised by royalty, along with their trades union habit of calling each other 'cousin'. Debs also kissed each other when they met (not their partners). Others kissed only as a mark of specific affection rather than social gesture. It is true that if a French politician or general awarded you a medal, he gave you not just a buss but a positive smacker on each cheek: a fairly disgusting experience, we thought, from which you would emerge reeking of garlic and possibly covered in lipstick. But then the French were very forward in kissing. On an early visit to Paris I remember being shocked by the flamboyant way in which young lovers embraced in the métro, other Parisians paying not the slightest attention. But was not that just another example of French decadence, also then symbolised by the Olympia Press? Years before, a pious nun had told me that all indelicate words and indecent jokes were ultimately manufactured by the Devil in the *vieux quartier* of Marseilles.

Today, men and women greet each other with a kiss all the time. It is one of the few post-war examples of an upper-class habit filtering downwards (the use of 'loo' is another). As a rule it is the other way round: even Tory grandees now refer to voters as 'punters', and to judge by their behaviour half the Cabinet is composed of yobbos. But cheek-kissing, or what I call the double-buss greeting, which should be accompanied, on the male's part, by an appreciative *mmmmm* noise, as though one were enjoying a juicy steak, has spread steadily to encompass most of the middle class and is even (thanks to television) penetrating further. I would be very interested if someone could tell me when the decisive moment came. I first became conscious that the habit was established in the middle-Sixties, that decade of momentous innovation, when George Brown, then a senior minister, was criticised for kissing a female member of the royal family on both cheeks, at some government gathering, and then adding, 'And one in the middle too.' The fact that George, who boasted of having been born in Peabody Buildings, was taking advantage of the new custom was a sign of how far things had gone.

They have gone much further since, but it is still not quite clear what the rules are. When you come across a woman you vaguely know at a party, do you shake hands or buss? Mistakes are bound to occur. I sometimes have been kissed by a woman I have never set eyes on before; or, in my own confusion, find myself embracing a haughty matron I do not know. Not to kiss, in error or inadvertence, can cause offence, especially to ladies. 'Don't you like me any more then?' I received this ticking off from Edna O'Brien, whom I had failed to kiss at a crowded gathering last year. The room was dark, she had changed her hairstyle and, to be honest, I hesitated; and he who hesitates in bussing is lost. Shaken by this *faux pas*, I became a little disoriented, or buss-happy. The next morning, at a lunch, I kissed Margaret Thatcher, something I had not done all the years she was in power. I believe strongly that one should not kiss a prime minister, even if she is a woman, or perhaps especially if she is a woman: the dignity of the office must be considered. But a former prime minister is, I suppose, a different matter. Anyway, the deed was done and she did not seem to mind.

But there is a point about bussing which has received insufficient attention. Who ought to do the actual kissing, the man or the woman? Or does it depend on the way the two people feel about each other? The French, who naturally have thought deeply on such matters, have an old saying which applies more widely than to the embrace itself: '*Il y a toujours un qui baise et un qui tend la joue.*' Very true. Drusilla Beyfus, our leading authority on manners, tells me: 'There are no clear rules whether the man or the woman kisses, or whether it's first on the left cheek, then on the right, or vice versa, or only one, or both.' She thinks that, where there is special affection, one in the middle is quite OK too, though it doesn't exonerate the late Lord George Brown. She believes that the element of uncertainty 'adds to the fun'. So, come to think of it, do I.

23 January 1993

ART

A NEW AGE FOR ART

Giles Auty

In my first *Spectator* article of this year, I made a statement with an accompanying challenge. What I wrote was that an almost total modernist hegemony exists now in the administration of the living visual arts in Britain. This lop-sided domination has come upon us by the steady accumulation of all key jobs in this field by those of an often hard-line modernist persuasion, e.g.: Nicholas Serota as director of the Tate Gallery, Lord Palumbo as chairman of the Arts Council, Henry Meyric Hughes – who was formerly head of visual arts at the British Council – as director of exhibitions at the South Bank Centre (with responsibility for all Arts Council touring exhibitions), Norman Rosenthal as exhibitions secretary at the Royal Academy, Bernard Cohen as principal of the Slade School, Paul Huxley as professor of painting at the Royal College of Art, Waldemar Januszcak as commissioning editor at Channel 4.

But such names are only the tip of a modernist iceberg. What about the directors and senior staff at the Whitechapel, Serpentine and ICA galleries or all the other national and regional galleries of living art which receive public funding? Outside journalism, almost every job of significance in living art in Britain is the exclusive preserve now of the modernist faithful: regional Arts Boards, Arts Councils, the British Council, national and regional museums of living art – to say nothing of their boards of trustees – art schools, art broadcasting at the BBC, universities which run courses in contemporary art history . . . the list goes on and on. Not surprisingly, the system has become hermetic and absolutely self-perpetuating; no hint of daylight or fresh air can get in. My challenge was for anyone in authority to deny that this state of affairs exists. Nobody has done so. I suggest this is because everyone employed in art above a certain level knows perfectly well that what I wrote is true.

Given this is the case, what are the effects on a living art form of such a one-sided régime? Does anyone really think it can be a good thing? Or is it a malign influence on the free development of national and international culture? More to the point, perhaps, does such extreme bias enjoy the support of the country at large or the backing of any kind of official or legal sanction? To quote merely one example, what gives the Tate Gallery the right to promote artistic avant-gardism so heavily – at the expense of other forms of living art – not just through widely questioned events such as the Turner Prize but also through long-term purchasing and exhibiting policies?

Clearly, if the business of living art were simply a privately organised club one could not cavil at the rules and objectives set by its members. But, of course, this is not at all what I am describing here, for most of the senior administrative posts in contemporary art in Britain fall squarely within the public sector. Effectively it is we who pay for the nation's leading museums of living art, Arts Councils, regional Arts

Boards, the South Bank, the BBC and British Council, to say nothing of our art schools and university courses in art history. If all are dominated, in effect, by what amounts to a narrow and self-interested faction, then one imagines that the sanction of the general public, through the persons of its elected ministers, would be a first necessity. Where the public pays there has to be public approval or, at least, public accountability. In fact there is neither. Through strict adherence to an arm's-length arts policy, successive governments have effectively created a train without a brake: they have divested themselves of any power to stop art steaming off headlong now in dangerous or even fatal directions. Such lack of government safeguards strikes me as reckless and short-sighted.

In my New Year's article I compared the current control by modernists of jobs in living art in Britain with that exercised formerly by Communist Party members in Marxist states. Oddly, modernism and Marxism have had broadly similar lifespans. Both arose in response to what may have been, at least originally, justified needs. But when the ideological masters of Marxism and modernism found they could not deliver the revolutionary utopias they had promised, both régimes hardened, relying thenceforward more on *realpolitik* than on intellectual arguments or quantifiable performance to maintain power. This is the state of affairs still prevailing today.

But while Marxism has crumbled, modernism in art persists in the West as an imposed culture, in spite of its ever increasing unpopularity. Eastern European Marxism was destroyed finally by its own economic ineptitude. Modernism hangs on simply because it is underpinned by a major commercial, capitalist enterprise: the vast industry of creating, promoting and selling what most people are conditioned to think of as modern art. Most of the artistic values which pertain to this industry are so vague that the industry depends very heavily for its continued existence on the endorsement of its values by modern museums. The views of the public which pays for the museums in the first place do not come into this equation. The relationship between dealers and museums is a cosy arrangement which relies for its continued success on an absence of dissenting voices from within the system itself. Hence the modernist obsession with hegemony – the effective control of all key positions. In this way dissent can be confined to the outside, where it can be dismissed as philistine or uninformed and as motivated solely by failure to rise to the supposed challenge presented by avant-garde art.

Today, the most influential dealers in avant-garde artefacts are located in the USA, Germany and Britain. So, by pure coincidence, are many of the most influential modern museums. Do you ever wonder why such a high proportion of contemporary artists who appear in major exhibitions in Britain's halls of living culture hail either from the USA or Germany and so seldom from other artistically active nations – Spain, for instance? German and American galleries, which are in a position to promote their artists heavily, expect to be able to get works by them exposed in Britain's modern museums. But often when they do, this country's artists and critics can detect little or no merit in the imported art which has been thrust upon them. The American painter Julian Schnabel is an excellent case in point: a few years ago he was the subject of major exhibitions at the Tate Gallery and Whitechapel. Yet at much the same time all the modernist directors of New York's modern museums flatly turned down an exhibition by Britain's – and arguably the world's – pre-eminent figurative painter, Lucian Freud. This extraordinary snub could hardly have been on grounds of the works' quality – unless all the directors were blind – and arose simply because Freud's painting fails to conform obviously to the prescribed canons of modernism.

Not surprisingly, modernists act as though the condition of modernism – art manifesting as little evidence as possible of any traditional thought, practice or qualities – is a virtue in itself. Yet clearly artistic radicalism, modernism – call it what you will – cannot ever be a virtue in itself, since any change, let alone change for change's sake, can as easily be for worse as for better. It is a little remarked on fact that a majority of Britain's foremost artists of this century – Sickert, Spencer, Bomberg and Freud among them – have not been modernists at all in any accepted sense. Modernism is essentially schismatic in nature, severing itself from the guidance and values of traditional practice and dismissing these as irrelevant to the needs of a truly modern society. But who is to decide on what the true needs of contemporary society may be? Indeed, are these needs known only to a few avant-garde artists, who often have only the haziest contact themselves with the realities of life? Might not art which celebrates extraordinary human skills, beauty and humanity have something to say in our lives?

It is significant that the three art movements most in favour at present with the controllers of modern museums in the West are those most opposed to the known values of art itself and to all traditional thinking: Dada, Pop and Conceptualism. Total modernist domination of professional opportunity means effectively that art can develop or flourish now only in directions which ruling modernists specify. One has only to think here of Lord Palumbo's recent initiative in trying to raise and spend £20 million on 'experimental' art, or the Tate Gallery's recent bid for virtually unlimited expansion and powers. Clearly the carrying out of practices other than those specified from on high becomes the artistic equivalent of swimming against the tide.

In the comparisons I have made between the radical totalitarianism of Marxism and that of modernism one element was missing: the systematic oppression of traditional beliefs and practices. But a surprisingly apt parallel can be drawn here between the discrimination employed by modernists against traditional practice and forms of training in art and that used by Marxist régimes against Christianity. In both instances it is the possibility that longstanding traditions may still be relevant that artistic and political radicals seem so desperate to deny. While Marxists closed and destroyed churches and seminaries, modernists have had to content themselves with denying gallery space, professional opportunity of almost every kind or the right to a proper training to those who wish still to belong to the great, unbroken traditions of European art. In each case opponents of a major tradition hope that the tradition will be damaged irrevocably at its roots through their actions and so will become, in time, unsustainable.

Modernist domination of art schools is possibly the most sinister consequence of the current hegemony. Clearly, if all public resources are given to radical forms of further education in art then no alternative approach is likely to flourish. In the history of further education in Britain, no courses can ever have been pursued in such an arbitrary and capricious way as those run in recent years in our art schools. Here, the modernist claim that no agreed standards exist creates ample licence for anarchy. Today, students who resist the familiar modernist brainwashing that takes place in virtually all our art schools are punished academically by being awarded poor degrees, while staff who try to make the case for alternative and more durable values usually end up getting the sack. Unsurprisingly, all but the most resilient students are crushed by a system which is driven, in the final analysis, by the greed and paranoia of the modern art industry. For even art students are discouraged from querying the values promoted by this industry, since serious questioning from almost any source could trigger the collapse of a market sustained by the enforcements of a régime rather than by intellectual arguments.

Foreseeably, students become cynical and disillusioned as a result of such pressures, believing that the only route to success under the prevailing modernist régime lies in attracting attention to themselves by the extremism of their work or actions and through being taught to exploit all forms of publicity. Last year's short-listed Turner Prize artist, Damien Hirst, could hardly be improved on as an example of this trend. The college he attended – Goldsmiths' – runs courses in how to manipulate the media as a central part of fine art studies there. It is hard not to reflect on what a repellent world the prevailing modernist domination has created.

As we must realise by now, the objective of those employed in our publicly financed galleries of living art has little to do with either public pleasure or admiration. Real kudos is gained by administrators of those galleries who put on exhibitions which public and critics dislike. Dislike proves simultaneously the ignorance of public and press and the supposedly challenging nature of the art on view – as well as the good party mentality of the curator. This kind of action is the most certain route to success in our modern museum hierarchy. Low attendance figures or the irritation of public and critics merely prove the curator's moral superiority. Clearly, wherever modernist rules apply, the unfortunate paying public has little chance of winning.

Two years ago, a young modernist administrator put on the London version of *The British Art Show 1990*, one of the most poorly attended and critically slammed shows ever presented at the Hayward Gallery. Last year he got his own avant-garde show there, possibly as a reward. If anything, this turned out to be even worse. In an end-of-year survey conducted by *Arts Review*, five of the nine established art critics approached by the magazine voted this particular hugely costly show, *Doubletake*, the worst exhibition of 1991. Nonetheless its organiser has since been elevated to the Arts Council's buying panel, empowered to recommend on purchases made in the public's name. You may sense some irony here. In what other career can one possibly gain promotion or reward by actively displeasing the client who pays? How can we even begin to find a way out of such enveloping darkness?

From what I have written it should be plain we must find a way of loosening the current modernist stranglehold. Until this stranglehold is broken, art cannot breathe, nor artists – or even administrators – develop naturally. Justice and the long disregarded wishes of a majority of thinking people demand an overdue levelling of this particular playing-field. At least a proportion of public funding in this country must be removed now altogether from modernist control and channelled into a new initiative. While the Tate Gallery blithely demands from the nation a huge increase in annual funding plus a brand-new museum costing £100 million as an extension of its already totalitarian powers, such money could not but be better spent elsewhere fostering a revival of the great craft, tradition and values of art which modernists have tried so hard to stifle and ridicule.

By starting a centre for living art of a non-avant-gardist nature and an attendant art school devoted to the development of real and necessary skills – rather than merely of attitudes – a rallying flag would be planted for everyone tired beyond belief with the present modernist hegemony. As more and more artists and students renegotiate their pacts with the past, they need do so no longer in the certainty of acute professional disadvantage. The proposed centre might devote itself initially to showing the vast range of excellent living art from this and other countries which the restrictive canons of modernism exclude at present. Catalogues accompanying these exhibitions would aim at sense and lucidity – another revolutionary suggestion. The projected centre could show us what we have been missing in art; the validity of an alternative viewpoint to modernism demands at least this minimum of recognition. Of course, galleries devoted to modern art as we think of it could continue for so long as anyone wished to visit them. What we need is the provision of a greatly overdue alternative and the recognition that the reasonable needs of a great many artists and gallery-goers do merit attention.

The Italian Renaissance was triggered by a look back to a golden age and standards. Faced by current avant-garde excess, it is difficult for many not to look back to artists such as Titian and Veronese, Velazquez and Goya, Rembrandt and Vermeer with an acute and justified nostalgia. Yet we should never lose sight of the fact that even these great masters were mere human beings, as we are. What we can learn from their example is that given the right conditions in art great achievements were possible once – and could be again.

23 January 1993

LOW LIFE

GONE WITH THE WIND

Jeffrey Bernard

There were a few of us in the bar of the Groucho Club the other day talking about Camillagate when, during a pause for reflection and a sip of our drinks, a lurking waitress suddenly said, 'I wish I was a suppository inside Prince Charles.'

'It's no good – the kidney's rejecting him!'

I couldn't afford to choke on my drink, not at £4 a shot, but I did pause to think that my own ambition to be an engine driver when I was not that much younger than she was a pretty meagre and unambitious dream. Some strange dreams and fantasies have been manufactured in this head of mine but I have never hoped to be medication in an orifice, royal or not, to melt and then be gone with the wind. To want to be the bee in Saddam Hussein's bonnet would be reasonable enough, or to have been the bullet that killed Hitler in the end would have been a worthwhile dream, but to end up as a fart is an appalling thought.

I didn't realise that women waited on tables thinking such things. Oh well. There was a man once who said that he would like to be stabbed in the back by Carlo Ponti and you can see his point, but how could a seemingly sane Liverpudlian girl want to go for a dip in brown Windsor soup? Our obsession with royalty really does know no bounds.

I remain content to know that the Queen used to read my column in the *Sporting Life* every Wednesday and Saturday some 20 years ago and that was as close as I ever wanted to get to the Palace.

Meanwhile, life ticks by for this commoner and pretty boring it is too, although letters from readers in Australia of all places would indicate that they think I live in a bowl of cherries. Last night was OK, though. I went to see Peter O'Toole in *Our Song*, liked it, liked him, and went around to his dressing-room after to have a drink with him. He autographed a picture of himself for the sainted Vera, who is about to turn up at any minute. She will be well pleased.

So will I be to see her. Her stand-in last week was a young man, unsuitably named, I think, for a home help, Craig, who wears a Russian fur hat while he washes the dishes and who studies fine art in Holland when he isn't elbow-deep in the sink. He is rather formal, as befits a Craig – a Tom, Dick or Harry would tell me to get stuffed – and he says he doesn't mind working his way through college at fairly menial tasks. I don't get that. Washing up dishes and hoovering for crocks can't be fun. By the same token he finds it hard to understand that thumping Monica electric de luxe is loathsome to me. I think Olympia typewriters should bring out a new model and call it Camilla electric de luxe. I would like to be the ribbon in her.

Anyway, last Friday I had to buy a sofa in the sales. It is essential. I haven't actually sat next to anybody in this flat since I moved here a year ago. It is a very flashily upholstered job, as bright as a Henley Regatta blazer, and bloody expensive too. I moaned and whinged about the price of it for hours and the very next morning I received a cheque in the post covering the cost with a little bit over. To my amazement the cheque was for royalties for a short run of *Jeffrey Bernard is Unwell* in Copenhagen. What on earth could the Danes have made of it? Keith Waterhouse and I must speak in Esperanto. Gabby who runs the delicatessen in Old Compton Street tells me he read good reviews of the play as well in the Italian paper he buys. Considering the Italians are tantamount to teetotallers I should have thought it would be absolute Greek to them.

But it bodes well. I need a new cooker as well as a sofa on which to chat up young gullibles. Perhaps 1993 might not be as disgusting as I had thought. And don't tell me about small mercies. The big one is not being a suppository.

23 January 1993

YOUR PROBLEMS SOLVED

DEAR MARY...

Mary Killen

Q. I have a mistress to whom I regularly make late night telephone calls. The trouble is that neither of us wants to be the one to hang up or the last to say goodbye so we spin out the goodnights for, sometimes, ten minutes. How can I put a stop to this, without causing offence?

Name and address withheld

A. Why not suggest to your mistress that you take it in turns to be the one to hang up?

Q. A bet-hedging friend of my boyfriend and mine is always letting us down by not turning up for things. He is definitely fond of us, but suffers from a sort of social promiscuity. This means that, when invited somewhere, he says, 'Yes. I think I'm going to be able to make that', but then chucks at the last minute if he gets a better invitation. Clearly some kind of psychiatric treatment is indicated but, in the meantime, how can I ensure that he does not chuck a forthcoming shooting weekend that we want to invite him to? It will be no fun without him.

Name and address withheld

A. Issue the invitation formally, i.e., in writing. No doubt your friend will fail to commit himself to a written response. This means that, after a suitable lapse of time, you can ring up his parents and say, 'I'm frightfully sorry to trouble you. I'm looking for Hugo, (or

Desmond ... whatever his name is) and thought he might be with you. You see, I haven't had a reply to my invitation for this weekend that I'm setting up virtually in his honour, because it will be no fun without him, and now I'm going to be out of contact myself for a few days.' You may then leave it to his flattered parents to track him down and insist that he commit himself to a formal acceptance of your invitation.

Q. What should one say, if one is a friend of both HRH the Prince of Wales and Mrs Parker Bowles, next time one meets them? One cannot pretend one has not read the transcript of the call and the references to internal protection.

Name and address withheld

A. If you genuinely are a friend, then you will be aware that, in upper-class circles, light-hearted banter to do with bottoms, lavatories, being sick, et cetera, form the central core of most friendly telephone calls. Though the two might be angry that their conversation was taped, they will not be embarrassed by any of the lavatorial aspects of it. One suitable opening gambit for genuine friends of the two might be to say, 'I am sorry you've had such a horrid time recently', then proceed immediately to some news of your own.

23 January 1993

THE MAGIC REALISTS

Francis Harvey

Tonight, all over this divided city, where
people in small terraced houses are

viewing the big gangster movie on
BBC, one family, watching a mobster
riding shot-gun in a stolen car,
hears him come raging through
their own front door.

23 January 1993

CITY AND SUBURBAN

RUPERT GETS A JOB IN THE BANK – IT'S ALL PART OF THE HOGG SERVICE

Christopher Fildes

I am sure that Rupert Pennant-Rea can spell 'potato', which makes it all the odder to see him set up as the J. Danforth Quayle of Threadneedle Street. He is on his way. A wave of the Queen's wand, with the Prime Minister holding her hand, has translated him from the editor's chair at the *Economist* to the Bank of England as the Deputy Governor. Truth to tell, and bored though he might be, he would be better placed in Washington. What a vice-president has to do is to preside over the Senate, represent the President at funerals, and, at the President's funeral, represent himself. A Deputy Governor has a more searching job specification (and a £164,910 salary to match) and it is no fault of Mr Pennant-Rea if he does not obviously meet it. The Deputy is now the nearest thing the Bank has to a chief executive. He is also the man in charge of the engine-room. The Governor is on the bridge. He is the Bank's public face and voice, at home and abroad, and he travels widely and often. When he is away, the Deputy is required to stay at home and take charge. If there is a sudden crisis, he must handle it – the present Governor has something of a gift for absence, and was out of the country for the Johnson Matthey rescue and again in 1987 for the stock market crash. The Bank itself employs as many as 4,500 people, in such different skills as trading bullion, issuing stock (at £1 billion a week) and printing banknotes. It has a large economic department and advises on policy, but it is not a department of state or a think-tank. It is, as it always has been, a bank, with a highly specialised business, an unrivalled customer base, and a £5½ billion balance sheet. These are risky days for banks, and they need professional management.

Whose bright idea is that? The first response, where I sat, was a cry of shock, and the second was: 'It has to be Sarah.' Third thoughts have gone no further. The appointment bears all the marks of Sarah Hogg, head of the Prime Minister's policy unit and upstairs eminence in Downing Street. In Evelyn Waugh's *Scoop*, Mrs Stitch presses the buttons which bring jobs and honours to the Boots – the wrong Boots, as it happens, but never mind – and passes it off as all part of the Stitch service. This must be all part of the Hogg service. Mrs Hogg is herself an old hand at the *Economist*. There, Mr Pennant-Rea was her protégé. He worked for her when he first joined the paper, and worked with her thereafter in a group which modestly styled itself the Magic Team. There could be no two more natural members of a mutual admiration society, for no one could be *plus bien pensant* or closer to the heart of Europe than Mrs Hogg. In such matters the Prime Minister relies on her judgment. In much the same way, Neville Chamberlain came to rely in Sir Horace Wilson, nominally his chief industrial adviser but in practice a backstage whisperer and confidant on anything from absenteeism to appeasement. A courtier's power is by its nature insecure (as Sir Alan Walters discovered) and the art, so seldom practised, is to quit while still ahead. If, as I think, this appointment represents a serious error of judgment, I would advise Mrs Hogg to take it as the gypsy's warning, and move on. She could always rely on the Hogg service.

30 January 1993

NIGEL'S CZECH MATE

Dominic Lawson

Grandmaster Josef Dorfman, ex-captain of the Red Army chess team, former coach and second to the world chess champion Gary Kasparov, is not easily amused.

But ten years ago, when he visited London with Kasparov, I reduced the normally po-faced Dorfman to hysterics. I had asked him, over lunch at one of London's gloomier restaurants, 'Do you think that Nigel Short could become world chess champion?' Dorfman's forkful of steak stopped on its otherwise mechanical progress to his mouth. From that mouth came a low gurgle. The gurgle got louder. After a minute of gurgles I finally realised that the man was laughing uncontrollably. I pointed out, patriotically, that Nigel had recently become the world's youngest grandmaster, and that in the previous year he had come second to Kasparov in the world junior championship. Dorfman finally summoned sufficient composure to reply. 'No Westerner will become world champion. All your players are on their own. They have no support from the state. Who do you think pays me – and two other grandmasters – full-time to help Kasparov? Who do you think paid for Kasparov's chess education from childhood? Nigel Short is very talented, but one man cannot beat a system. Forget it.' I did.

Six years later, in 1989, however, I was sitting next to Nigel Short's wife, Rea, on a flight from Barcelona. Nigel had just been competing there in the Chess World Cup. As was usual for him at that time he had scored some dazzling victories, but suffered some pathetic defeats, including his customary drubbing at the hands of world champion Kasparov.

What, I asked Rea, could be done to help Nigel – and the hopes of British chess – reach full potential? She echoed Dorfman's remarks of six years earlier. What her husband needed, she insisted, was back-up, preferably from a grandmaster of vast experience, who could accelerate Nigel's development by passing on that wisdom in concentrated form. The problem was that such wisdom was not so much priceless as very pricey, and Nigel's earnings as a chess player could not cover it. A week later I recounted this tale to Sir Patrick Sheehy, who, apart from being on the board of *The Spectator*, spends most of his remaining working hours as chairman of British American Tobacco. Pat is a man of action. Within a month Eagle Star, BAT's insurance arm, had agreed to fund the acquisition for Nigel of the grandmaster coach of his choice.

Nigel's initial choice was Boris Spassky. Who better for a putative world champion to have as a coach than one who himself has held the highest title? And besides, the two men were – and remain – very good friends. But it didn't work out. These days Boris's talent is matched only by his laziness, and Nigel needed someone who would be as motivated as he to wrest the world championship from Russian hands, for the first time since Bobby Fischer did so – against Spassky – in 1972.

The answer was, in retrospect, obvious: hire the man who had himself acted as Fischer's second in that match. His name is Ljubomir Kavalek, known as Lubosh. He has a particular hunger to bury the remnants of Soviet success – and he sees Kasparov as very much part of that system. Lubosh fled his homeland, Czechoslovakia, shortly after the Russian invasion of 1968 (but not before putting on a black armband in the 1968 Chess Olympiad, when he represented Czechoslovakia against the Soviet Union). After Fischer's retirement, Kavalek became the dominant chess player in the United States, winning the US championship on three occasions. According to Kavalek, in an article he wrote for the *Washington Post*, Nigel turned up on his doorstep and said, 'Lubosh, I want you to make me world champion like you made Bobby Fischer world champion.' Nigel denies he said exactly that, but it certainly made good copy.

And it is true that Kavalek has helped to turn the British grandmaster into a lethal match player, most notably when he astounded chess players and bookmakers by knocking out the former world champion Anatoly Karpov in Spain last April. It is not just that the bald, bearded, and slightly sinister-looking Kavalek is fantastically hard-working. It is not just that he has an unequalled database of almost a million chess games, logged into a 120 megabyte computer. It is more, as he put it to me recently, that he knows 'the way these specimens of the Soviet school of chess think, how they have been taught to think. Once you understand that, they become very predictable.'

But none of this should detract from Nigel Short's great achievement, which is to become only the third non-Russian since 1927 to qualify to contest a match for the official world chess championship. Once the theatre lights dim, and the clock starts ticking, it is Nigel alone who engages in brain-to-brain conflict with the most advanced products of the greatest chess factory the world is ever likely to see. And Kavalek, himself a modest man, knows this. I recall a moment after one of the games in Nigel's triumphant final eliminator match against the Dutch champion Jan Timman last week in Spain. Nigel, Lubosh and I were in Short's hotel suite, analysing that day's win over Timman. Lubosh thought he had found a move for Timman which would have turned the game around. It certainly looked terrifying. 'I saw that,' said Nigel, quietly. 'But look.' And then in a blur of hand movements he played four further moves for each side: 'Now black must resign.' Kavalek turned to me with a strange grin, half sheepish, half triumphant: 'Did you see that? That is why Nigel is special, why other grandmasters are afraid of him.'

Gary Kasparov is not afraid of Nigel Short. He has already, punning fluently in English, declared that their match 'will be short'. And in his autobiography *Child of Change*, Kasparov stated, with his customary lack of false or genuine modesty, that, 'it is Nigel Short's misfortune to have been born only two years after me'. We shall see how unfortunate, when the two lock cerebella in seven months time. Meanwhile I prefer to carry with me the memory of Nigel in his hotel room half an hour after he had won his match against Timman. He had just told some reporters, to their disappointment, that he 'felt nothing'. But here he was in front of a few close friends and family, hurling himself through the air, then lying on his back and kicking his legs in a paroxysm of delight. I wondered what Josef Dorfman would have said. Probably, he would have laughed.

6 February 1993

THEATRE

INTO THE WOODS

Sheridan Morley

ROBIN – PRINCE OF SHERWOOD
Piccadilly

LA MUSICA
Hampstead

WORLDS APART
Stratford East

'Uppers or downers?'

To hail a new West End musical by proclaiming that it is not a fiasco
might seem to be damning by praise so faint as to be invisible, but at
a time when most of my colleagues are lamentably failing to do so, it
seems to me that distinctions have to be drawn even among dross.
Musical fiascos are shows like *Which Witch?*, high above glacier level
in the realms of Norwegian camp, or *Troubadour* which was financed
by the Japanese, arguably the worst thing they had done since Pearl
Harbor, in which one of the chorus girls, told to improvise during a
battle scene, memorably announced in my hearing that 'These Crusades are spreading like wildfire'.

By such immortal standards, *Robin – Prince of Sherwood* is not
a fiasco at all: instead, it's an inexplicably leftover 1959 Palladium
pantomime of the kind which used to star Frank Ifield, a wonderfully
middle-of-the-road pop singer of, I think, Australian extraction whose
idea of a dramatic climax for *Babes in the Wood* was to turn to the

audience in subdued amazement and say, 'Good heavens, no Babes', thereby indicating their loss in the wood.

Quite why Bill Kenwright, as director and producer, has seen fit to revive the tradition in early February 1993 remains unclear, unless he has some mysterious arrangement with the theatre owners whereby if he keeps the premises warm a better score will be along in a minute. This one compares very favourably indeed with the last musical venture into Sherwood Forest, which was, as I recall, Lionel Bart's catastrophic *Twang* about 30 years ago.

This is in no way *Twang 2*: it has an amiable if anonymous company, most of them considerably jollier as Merry Men than those Kevin Costner recently managed to gather round him for a turgid Hollywood camp-around-the-camp a couple of years back. It has more of a pamphlet than a book by way of plot, and is built on the touring *Joseph/Dreamcoat* principle, which is that if enough people rush towards the footlights baring their teeth at you all criticism is made to seem as irrelevant as at a revivalist meeting of Bible-belters in the Mid-West.

The whole show is a kind of perpetual finale, designed for the very dim: 'Here's Richard,' the chorus shouts as the King enters from the Crusades, whereupon, in case you had missed the point, his first line is 'I'm Richard'. Behind him the company is forever lining up for their team photograph, but the dialogue has a kind of surreal charm: can I really have heard, and written down, such lines as 'Morgana, get a move on' or 'Buy a leg of lamb, Give yourself a treat', and if so who on earth says them? More mysterious still is a couplet which, depending on the accuracy of my marginal hearing, either runs, 'If you've got a cause/You can bet that they'll endorse it' (presumably referring to Robin's Merry Men), or alternatively, 'If you've got a cause/ You can bet that they're in Dorset'. All in all a collector's evening, and not to be missed.

Which is rather more than can be said for *La Musica* at Hampstead. With all due respect, Marguerite Duras is, like the other one who married Jean-Paul Sartre or possibly never did, the kind of thoroughly tiresome old French bat who has always put the English off crossing the Channel. She comes back to us with an extended version of a one-act piece first seen 20 years ago; it now runs 80 minutes going on several hours, and still concerns a couple of near-divorcees meeting on the eve of the final decree to rake over the embers of their past love. All other guests having presumably vacated their hotel in terror lest this self-obsessed couple pin them down in the lounge with yet another recollection of how their marriage went wrong, we are left with a duologue of stunning tedium and mirthlessness. Harriet Walter and Larry Lamb give hauntingly powerful, emotional performances in a production by Joseph Blatchley which would have been even better if someone had bothered to find them a play.

At Stratford East, Paul Sirett's *Worlds Apart* is in the fine old knock-about tradition of Joan Littlewood's social-conscience comedies at that address. In the course of a day at the Heathrow Airport Immigration Centre, we are treated to several case histories of despair, corruption and crisis, and that's just among the staff. The immigrants themselves are an equally mixed and troubled crew, and if Sirett has a message for us it is the most cynical of all: that immigrants are the kind of people who will keep trying to immigrate.

13 February 1993

MISCHIEF, MURDER AND MULTIPLE ADULTERY

Simon Courtauld

> Here's to myself and one other
> And may that one other be she
> Who drinks to herself and one other
> And may that one other be me.

Written by someone who had just confessed to a 15-year-old girl that he had murdered his wife's lover, these words could hardly be more poignant. They were disclosed to me for the first time last week by the 'girl' in question, Juanita Carberry, as she talked about the murder of the Earl of Erroll in wartime Kenya and the man, Sir 'Jock' Delves Broughton, who confided in her that he had done the deed.

It all happened a long time ago, but this irresistible story of sex, violence and the aristocracy has been stirred into life again. Now aged 67, Juanita Carberry lives in a London flat overlooking the Thames, not far from Chelsea Harbour. She is small-framed, wears glasses, has her hair swept back and pony-tailed – and she is the last survivor of the principal characters in what has become known as the White Mischief affair.

Erroll had been having an affair with Broughton's second wife Diana, a creamy ash-blonde from Hove, to whom he had been married for no more than a few weeks. Broughton was tried for the murder and acquitted; he returned to England and committed suicide at the Adelphi Hotel, Liverpool. In his enjoyable book, *White Mischief*, published in 1982, James Fox concluded that Broughton was guilty, producing Juanita in the final chapter, 'The End of the Trail', when she reveals to Fox the secret – Broughton's 'confession' – which she had kept for nearly 40 years. Fox's verdict was persuasive, but he devotes barely a page of the book to this crucial conversation, three days after the killing, between Broughton and Juanita.

At the time of the film of *White Mischief* in 1988, I wrote an article reviewing the evidence against other suspects, which prompted Broughton's son, Sir Evelyn, to write a letter declaring his father's innocence and pointing an accusing finger at Diana. When Sir Evelyn died a month ago, I repeated his claims in his obituary in the *Daily Telegraph*, which persuaded Juanita to write to the newspaper, reiterating Broughton's guilt and refuting Sir Evelyn's theories.

Nearly two weeks elapsed before Sir Evelyn's widow waded in with a stinging response. Sir Jock's private papers, she wrote, were very revealing; had they been produced, 'that ridiculous book *White Mischief* could not have been written'. Diana is now portrayed as a gun-slinging nymphomaniac: she 'was having a passionate affair with an Italian during their supposed engagement. She had another lover on the boat to Africa and had asked another man to join them on their honeymoon . . . [Broughton's] letters show that, once married, he despised Diana . . . Diana shot her farm manager some years later.'

James Fox then entered the correspondence last Monday, saying that these letters from Broughton written after his trial were being used 'to blackmail Diana over an insurance fraud committed by Broughton, possibly with her knowledge, before the war'. 'Whether it was love, jealousy or, by now, obsession, he was blackmailing Diana to get her back.' Fox also wrote that the Broughtons had never produced any evidence to discredit Juanita's story.

What else, I wondered, could she tell me of that day when Broughton came to the Carberry house at Nyeri to see his wife and found Juanita there alone? He told her he had killed Erroll and then, as I knew from Fox's book, he wrote something in her autograph book about his likes and dislikes. Fox had not seen this album, but Juanita now showed it to me – and there, in Broughton's hand, was the verse reproduced above.

At the same time Juanita also asked Broughton to write down his favourite animals ('Horses and Bears'); pastimes ('Hunting'); sport ('Hunting'); subject ('Roman history'); career ('Landowner'); books ('*Mr Pickwick*'); country ('England'); film ('*Ben Hur*'). She asked him, 'What is better than Love?' – he wrote 'Anticipation' – and, 'What do you Fear most?' 'Loneliness'. Beneath that word is the signature, 'Delves Broughton' and the date, 27 January 1941.

It is an extraordinary document, never shown to the police, never produced at Broughton's trial, never published. I could detect no evidence of stress in the writing, but I wonder what a graphologist would make of it. Those who still reject the 'Broughton did it' version of the murder ask why on earth he should have admitted his guilt to Juanita. It is a puzzling question – Broughton was supposed to dislike children – but the poem which came to his mind when Juanita asked him to write something, and the fear of loneliness, surely provide the clue.

Broughton had come to Kenya with Diana in November 1940 (they got married in Durban, on their way up the coast to Mombasa), and by the end of the month she had fallen for Joss Erroll. Their affair was flaunted openly in the small circle in which they moved, revolving always round the Muthaiga Club. Broughton was humiliated and realised, by the time of the murder, that he had lost his bride of 11 weeks. (He was then faced with honouring a curious marriage pact with Diana: if she fell in love with a younger man, he had agreed to give her a divorce and a healthy income.)

Just as the cuckolded Broughton was now something of an outsider, so too Juanita was out of place – a schoolgirl in this selfish, hedonistic society in which children were ignored, if not despised. She suffered the additional disadvantage of living with a father, stepmother and governess who, by Juanita's gruesome account, were all practitioners of the arts of physical and mental cruelty.

Broughton and Juanita shared an interest in horses. At a tense lunch a few hours after Erroll's body was discovered – at 3 a.m. at the wheel of a Buick, with a bullet through the head – Broughton asked Juanita to walk with him to the stables. Three days later, after the inquest, he drove up to Nyeri and, finding Juanita alone, they walked together through the gum trees to the yard where she kept her pony, Springbok.

'I remember clearly how uptight he was,' Juanita told me last week. 'He said I shouldn't be frightened if the police turned up, because they had been following him.

'"Why?" I asked.
'"They think I killed Joss."
'"But why?"
'"Well, I did, actually."

'He told me how he had hidden in the back of the Buick [when Erroll dropped Diana back at the Broughtons' house at Karen], and when the car slowed up at the junction with the Ngong road, Jock shot him and the car nosed down into a murram pit. Jock hung on by the arm-straps in the back, which the police found were torn off. I had been in the car the day before, and I know the straps were in place then.'

Broughton and Juanita went back to the house, he wrote in her autograph book, and a little later Diana and June Carberry (Juanita's stepmother) returned from a visit to Nanyuki. Diana hurled abuse at Broughton, calling him a murderer. June slapped her face and took her to her bedroom, where photographs of Erroll, and his uniforms, were spread over the bed. Juanita made herself scarce. She never saw Broughton again.

Broughton's defenders say that he was drunk on the night of the murder, also lame, and could not have walked home the two and a half miles from the road junction where the body was found. But he was used to walking on safari, he rode frequently, and was in fact a pretty fit 57-year-old. It would surely not have been beyond him to walk that distance along a straight, flat road at night – even if he had had a few drinks to drown his sorrows and stiffen his resolve to get rid of lover-boy. Not only is Juanita's story entirely convincing, but it is said that a letter exists – written after the trial by Broughton to the Attorney-General – which in effect admits that the jury reached the wrong verdict.

Juanita was served with a subpoena to attend the trial as a defence witness on 4 June 1941, but she was not called (though Broughton's barrister, the South African Harry Morris, did sign her autograph book on that day). Perhaps it was feared that she would crack under cross-examination; June had warned her not to say anything to the police. But, as Juanita made clear to me last week, she did not need to be told.

'A grown-up had told me a secret. I liked him and he had trusted me. I was not going to let him down.

'As a child I had had to learn to lie, in order to save my skin.'

Child abuse may not have been the term used in those days, but that was what Juanita suffered. Her father John Carberry would force her to swim round his boat in the shark-infested waters of Mombasa harbour – a few hundred yards from where the Kenya Meat Commission tipped its offal into the sea. She was beaten, often with a rhino whip, not only by her father but also her stepmother, June, and governess, Isabel Rutt.

There was a bit of sexual abuse too.

'When June was alone she would ask me to sleep in her bed, and her hands wandered when she thought I was asleep. I can remember that horrible bedroom – the walls were the colour of raspberry ice-cream and the bed, door and window-frames were all black.

'Rutt used to bring her boyfriends to the room which I shared with her. She was often rutting away while I was there.'

(By a remarkable coincidence the egregious Rutt had previously been governess in England to a family called Binnie. She was sacked for allegedly mistreating their daughter Joy, who is married to Lord Carbery, John Carberry's nephew.)

Juanita refers to Carberry as 'my alleged parent', preferring to believe she is the daughter of Carberry's neighbour and business partner, a white Jamaican called Maxwell Trench (she still keeps in touch with the Trench family). The game of 'musical beds' in Kenya during the Happy Valley era can get confusing: Juanita's mother, Maia Anderson, may have been the daughter of Rudolf Meyer, sometime owner of the *East African Standard*.

Carberry was born John Evans-Freke and inherited the Irish title of Lord Carbery – he had his 21st birthday party at the family seat of Castle Freke at Rosscarbery, County Cork. He sold it after the first world war, having apparently gouged the eyes out of all the family paintings, disclaimed the title, assumed an American accent and became an ardent supporter of Hitler.

Photographs of Carberry in the 1920s show a man of arrogant, supercilious good looks, with more than a hint of cruelty in his half-smile. I asked Juanita if he had any redeeming qualities. 'No, I can't think of any.'

Carberry's third wife, June, was 'a drunken tart, and common with it', as one contemporary described her. She also took drugs – 'there were plenty of needles lying around,' Juanita remembers. In 1972, when June was unwell and living in Johannesburg – they had not seen each other for 30 years – Juanita wrote her a sympathetic letter offering to come and see her. Juanita had not remembered getting a reply, but as we looked together through some of her old papers, she found one letter from June. It was typewritten, civil but noncommittal, and there was no suggestion that they meet again. June died, aged 63 and an alcoholic, in 1975, and left most of her money to her hairdresser and a dogs' home.

Erroll and Diana were said by some to be more attractive characters

– though one acquaintance in Kenya in the 1930s told me recently that 'if anyone really needed killing, it was Erroll. He was an appalling shit'.

Diana became a *grande dame* in Kenya, marrying Lord Delamere and staying on until shortly before she died in 1987; and it is clear from Fox's book that he was mesmerised by her. Broughton had 'adored' and 'worshipped' her, as he wrote after the trial, but now we learn from Lady Delves Broughton's letter that Diana spent more time in bed with other men than with her husband – which was not so uncommon among the Happy Valley set in those days. Perhaps it is not surprising that she was such a close friend of June Carberry.

They were certainly an odd bunch. Broughton must have appeared to Juanita to be the only person capable of conventional behaviour. At least they could talk about horses, and Juanita was flattered that someone should pay attention to her. He took her into his confidence, and she probably saved him from the gallows – which Broughton's family still refuse to accept today.

Soon after the trial, Juanita left home, following a particularly brutal beating from her father, and went to Nairobi to live with her uncle, Gerald Anderson. It was quite a change from the Carberry household: he was a member of Moral Rearmament and 'confession groups' were held in the house. Juanita recalls someone asking to be forgiven 'for being short with my wife while she was having her period'.

As soon as she could get away, Juanita joined the army, becoming a corporal in the First Aid Nursing Yeomanry (Fany), and after the war was briefly married to a telephone engineer, Wally Evans. For much of the past 30 years she has been at sea, working in the merchant navy as 'anything from mess-girl to third mate'. She travelled for some time with a ship's master called Ron – 'I was his concubine and I worked unpaid' – and worked for the Mission to Seamen and the World Society for the Protection of Animals when she was at home in Mombasa. But the endemic corruption in modern Kenya began to get her down and she decided, in 1991, to settle in London.

Sitting in her flat, surrounded by photograph albums and memorabilia from her life in Kenya, I found it hard to believe that this woman had come through it all and survived. But she is *nyawera* (a worker), the name given her by the Carberrys' Kikuyu servants, and she has worn well. These days she works out on an exercise bicycle every day and drinks skimmed milk.

When I made the mistake of referring to her having come home, Juanita told me not only that she will always regard Kenya as home but that she also likes to think of herself as an honorary Kikuyu.

'I was expelled from a school in England because I refused to speak anything but Swahili,' she said. 'When the Carberrys used to lock me in my room, without food, the Kikuyu servants would look after me. There was a bond between us.' Whether or not she is the daughter of John Carberry, Juanita is surely a true daughter of Kenya.

And the person she remembers most fondly from her teenage days – the 'one other' in that haunting poem, to whom Diana sadly would not drink, but to whom Juanita is happy to raise her glass – is Jock Delves Broughton.

13 February 1993

DEAR DEAD UNHEROES ...

James Michie

Dear dead unheroes and unheroines
Who mangled your own selves – and I've known ten,
Hectic, vivid, amusing women and men –
What's your verdict now? Are you damned for your sins?
Some said so; others shrugged kindly; a few cried
For a dislocated day or month or two
And scratched the scab of no-guilt, as friends do
(As I did) who are abashed by suicide.
But now that an old colleague of sixty-five
Has blown his brains out, I'm inclined to call
A halt to pity for self-pity. All
Those guns, ropes, razors, ovens ... Why not contrive
    Some evanescent exit, in a style
    That will raise at least the ghost of a half-smile?

13 February 1993

A MAN OF MANY SURPRISES

Bernard Levin

Brian Inglis, who died abruptly last week at the age of 76, was deputy editor of *The Spectator* from 1954 to 1959, and editor from 1959 to 1962, when it reached its highest circulation to date. Backed by Ian Gilmour, who had edited it from the time he bought it in 1954, and who had broken sharply with the genteel version of the magazine that had been tottering to its end, he brought in a gallimaufry of iconoclasts: Alan Brien, Katharine Whitehorn, Rory McEwen, Cyril Ray, David Cairns, Philip Oakes, Peter Forster and me.

How we ever got any work done none of us can now remember. Lunch-time was spent drinking, the afternoon arguing, and the morning drifting in. But we did get the work done, and that was because Brian, who lifted his elbow higher than any of us and reminisced long and fascinatingly, was the most gently cunning coaxer of any staff of writers. His imperturbable façade (which in fact hid an extraordinary shyness and effacement) infuriated us so much that we were constantly hatching murder plots, while his Cheshire Cat smile enraged us further.

Journalists – real ones, anyway – cannot start anything until the last possible minute. Brian, who was a very real journalist, broke that pattern; he would have an in-tray and an out-tray, and steadily reduced the pile on his right and as steadily augmented the pile on his left. When all was finished he did no rubbing of his hands, no sighing, 'Well, that's done'; he would simply murmur, 'How about a jar?' and off we went to the pub.

He left us all to our own devices, our own styles, our own King Charles's heads; or rather, he hypnotised us into thinking that that was what we were doing, and even when there was real heat in an argument with him, his voice never took another decibel; an outsider might have thought that he was a *fainéant*, or even dull, but we knew better – oh, we knew very much better – this was a man of many surprises, and his greatest surprise was what lay behind the façade. He was a man with an exceptionally well-stocked mind, and on some issues – Ireland, of course – he could be truly passionate. Yet his sense of perspective was perfect.

'Have you a humour section?'

There was a fraudulent libel action brought against the paper by three Labour money-grubbers, abetted by a shockingly biased judge and a defence counsel who entered the court without the slightest knowledge of what the case was about; Gilmour was deeply wounded – not because it was his money that was lost, or even because of the odious handling of him in the witness-box by that old rogue Beyfus, but because of the shamefulness of the injustice that had conquered truth. Brian certainly felt the pain, but he shrugged and murmured 'cod', and got on with his life and the magazine.

That word 'cod' was often in his mouth. It had many meanings, but they all added up to a kind of gentle scorn; someone who overstated a case, who boasted too loudly, who claimed intimate friendships where there was nothing but acquaintance – this was cod, and for emphasis, 'codological'.

Cod was a mild term; 'chancer' was more powerful. A chancer was near to a crook, and someone to be avoided. But Brian was very parsimonious in his use of the word; the villain had to be a real one, and for Brian to condemn anyone as without any redeeming quality was very rare indeed.

Come to think of it, he very rarely condemned anyone or anything; I have never known a man with so few grumbles, and certainly never a grudge. He died as he would have wished; in an instant, with no lingering. I can hear him now, with that engaging touch of brogue, saying, 'Ah, Bernard, don't be so codological.'

I think I'll take a jar now. He would have wanted me to.

20 February 1993

WHEN NICENESS IS NOT ENOUGH

Matthew Parris

The courtship ritual being danced on the White House lawns by President Clinton and Prime Minister Major was, as Peter Riddell wrote in the *Times* on Monday, 'doomed to succeed'.

One could guess on Tuesday that before Wednesday was out it would be 'Bill' and 'John' and smiles all round. By Thursday Foreign Office officials would be privately briefing journalists on the quite extraordinary warmth which Mr Major had already succeeded in injecting into the bonding. By the weekend we would know that the Special Relationship is – well, extra special, for John and Bill.

A few disagreements of a practical kind remain, of course . . .

The greater part of all this hyperbole is pre-scripted and could be press-released with impunity, before any meeting of any British premier with any American counterpart, however cordially they detested each other. The performance takes on the air of an old *Daily Mail* report of one of those matings of Mr Heath's panda, flown abroad for a rendezvous with a foreign sweetheart. As grumpy as the beasts may appear, it is necessary to find something joyful in the occasion.

Only later, when the offspring fails to appear, or does appear, to be rolled on and squashed by one of its parents, do we find it all mattered less than we thought. (In this case, the mating gets off to the worst of starts as the whole zoo knows that sources close to the British panda did their best to keep the American one out of the cage. There was another panda in John's life at the time: George.)

Reports of John Major's success at building personal friendships in the political world are not all hype, nor are they entirely routine. They are the distinguishing mark of his career. He would never have won Lady Thatcher's affection (plenty had her respect) if he had not been nice as well as clever. He would never have been elected to replace her as leader without the intervention of so many friends, and the notable absence of enemies, on the backbenches. He would not have kept Lady Thatcher's support, and later her neutrality, and later her silence, and now her ambivalence, for as long as he did without effort and charm.

The charm was deployed from day one. When, early in his prime ministership, John Major went to Bonn to forge the first link of what was meant to be an Anglo-German alliance with Helmut Kohl, the personal chemistry fast established between both men provoked what Boris Johnson described, on these pages ('After you, Helmut', *The Spectator*, 1 August, 1992), as little whoops and squeals of excitement among Foreign Office officials.

Even with M. Mitterrand he managed to calm the open hostility which had existed between the French President and our previous Prime Minister. Then there was the relationship with Mikhail Gorbachev, only a few meetings old when he wrote to his friend in captivity after the attempted coup: '. . . Above all, Norma and I are desperately anxious about you and Raisa's well-being. We send you the love and heartfelt good wishes of the British people . . .' This was an intimacy (I think sincere) acquired with remarkable speed.

These may have been strengths. But friendship imposes debts, too, and John Major has been willing to honour them. To his obvious political cost, he has supported Cabinet chums in difficulty. The personal relationships in John Major's political life are plainly quite central to him, not just as a career strategist, nor only as a negotiating tactic but as a man. What kind of man? Having observed him from the outset, when we both entered the Commons in 1979, I am certain that the ambition to be on good terms with people is quite instinctive. He pursues it with persistence and skill. He succeeds (where so many careerists fail) because his friendliness is genuine.

Added to sincerity is technique. The squeeze of the shoulder, the care he takes to give you his whole attention, and all the small civilities that accompany a natural gentleman, are carefully employed. Major can be generous with his time. He can take pains not to regulate his civility according to how much he thinks someone matters. People who do matter notice this. People who didn't matter have a way of mattering later. All this he knows. And in dealing with equals or political superiors he knows how to balance familiarity with respect.

Most important, he has the good manners and the brain quickly to grasp and properly to engage with the argument another puts to him. It is both flattering to those with whom he negotiates, and expeditious of the business in hand. It was something Lady Thatcher never would do. Just as her insolence had its strengths, so his intellectual courtesy carries its dangers. To these I shall return. But his reward is that, whereas a discussion with Lady Thatcher would leave you worried that at least one of you must be mad – and not at all sure which – the meeting of minds which Major promotes comforts with the thought that you are both clever, sensible, decent fellows.

I have emphasised technique because he so conspicuously has it. But I began by saying he was genuine. John Major sets store by personal relationships not just because he is a good and nice man, which he is, nor only because it works well for him, which it does, but because he can't help it. I honestly don't believe Major is capable of planned rational aggression. The consequence (of which more later) is that when he does turn nasty, he doesn't handle it at all well. We psychoanalyse at our peril, but it does seem that Major's childhood and adolescence were such as to drive a youth to choose one of three roads: defeat, rebellion or collaboration.

Major chose collaboration: a careful (perhaps unconsciously studied) strategy to build security and win friendship in a world which might naturally have rejected the likes of him. It was a good strategy, perhaps the only one available. He would never have reached the House, and never have prospered there, without it. Practically speaking, he has needed friends.

Whether, beyond that, he has any emotional need to be liked by others, or any unreasoned fear of their dislike, it is impertinent to speculate. I'll risk the impertinence and temper it by remarking that it's certainly a problem I've had myself. To want to be liked by more than a few people, and by people one knows to be inferiors, *is* a problem. Fear of disfavour actually blocks the development of the few real friendships we do need.

Popularity is useful in politics but can be achieved by cynical means and dispassionately. However useful, you should never need it personally. Whips and Tory constituency associations can smell insecurity like dogs. More dangerously foreigners can smell it. Elevated to the status of policy, personal friendship has certain costs and limitations. The limitations of this strategy are, first, that it is not a strategy, but a screen. Though friendship may be the method by which you proceed, substantive differences will always surface in the end. There was no way, for instance, that the natural tensions between Lady Thatcher's view and Mr Major's could forever be hidden, nor her anger stifled. It might have been better to get the shoot-out over with early on. It might still.

In the end, Major got no further with Mitterrand than Thatcher. In the end, when Britain's interests (as Major saw them) diverged from those of Germany (as Kohl saw them), all that personal chemistry came to nothing – fizzed, indeed, into something toxic. And, in the aftermath of Black Wednesday, Mr Major could be heard in the members' dining-room at the Commons, soundly castigating his former German 'friends' for letting him down. Had he not learned that, at the heart of policy, foreign as well as domestic, must lie the conflict of interests? When these collide, friendships fly away like morning mists. Good relations can help avoid the unnecessary arguments, but are helpless in the face of the necessary ones. Some of the arguments at home, in the EEC, and across the Atlantic seem to me to be of the necessary kind.

Too great an emphasis on personal relationships between statesmen can exaggerate an impression of the freedom of action of either. In the end, Kohl had to bow to the Bundesbank. In the end, Major's Maastricht stance (in my view a very arguable one) was wrecked by his own recalcitrant backbenchers. In the end, differences over trade, over military deployment and in our two world views will dominate the agenda of Anglo-American dealings. Friendliness in Washington this week can help, but how much?

These are limitations to friendship, not arguments against it. But arguments against it do exist. A statesman too concerned with good personal relations can end up losing the respect even of friends. It was interesting that Mr Major stayed out of the Chamber of the Commons when Douglas Hurd came in to stand on his head last week. His coyness over Europe with colleagues, junior and senior, is coming close to infuriating the rebels, disappointing the loyalists, and baffling the undecided.

And there is another problem. Concentrating on Europe has taken him away from his own troops. Not just because he must be physically absent often (though he must) and preoccupied (though he is) but because backbenchers who had expected from him the tender loving care they missed with Lady Thatcher see, in his frantic attempts to keep Britain's allies on side, evidence that he loves foreigners more than he loves them. It's all smiles for Helmut, they complain: then he comes home and snaps at us. Backbenchers are complaining that the famous shoulder-squeeze has become rather peremptory, since the last election.

Further, a political past spent avoiding conflict with associates and counterparts leaves you all at sea when the inevitable conflict comes. Fighting in the playground gives us useful maps of our own strengths and weaknesses, and those of others. It helps us guess who are our best allies, and where our secret enemies may be found. It teaches us how to win, how to advance and how to retreat. It teaches us how, and how hard, and where, and where not, to press others – and when to hang back. It teaches us how to give in, how to kiss and make up. I am not sure that Major possesses these maps. I wonder whether over the last decade he did enough fighting on the backbench playground. Like a cat at play, Lady Thatcher used to fight just for pleasure, sharpening her claws, pouncing, sparring – all for practice.

But Mr Major sometimes looks like the Jeff of a Mutt-&-Jeff team who has lost his Mutt and is finding that the brandy and cigarettes alone are not doing the trick. This has seemed especially so in recent months in Europe, where memories of Lady Mutt are fading.

Finally, those who have set great store in keeping relationships sweet are often unpractised at being hurt. Mr Major tries hard, sometimes too hard, to stay friends with people; but there comes a point when something snaps. He can then become disproportionately angry. He feels betrayed and enormously aggrieved. The press call it peevishness or petulance but it reflects real hurt. He then gets seriously ratty with people and ends up making lifelong enemies of colleagues who had been no more than tiresome, or silly. Nice guys, when we turn nasty, can make a terrible mess of it, usually because we've had so little practice, and have bottled it up for too long.

I hope America turns out better than Germany, or France. It is sad that, having intended to become the bridge-builder between the American President and Chancellor Kohl and his friends, Major has lost Kohl to the Bundesbank, Bush to the US electorate, and now starts with the legacy of the Tory party's pro-Republican intervention in the US presidential campaign to clear up.

Incidentally, despite Number 10's protestations, I don't believe Norman Fowler, the Conservative Party chairman, would have acted without the express or implied permission of his boss. If he did, Major should sack him. But then Norman's his friend. And it wouldn't have happened if he hadn't wanted to be George's friend. And now he wants to be Bill's friend, and . . . oh dear. There you go again, John.

27 February 1993

LONG LIFE

LOVABLE LUTYENS

Nigel Nicolson

The sweetest man I have ever known was Edwin Lutyens, the architect. In his middle life he became the intimate friend of my grandmother and was constantly in and out of her houses, adapting them, extending them, even building them, and as she was extravagant far beyond her means and he, like all artists worth the name, encouraged extravagance in his clients, they planned and sometimes executed absurd architectural fantasies, like a terrace composed entirely of slates set on edge (it took 10,000) or throwing three large Brighton houses into one, laughing together when she found herself landed with three main staircases, three ballrooms and 15 bathrooms in a house that she inhabited alone.

My earliest memory of it is carrying pails of pebbles from Brighton beach to form the dark squares in the chessboard that he patterned in her garden. How I hated it! 'But McNed,' I protested, 'there are only 32 black squares in chess. Here you have 64!' 'It's called double-chess,' he replied. 'Quick, another 12 pails-full!' Then he would reward me not with hugs or sweets but little drawings, of an egg which when unfolded revealed its parent chicken, or of a small boy peeing, which when my mother approached he quickly changed into a tulip growing from a pot. Once he showed me his plans for a great country house and I asked him why the nursery was round. 'So that the children can't be stood the corner,' he explained. In another of his grand houses he pierced a peephole from the nursery into the hall so that they could watch the guests arriving. He adored children, and we adored him.

His quarrels with my grandmother were always one-sided, her side.

She would loudly complain when his clerk submitted bills for work completed for her, eventually paid him not in cash but in tapestries, and then declared that he had stolen them. Patiently he would explain that architects like peeresses have to eat sometimes and push a propitiatory sixpence under her bedroom door when he left next morning. Once she needed a blind to shield her loggia from the sun and pretended that she could not afford it. He suggested that she should put a box in her hallway for contributions from tradesmen and her guests, labelled 'For the Blind'. This sort of thing delighted her, like his puns: 'Toute Suite' for her private apartment, or 'Is Lady Ida down?', when visiting the Sitwells at Renishaw, or to a priest, 'Do two 'Aves make one 'Oly?' And his playful impertinence, as when he showed Queen Mary round her Doll's house and she asked him the meaning of the initials M. G. and G. M. on the pillows of the royal bed. 'The first one, ma'am,' he replied, 'stands for "May George?" and the other for "George may".' The point, it is believed, escaped her.

His extraordinary originality is evident in everything he touched. I was reminded of it last week when I visited one of the gardens he designed with Gertrude Jekyll at Buckhurst Park in Sussex, now beautifully restored. As the house stands on a hilltop, he sunk part of the garden to protect it from the wind and created within the hollow a long, stone-lined pool buttressed by walls and approached by semi-circular flights of steps counterswirling like the skirts of contiguous ballerinas. In miniature it anticipates the wonderful gardens that he designed for the Viceroy's House in Delhi.

It was there that he behaved in a way that I find most characteristic of this lovable man. The story is told by Christopher Hussey in his Life of Lutyens. When he was showing the Vicereine, Lady Hardinge, round the finished house, he either broke something or offended her in some other way, and was sent to his room in disgrace. There he wrote her a note of apology, ending, 'I will wash your feet with my tears and dry them with my hair. It is true that I have very little hair, but you have very little feet.'

27 February 1993

DIARY

Dominic Lawson

The tabloid papers generally refer to youth crime as 'an epidemic'. If this is really so, how is the virus transmitted? I consulted Doctor Theodore Dalrymple, well known to *Spectator* readers for his regular medical reports from one of Her Majesty's prisons. The good doctor advised me not to sneer at the hyperbole of the tabloid press. 'It has often occurred to me', he said 'that criminality is indeed a virus, spread by an infected tattooist's needle. There is much circumstantial evidence for this.' The link between loutish or criminal behaviour and the wearing of tattoos has been made much of recently, notably by Mr Tony Parsons' *The Tattooed Jungle* – a televised tirade against the working classes. But the maligned working classes are merely following a fashion set by the highest in the land. These days it is scarcely possible to open a page of the *Tatler* without seeing a photograph of a Duke's daughter sporting a tattoo on a deliberately bared shoulder. And as for the royal family! I have recently been reading Kenneth Rose's marvellous biography of George V. Mr Rose reveals how in 1879 both Prince George and his elder brother Albert spent three hours each under the needle of a Tokyo tattooist. 'Further designs,' writes Mr Rose, 'were added in Kyoto and Jerusalem . . . George Burchett, the doyen of British tattooists, many years later inspected the ornaments which Prince George carried for the rest of his life; "I was honoured", he wrote demurely in his memoirs, "to be called upon to make certain improvements to them which the King instituted on Queen Mary's suggestion."'

6 March 1993

THE LOSS

Beatrice Garland

Dismay and grief contend
for room. The upper hand
is gained at first by grief;
this much I understand.

It has colour and a shape
familiar to the eye.
The taste is sharp: the earth
breaks open; grief says cry.

Grief is for something lost,
a place where someone stood.
Its dimensions are the same
as the vanished good.

Out of it may come
a thought, a fresh resolve;
endured and done with,
it allows for love.

But the future, not the past
is the dominion of dismay.
In this bleak emporium
nothing is on display.

Just vacant shelves and long
cold sweating floors.
Nothing belongs, nothing
fits. Are there no doors?

If it were grand, heroic,
demanding an attitude,
I could be decent or brave,
make choices, stand unbowed;

but dismay is private,
unpromising and small:
things that have gone badly;
a face turned to the wall.

All you might notice –
no origin, nor sound –
is something darkish, bruised,
spreading underground.

Can you be accompanied
in this unquiet domain?
I think not. Its nature,
uneasy, not quite pain,

is only made for one.
And almost as relief
I would embrace the clean
exigencies of grief.

6 March 1993

'WE MIGHT AS WELL MAKE LOVE'

Anne McElvoy

I am hopelessly prudish, petrified of the sight of my own naked body, let alone anyone else's, and only interested in the bedroom peccadillos of my elected representatives because I have not come to terms with my own libido. Yes, I must be British. The awful truth about my warped and infantile attitudes to sex have been revealed to me in the German press over the last few months, but having lived there for several years previously, I long sensed their conviction that we are not good at It.

Relations between Us and Them are admittedly not at their most

'Boys will be boys, dear.'

friendly just now. We hit them with Nicholas Ridley, Robert Harris's *Fatherland* and the conviction that the Bundesbank is responsible for our fiscal woes. Even the politically-correct *Granta* has just published an edition sensitively entitled 'Krauts!' There had to be a counter-offensive, and now they are hitting back below the belt with a spate of erotic defamation. It grieves me to report that *The Spectator* unwittingly handed them the first grenade to lob. Michael Lewis, leaving these shores for America last year, wrote a gently mocking article about his sojourn in London ('Oh, not to be in England,' 23 May 1992), concluding that he wondered how a nation as stand-offish as this ever managed to consummate its affection, and conjuring up the amusing picture of a bedroom contraption which catapulted the couples at each other in order to get the awful deed over with. I laughed, you probably laughed and the author doubtless let out the odd splutter of mischievous mirth as he wrote it.

But it was taken with deadly seriousness by Germany's leading news magazine, *Der Spiegel*, which intoned the following week, 'In the everyday life of this puritan island, the Victorian notion remains prevalent that sex must not be fun and is really only there for procreation.' A German television channel then devoted a half hour to our attitudes to nudity, giggling at the fact that we consider naturists to be odd, when of course everyone knows that it is perfectly normal to grill your sausages starkers while addressing your soberly undressed neighbouring sunbather as 'Herr Doktor'.

With the bit between its teeth *Der Spiegel* refused to let go, and unleashed its considerable investigative expertise in search of British sex. An unnamed female correspondent drew the office short straw of 'trying out some Englishmen'. Her conclusions were shrivelling. 'Lights out, then they climb on top of you and after three minutes they spring out of bed covering their genitals with a towel.' I hope they gave her compassionate leave afterwards to recover from the experience. Another seeker for truth, this time from the liberal *Die Zeit*, did the rounds of Christmas parties in London and marvelled that this repressed people abandoned its chastity with such gusto after two mince-pies and a Babycham once a year.

I could forgive all of this more easily if my years in Düsseldorf and Berlin – East and West – had left me swooning with memories of the sheer sexiness of my hosts, but they did not. It is not just the fact that I do not find horn-rimmed glasses and green and purple checked jackets particularly attractive, but it is also the unimaginative literalness of the younger generation of Germans when it comes to matters of the heart and loins.

I tried, I really did. There was the handsome television journalist with the mesmerising green eyes behind the horn-rims. A brief conversation of strange, prickly intensity, the establishment of abstruse common interests, an invitation to dinner the next night – such romantic promise. I turned up for the date to find Eros already half undressed. 'Let's just take off our clothes and go to bed,' he drawled. I said I thought we were going out to dinner to discuss the crisis in East German literature. He looked momentarily confused. 'But why bother talking when we could just go to bed?' he said.

Being hopelessly prudish and alienated from my own libido, I related this woeful episode to another English friend in Berlin. 'Yours was quite romantic by usual standards,' she said grimly. Her dreamboat had lured her back for coffee, bemoaned the late-night television schedule and said in a tone of bored resignation, 'Well, now you're here we might as well make love.'

All cultures have their own peculiarities about courtship. The average British male, unless roaring drunk or ill-socialised, will approach cautiously throughout an evening until he is within striking distance, stroke a hand or touch a shoulder to check that he is not inducing a feeling of revulsion in his prey and, if he feels the climate is right, lunge and hope to encounter a willing response. I have nothing against this, as it gives the woman ample chance to skip nimbly out of the way before it is too late.

The German approach of direct verbal petitioning does not leave that option open and causes embarrassment and illfeeling if the answer is no. I don't quite know how to mend fences with a young politician who in the middle of a discussion on the flaws in the unification treaty said, 'I think it is time to continue this conversation lying down,' and then stormed off accusing me of being (you guessed it) prudish when I declined, but I rather feel that he broke the fences of delicacy in the first place.

All the odder, then, that they look with particular distaste on our interest in politicians' sex lives. According to *Der Spiegel*, whose coverage of this land is limited to two basic stories, 'Britain's Economic Decline' and 'The Island of Puritans', the case of David Mellor 'reminds Britons of what a wide discrepancy yawns between national sexual prudery and their inexhaustible sexual voyeurism'. A letter to the *Berliner Zeitung* berates the British habit of 'snuffling under MPs' beds' and concludes, yet again, that this is a mere reaction to our miserably unfulfilled love-lives. The obsession with our mating habits has become so advanced that it has taken on a fantasy life of its own. The usually sensible Berlin *Wochenpost* this month reports that we suffer more from premature ejaculation than any other western Europeans (what ghastly research that must have entailed for some poor reporter) and that it is 'quite usual for Tory politicians to dress up in baby-doll nighties and have themselves whipped . . . allowing the sadistic Super-Ego to punish the Ego of lust'.

Not that there is much chance of our catching Helmut Kohl or his ilk in a baby-doll nightie. When a magazine alleged that the prominent Social Democrat Oskar Lafontaine frequented Düsseldorf brothels, it rather than Herr Lafontaine became the subject of opprobrium in Bonn. If this were to continue, a sonorous newspaper leader remarked, the country could end up with the 'British disease' of the tabloid press 'relentlessly snuffling in the intimate spheres of politicians' lives', and wouldn't that be awful?

A propos of brothels, the *Wochenpost* proffers the valuable piece of information that there are four times fewer of them in Britain than in the old Federal Republic, a discovery which no doubt is a sign of our economic and sexual weakness rather than reflecting an excessive liking for prostitutes on the part of their countrymen.

Scandals in Germany are always of a financial rather than a sexual nature, which is very convenient for the politicians but makes for inordinately boring newspapers. It also strengthens rather than diminishes the blackmailer's hand. The late Willy Brandt, a notorious womaniser, was closely watched by the internal security service, and the material they garnered on his misdemeanours was almost certainly used in the internal party trickery to oust him from office in 1974, behind the smoke-screen of the discovery of an East German spy in his office. Attenuated secrecy makes mountains of molehills much more effectively than a prurient press.

Sex, like a lot of other facets of German life, is riven with contradictions. The society which prides itself on a 'natural' approach to the body has satellite television channels like RTL which pump offensive pornography into every living-room. These are remarkably horrible even by the standards of the industry, with many so utterly weird that one wonders who on earth gets the remotest pleasure from watching them.

Like the series of tales from a gynaecologist's surgery, a nightmarish mixture of cod 'medical advice' (which I will spare you), interspersed with sex scenes and shots of the ghoulish doctor peeling off his rubber gloves and casting them into a pedal bin. Very high viewing figures.

East and west, they like their naughty films. Erich Honecker, when his senile dementia allowed the recognition to permeate that the régime was not entirely popular with its subjects by the mid-Eighties, spent precious currency reserves on importing *Petites Folies*, a charmingly dated French porn series full of buxom chambermaids, well-hung plumbers and not a gynaecologist in sight. It was calculated to distract the plebs from the lack of citrus fruits and stimulate the falling birthrate at the same time. When Honecker's cupboards in the Wandlitz compound were opened to the public gaze, it was discovered that he had the whole set and other similar offerings not considered suitable for the working class in his tape library.

You can hardly fail to become rich in Germany by peddling sex aids, particularly now that the market has expanded to the east. As I travelled through the blighted small towns of Saxony soon after currency union in 1990, I drove down a main street which had but one new western investor to enliven its dreary frontages: Dr Müller's sex emporium had arrived. The population was understandably aggrieved that while they couldn't get fresh vegetables or a pizza in a 25-mile radius, they had 35 potency cures on their doorstep.

A befugged Teutonic view of life in Britain persists in Germany which seems to have been forged somewhere about 1890 and has altered little since. Along with the lore that we all sit down to tea and toast at four o'clock sharp before making our way home across cobbled streets in a pea-souper fog, stopping only to address our fellows as 'Sir', goes the iron conviction that we are *verklemmt* – uptight. Has no enterprising London correspondent of a German publication seen

Margi Clarke interviewing deadpan Liverpool housewives about their favourite positions on *The Good Sex Guide* or twisted his neck trying to follow Jeremy Irons' sadomasochistic exertions in *Damage*? I suspect they have, but can't bear to let their readers in on the secret of our enlightenment and spoil the fun.

While I was mulling over these peculiarities, another girlfriend called from Berlin to relate an evening of heavy-handed banter from her hosts about the British preferring hot-water bottles/cricket/a cup of tea to Doing It. As they left the café, one young stud whispered to her with the magnanimity of a philanthropist in a poor-house, 'You can sleep at my place if you want.' But hang on. If we are all so bad in bed, why do they proposition us with such desperate regularity? And if they are all so good at it, why do they need to?

13 March 1993

IF SYMPTOMS PERSIST . . .

Theodore Dalrymple

One of the questions which the doctor is enjoined to ask prisoners as they are received into the bosom of our penal system is whether they have ever had any serious injuries. The answer to this question is almost always no. Three questions later in the doctor's *pro forma*, the prisoners are asked whether they have ever been in hospital. The answer to this question is almost always yes.

'What for?' asks the doctor.

The most usual reasons given are a car crash or an assault.

'And what happened to you?'

'I had a fractured skull, two broken ankles and a punctured lung.'

One might mistake the denial of these injuries as serious for admirable stoicism, were it not that the prisoner who considers a slash in the neck with a machete but a normal hazard of life is inclined to be ferociously querulous over the lack in prison of marmalade for his toast in the mornings. Among British criminals, sugar in tea is a human right, but a stab in the stomach is a rite of passage.

The acceptance of injuries as part of one's cultural heritage is widespread. I was speaking last week to a lady with a black eye.

'Is your boyfriend violent?' I asked.

'Sometimes,' she replied.

'Have you ever been to hospital because of him?'

'Only to out-patients.'

She was one of three women whom I saw in two days last week who had between them 26 children, not a single one of whom was supported financially by any of the six fathers. Four of the children were in prison, as were two of the fathers. The husband of the lady with 12 children, it is true, had stuck by her: but he was drunken and insanely jealous, violent both in and out of drink, accusing her of making assignations everywhere.

'I've had concussion off him ten times,' she said. He'd been unemployed for 20 years because of a strange heart condition, which left him just enough energy to beat his wife regularly, but none for work. I asked her why she had never left him.

'I've tried, but he always finds out where I've gone.'

Once he had run her down in his car and broken her hip and pelvis, but she had dropped the charges against him, and the police, supine as ever in such matters (because 'it's a domestic'), proceeded no further. As for her plans for the future, she would return to him.

'I've been with him for 30 years, doctor, I may as well stick with him now. What else can I do?'

One of the ladies had just given birth to her seventh child: two of her previous offspring were in local authority care (the word 'care' in this context meaning, of course, degradation and brutalisation), and one had been adopted. The permanently unemployed father of the new baby was angry that the hospital thought the mother should stay a few more days for the sake of her health. She had a large cut on her forehead: with the frankness of childhood, her four-year-old son revealed that she got it when daddy throwed her down the stairs.

As soon as he learned that we wished to keep the mother in hospital, the father phoned a solicitor. No prizes, dear reader, for guessing for whom the solicitor's bill comes: it comes for thee.

13 March 1993

LONG LIFE

THE ANGRY BRIGADE

Nigel Nicolson

I only once met Nicholas Ridley, when I was 21 and he was nine. I was staying the weekend at his father's house, Blagdon, in Northumberland, and came down to breakfast on Sunday morning to find that little Nick and I were the only ones to get up punctually. At that age I was the shyer of the two, but thought it my business to open a conversation. The theme I selected was, by misfortune, the deplorable record of the local football team, one of whose defeats I had watched the previous week. I was not to know that Newcastle United were as sacred to Nick as the Twelve Apostles, and that any abuse of them was a sin against the light. He said nothing, walked to the sideboard, took up the steaming coffee-pot and poured its contents down my brand-new suit. At that moment his mother Ursula came into the room. 'Good heavens, what has happened to your suit?' 'I stupidly upset the coffee-pot over it,' I replied, thinking that this would make Nick Ridley my slave for life. I never met him again.

There are various questions raised by this story. One is the propriety of telling it at all, only a week after his death, when at first hearing it sounds as if I come out of it much more creditably than Nick. But that is not so. My credit is diminished by the very act of claiming it, and Nick's discredit is salvaged by his instinctive reaction at so young an age to an attack on what he held most dear. Two other questions emerge from this. Is it true or false that 'men are but children of a larger growth', that character is seeded so young that it is ineffaceable in later life? Secondly, is anger a virtue or a fault?

I have not known many angry men. I have known rude men, like Randolph Churchill, who would have excused himself by saying that his rudeness was simply a display of mettle which his father extolled as one of the most desirable of human qualities, and that he was equally rude to waiters and Cabinet Ministers, which was true, because I once heard him accusing one of the latter of cheating at poker, and the Minister gathered up his cards and wife and left the house. Rudeness is not the same as anger, and less defensible. I like to think that Lord Scarman, for example, is capable of anger but incapable of rudeness, and I do not suppose that John Pope-Hennessy was particularly nice at the V & A, or Jocelyn Stevens at the Royal College of Art, but both had the courage to risk unpopularity in an excellent cause.

So I argue that Nick Ridley's action with the coffee-pot was nobler than if he had simply called me an ignorant fool and turned away to help himself to kedgeree. That he never thanked me for saving him from his mother's reproaches showed not ingratitude but a certain dignity, as if he found it contemptible of me to curry favour with him by a lie. It was a quality that survived in him from childhood, 'a refusal to bow to fashion or expediency', as Patrick Cosgrave put it in his *Independent* obituary. He would not have poured coffee over a colleague who annoyed him, but the desire to do so would have been evident. It was his *capacity* for anger that gave him strength, a subliminal passion that reinforced his integrity and was the expression of it. I wish I had known him in later life. But if we had met, would I have reminded him of that scene at Blagdon? I think not. Once all anger about Newcastle United had long ago been spent, he would have thought it an act of insufferable incivility to recall it, and Nicholas Ridley was, above all, a most civilised man.

13 March 1993

EATING POP TARTS, WATCHING POP VIDEOS

Emma Forrest

A recent survey enthused that people are reading more than ever. I'd like to know, first, what it is they're reading (I fear a boost to Lord Archer's bank balance) and, second, who exactly these avid readers are. I've seen no reference in this survey to teenage readers. Is this because we don't exist? I can tell you only what I see every day at school. A teenager who reads is a rarity.

Our school library has recently and beautifully been refurbished and now boasts a catalogue ranging from Austen to Zola (before then I think it started with Kingsley Amis and stopped at Martin Amis because there wasn't any more shelf space). And whilst the computer-

'Do you think he's trying to tell us something
with his body-language?'

room is packed every lunch hour, the turn-out in the library is sparse at best. Occasionally, people come to stick discarded bubblegum on the radiator. Possibly the non-visitors find the studious atmosphere intimidating, but I think it's simpler than that. Reading is hard work. For a long time children believed their parents when they were told that something that took effort was more worthwhile than instant gratification, that hard work is eventually pleasurable: 'Taking time to clean and boil spinach, good. Using finger to eat peanut butter out of a jar, bad.'

It seems that mine is the first generation to reject this theory. My mother was genuinely surprised at my response when she asked if I didn't feel better for having cleaned my room and I said no. Why should I feel better? I stubbed my toe on the Hoover and it ate into time I could have used to watch pop videos on MTV.

When Marshall McLuhan prophesied in the 1960s that people would eventually stop reading and communicate instead through the electronic media, his work was considered as subversive as Darwin's. The notion that the printed word might be made obsolete terrified a generation of liberal intellectuals whose status within society was testimony to the importance of literacy. Looking back, we can now see that McLuhan's chant 'the medium is the message' was the original soundbite. I'm assured that hardly anyone actually read his work. Today his books are largely out of print. But it seems his prophecies might be worth re-reading. When he wrote *Understanding Media* –

The Extensions of Man, he was dealing with the radio, telephone and television. With microwaves, satellite dishes and fax machines to back us up, we seem to have proof that gratification must always be provided instantly. Because I and all the other children of the Eighties never knew a time when things took effort, we have a different slant on reading. Times may be hard but living is still meant to be easy. It's screens and sounds that link us and give us our identity.

Even the cult literature of angry young men (now dead or, worse, old) fails to persuade us that reading is worth the effort. What use is Jack Kerouac's *On the Road* when we have no desire to venture beyond the boundaries of our bedrooms with their view of the world via satellite? Which of us can relate to the teenage trauma of *Catcher in the Rye* when the cast of *Beverly Hills 90210* tell us everything we need to know?

These rebellious books, besides, are now on the school syllabus, immediately labelling them as duty and hard work. It is, after all, difficult to find personal pleasure in the *Catcher in the Rye* after you've had to write a 2,000-word essay analysing its use of slang. Books enjoyed by my parents' generation as subversive tales of adolescents battling against the establishment have been adopted by the establishment and I resent it.

It is especially puzzling to me that the Government which bemoans teenagers' unwillingness to read as a hobby is the same one that is pushing for tests at 14 as well as 7. Constant testing at school leaves us with no desire for anything that resembles effort when we get home. As the GCSE exams are based largely on coursework, there is pressure all year round. So now, more than ever before, we want to tune out in front of a television screen once we stagger home.

I can sit all day watching MTV, eating Pop Tarts heated in the microwave, drinking local, nutrient-free diet Pepsi, listening to electronic music created by people taking smart drugs. Sometimes, occasionally, it all makes me feel a bit queasy. It's then that I find myself tentatively reaching for a book to accompany my Pop Tarts. But much as I may enjoy a few stolen hours with black on white, I don't talk about my reading at school. It would be like saying I occasionally get the urge to sleep with fish under my pillow.

On the one hand, my school friends' uncompromising rejection of literature and reading disturbs me, but, on the other, I identify with it. Not reading is our way of alerting the intellectual establishment that we've moved on. 'Unliteracy' is our unique contribution to modern culture.

20 March 1993

OPERA

THAT DREARY OLD SAMENESS

Rupert Christiansen

PELLÉAS ET MÉLISANDE
Royal Opera House

There was a deranged – or perhaps uniquely sane – woman in my jam-packed Central Line carriage earlier this week. We were stuck in a tunnel, a fate which, being British, we endured in newspaper-rustling silence. But she could bear it no longer. 'Do you ALL have to come here, EVERY day?' she boomed in a tone of epic misery worthy of Sophocles. 'Is it ABSOLUTELY necessary?' At which I had to stifle an impulse to scream in hysterically grateful agreement. Then the train trundled grumpily into Holland Park.

The foyer at the Royal Opera House is beginning to provoke me to a comparable fit of claustrophobic heebie-jeebies. Because – poor darling me – I am only allowed a single press ticket, I enter the place in a cold sweat of anomic alienation, without a friend to hold my hand or distract my attention from the terrifying fact that the audience is ALL the same, EVERY first night: sitting in the ABSOLUTELY same seats, wearing the same clothes, drinking the same drinks in the interval, queuing for the same coats at the end. And, of course, I am part of that dreary old sameness too. Not him again, they mutter when they see me, Stalls H21 as usual; can't they put him a box for a change?

It felt much worse than usual last Wednesday, because the perform-ance of *Pelléas et Mélisande* on offer seemed like the same old opera production too. My friends know that I can bore for England on the subject of Debussy's masterpiece and am liable to go dewy-eyed and weak-kneed at the thought of the Stein-Boulez realisation for Welsh National Opera last year, but I'm afraid I found Covent Garden's effort routine and perfunctory. Let me begin with the evident lack of rehearsal. I know that there had been sickness and substitutions among the cast, but are we seriously to believe that a team had been working on the project for six weeks – the period that the Royal Opera manage-ment continually assures us is always expended on new productions?

If so, how can one explain the appallingly inept lighting ('*Viens dans la lumière,*' Pelléas begs Mélisande. '*Non, non, restons ici, je suis plus près de toi dans l'obscurité,*' she replies; but it was all *lumière*, there was no *obscurité*), and the fact that the singers had been directed only inasmuch as a traffic cop directs the traffic? I'll tell you how: this was not a new production at all, but a rather old one, borrowed from Vienna. Its original director, Antoine Vitez, died in 1990, and this revival – exhumation – was the responsibility of someone called Lorenzo Mariani. The lighting was the responsibility of some-one called Vanni Vannio. He has lit 6,753 shows in his career, the programme tells us, and I imagine by the time you read this he will have lit 6,758. I passionately feel that this sort of bargain-basement pulling in of other houses' discarded product is no solution to the Royal Opera's problems, or to the problems of 'international' opera in general.

Yannis Kokkos' sets bore certain superficial resemblances to the beauties that Karl-Ernst Herrmann unforgettably dreamed up for the WNO, but they were no more than pretty enough. The staging, as a whole, appeared totally innocent of the opera's deeper drama, its hard erotic and psychological realities, its emotional urgency. There was no characterisation to speak of and no sense of Maeterlinck's symbolism. I could only shut my eyes and remember how richly Stein had suggested the manipulativeness in Mélisande's childishness and the infuriating clot behind Golaud's good intentions, as well as the stifling inertia in Arkel's palace and the desolation of his god-forsaken kingdom. At Covent Garden there was just a grey void.

The musical interpretation was complementary. I admire Claudio Abbado enormously, but his conducting here seemed to me to miss the point entirely. It gave out a Debussy made Ravelian: all Berlin Philharmonic smoothness and sponginess, a tone poem or a landscape, but never an opera, never tense or ambivalent or catastrophic. All the colour and subtlety in the playing ended up completely meaningless, related to nothing except their own sonority. The cast was not to my taste either. I prefer the title-roles sung by a light young tenor and soprano; Abbado had gone for a heavier and older baritone and mezzo, François Le Roux and Frederica von Stade. Neither of them was up to much: Le Roux looked gormless and sounded mannered; von Stade is just too seasoned and healthy to play a creature as neurasthenic as Mélisande. Victor Braun's Golaud might have been interesting if there had been a director in the house to develop it. I hardly registered Robert Lloyd's Arkel or Yvonne Minton's long-awaited return to Covent Garden as Geneviève. The boy Yniold was sung by a vertically challenged lady, Patrizia Pace – in a curious way, she was the most engaging aspect of this dreary evening.

I was thrilled to catch BBC2's broadcast of Britten's opera *Owen Wingrave*, in the original production filmed for television in 1971. It is unquestionably only a minor work in his *oeuvre*, of no great musical import, but what a performance it gets and how immaculately theatrical and totally gripping it is! If composers writing opera today would only learn to handle narrative the way Britten does, contemporary opera would be a happier business.

3 April 1993

BOOKS

SIMPLE TRUTH HIS UTMOST SKILL

Kingsley Amis

PHILIP LARKIN: A WRITER'S LIFE
by Andrew Motion
Faber, £20, pp. 570

The author of this book consulted me repeatedly while preparing and writing it, and last year sent me a draft to check for factual accuracy where I could. If, as seems likely, Andrew Motion was as scrupulous with all his sources as he was with what I provided, then this must be one of the most truthful of modern biographies. Truthful, as I said, to fact; interpretation is a different matter.

As a volume of nearly 600 large pages, *Philip Larkin* is uncomfortable to hold on the lap, and, thanks to the method of binding, those pages will not stay lying down. The jacket design is repulsive. It consists mostly of a black-and-white photograph of about half of Larkin's face, blown up to about twice life-size and tilted over to one side, like a smart movie shot of about 50 years ago. Few would call him a handsome man, but he deserves better than such a distortion.

This is a critical biography, which is to say that it offers to explain

and pass judgment on the subject's works as well as recounting events
in his life, sometimes linking the two. As in biographies of other poets,
to link the two tends to trivialise and de-universalise individual poems.
Motion does not always avoid this danger:

> The precise source for 'Lines on a Young Lady's Photo-
> graph Album' is easy to trace, though Larkin altered
> some details. 'I mean,' says Winifred Arnott, 'there
> were in fact two albums, not one; there's not a picture
> of me wearing a trilby hat . . .' Behind such details, and
> behind the feelings which make them precious, lies
> another, less obvious, source. By covertly admitting to
> the pleasure it takes in fantasy, the poem connects with
> the other pictures Larkin liked to gaze at: the photo-
> graphs in pornographic magazines.

Of which more later. At other times a poem simply disappears under
an avalanche of biographical detail:

> Begun on 14 February and completed after 15 pages of
> drafts on 28 March, 'Dockery and Son' describes a visit
> Larkin had made to his old college at Oxford, St John's,
> on the way back from the funeral of Agnes Cuming,
> his predecessor as librarian at Hull, almost exactly a
> year earlier. [Agnes Cuming had died on 8 March 1962,
> and her funeral had taken place on the 12th]. The pre-
> cise circumstances help to explain why Larkin
> describes himself as 'death-suited' in the poem, as well
> as illuminating larger questions of theme and mood . . .
> [The poem] was a good last choice for the manuscript
> Larkin was preparing to send Monteith. On 11 June he
> made his final decision . . .

   In the same literalising, diminishing way, 'Reference Back', a poem
which in characteristic Larkin fashion moves from a particular
moment to a general view of life and age, and a chilling one, is taken
as merely the record of a single incident on a datable holiday from
Hull. When connections or contrasts between poems or novels are
suggested, they sink to the transatlantic-thesis level of the observation
that 'mouths, which yearned for fulfilment in *Jill*, are here [in *A Girl
in Winter*] punished,' meaning simply that there is an unsuccessful
kiss in the one and a visit to the dentist in the other.

It will be seen that the argument keeps shifting from the work to the life, and it is the life or the supposed character of Philip Larkin that Motion, no doubt properly, is most concerned with. The current popularity of biographies testifies to the existence of a large public interested only tepidly in what a famous person achieved in public, like climbing a mountain or writing a book, but avidly in what he or she got up to in private and was 'really' like. Unfortunately, in the present case the famous person, like most writers, led a rather dull life among rather dull people and, more unusually, wrote thousands of extant letters illustrating the fact.

This might not matter so much if Motion added to his qualities of diligence and conscientiousness others almost as desirable, such as skill, dash, ability to select, above all humour. By a second stroke of ill luck, he is deficient in all of them. These shortcomings, or others, see to it that the portraits of some minor figures in the story, like Patsy Strang, seem woefully out of drawing. But perhaps in cases like this what should rather be stressed is the danger of reconstructing a character entirely from letters and second-hand information.

No such lack of personal contact extenuates Motion's almost complete failure to understand and convey the large part that jazz played in Larkin's life. Here, as well as a whole book of reviews of jazz records (*All What Jazz*, 1970) and scattered references elsewhere, he could observe and discuss at first hand. But he appears not even to have looked at all closely when Larkin was listening to a favourite record, describing him for instance as capering round his Hull sitting-room with a spilling gin and tonic in one hand 'while the other mimed the drummer's part'. Philip spill an expensive drink like gin? Mime the drummer's 'part' with one hand? Boy, will you get off?

At least Motion mostly avoids taking any high moral tone on the jazz question. So much cannot be said for his treatment of Larkin's fondness for 'pornography', as it is invariably and tendentiously called here. In fact what Larkin was buying in the Fifties and later was porn only by courtesy, pin-ups, girlie photos, tit magazines with nothing pubic ever shown, page-three stuff on a good day. But Motion draws in his skirt in pious horror every time the subject comes up, talking about it with the shocked disapproval he otherwise reserves for Larkin's 'racist' political effusions. He goes further in an interview he gave in the *Bookseller* of 26 February 1993.

First suggesting in his insightful way that the women in Larkin's poems are 'cleaned-up' versions of what he drooled over in less right-minded moments, Motion reveals that the day he uncovered Larkin's cache of 'pornography'

> was the most important day in the writing of the book, because it was then that I realised that I had the opportunity to talk about a general truth, that the beautiful flower of art grows, on a long stalk, out of some very mucky stuff.

Oh, so it was only *then* that he realised it, was it? Pfui! It seems we are supposed to regard Motion with awed respect for having intrepidly ventured into the very depths of squalor and infamy on our behalf. So be it. If he has never leered, or even looked, at a photograph of a naked female, he is some kind of freak. If he ever has, then he is no worse than a medium-sized hypocrite.

3 April 1993

LETTERS

LARKIN ABOUT

Letters

Sir: This Be the Verse (Books, 3 April)

They f— you up your biographers,
they may not mean to, but they do,
they'll play your vices up for laughs
and worse comes out in the reviews.

But they were f—ed up in their turn
by old-style fools in corduroys
who half the time were quoting Auden
and half just plainly chasing boys.

Criticism sparks criticism,
it lengthens on the library shelf;
cancel all of your subscriptions,
and don't write anything yourself.

William Saunders
18 Dartmouth Park Avenue,
London NW5

10 April 1993

DELUSIONS OF GRANDEUR

Edmund Glentworth

In November 1991, Her Majesty's yacht *Britannia* steamed into the West African port of Dakar for a much publicised four-day visit. She was carrying no royalty. During the visit, the admiral in charge hosted a magnificent reception, to which the entire Senegalese establishment, along with Commonwealth and Nato ambassadors, was invited. The reception culminated in a display by the Royal Marine band, marching up and down the quay in their tropical whites, which would have brought a tear to the eye of the most unsentimental Briton. Not one member of the Senegalese government turned up.

Was this a protest against some heinous act by HMG? Had the ambassador's wife worn the same hat as the wife of the Minister of Natural Resources at the Camerounian National Day reception three weeks before? No. The Senegalese government was simply not interested.

This incident should destroy once and for all the delusion that pomp and circumstance are sufficient to earn Britain the respect she no longer earns by virtue of her wealth or power. If large parts of the world no longer care about Britain, why should we care about them? Why maintain a network of elegant and expensive embassies around the globe?

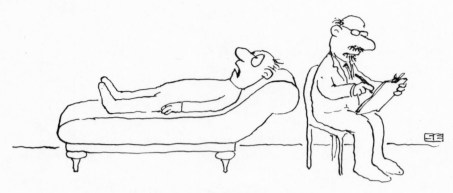

*'I had a wonderful childhood. It's life as an adult
that has traumatised me.'*

The answer, according to the Foreign Office, is that we have global
interests, and should therefore have a global presence. The first part
is true. We have still considerable overseas investments, economic
reliance on a free-trading system, the best and most exportable broadcasting in the world, the biggest international airline, an increasing
number of Britons travelling and working abroad. But to what extent
are these interests promoted or protected by the Foreign Office?

Not a lot. True, there is a consular service for distressed British
subjects, and a commercial service, staffed by career diplomats lacking
genuine commercial experience who have virtually no knowledge of
invisible exports, which now comprise a third of UK overseas earnings.
An unsatisfactory element of the Foreign Office's consular and commercial services is that it is wholly unclear to British citizens seeking
their assistance what level of service they are entitled to expect. There
is a role for the Citizen's Charter here. I discovered recently, while
trying to get up a seminar in Russia for a major group of City institutions (a process which required visiting a large group of Russian
officials in a short space of time), that our missions in Moscow and
St Petersburg will no longer help fix appointments with officials. So
what do they do?

The same question could be asked of the rest of the Foreign Office's
functions. Instant communications, the growth of international organisations and Britain's declining power have eroded its traditional roles.
Our bilateral aid budgets, however well targeted, are chicken-feed compared with those of the EEC and the UN (to which we contribute, but
over which we retain no control) and are in any case mostly adminis-
tered by the comparatively efficient British Council; major relief work
is carried out by non-governmental organisations; human rights are

monitored by the likes of Amnesty International; British language and culture are propagated by the excellent BBC World Service (paid for by the Foreign Office, but editorially independent) and increasingly by the wholly independent BBC World Service Television.

This leaves the Foreign Office with the traditional stuff of diplomacy: intelligence and government to government relations. This is what we are best at. The quality of our diplomats, says Mr Hurd, enables us 'to box above our weight', and to maintain our permanent seat on the UN Security Council.

One should always be wary of sporting allusions. Who are we fighting against? What is the point of maintaining close relations with countries in which we do not have the slightest intention of intervening? With the exception of Iraq and Bosnia, our recent record has been one of clearing out at the slightest whiff of trouble: we did nothing to stop the war in Somalia, part of which was once a British colony; we refused requests from Sierra Leone, a Commonwealth member, for basic military supplies (such as radios) to stop the incursions from Liberia which eventually toppled the régime; we closed our embassies in Afghanistan and Zaire and have not reopened them since. It may be sensible to behave like this. But, if so, we should stop posturing as a global power.

I was told once that our principal function was to disguise from our host government how much less we were doing by maintaining the appearance of activity. The context was a Foreign Office decision to cut all Overseas Development Administration-funded projects running at a budget of less than £1 million a year. This may have made sense in aid terms, but it was political nonsense: at a stroke all UK bilateral aid in several African countries (every one of which takes its turn at the UN Security Council) was cut as a result. With it went any residual influence the British Government might have had over them. The host government was not fooled.

One way of reducing the absurd gap between the outward show of our far-flung diplomacy (grand embassies, Jaguars, etc.) and its lack of real substance would be to match the level of our overseas representation to our needs. In particular, our smaller, far-off posts could be staffed by younger, cheaper and more energetic ambassadors with a smaller staff, often in conjunction with our EEC colleagues – in Dakar, there were no less than eight EEC embassies which all fulfilled the same function. Some of the more absurd security regulations could be dropped. For example, not every embassy needs a full-time UK employee eking out a life of staggering tedium registering papers in a windowless room; nor do all embassies need to resemble

Fort Knox. In one post in which I served (where there were no secrets worthy of the name), I had to unlock three doors with keys, as well as four sets of combination locks, in order to get into my office. The ambassador did not even know how to get into his. We were visited every fortnight by a Queen's messenger who, with his diplomatic bags, took up the three best seats on the plane down the coast and stayed two nights in a hotel. As often as not he did not have any mail for us.

In another post, we worked in a brand-new, purpose-built embassy which was designed to withstand a direct hit by a Scud missile. It was only when water poured through the roof after a snowfall that it transpired it had been incorrectly assembled.

Another example of the ludicrous obsession with security is the continuing bar on members of the diplomatic service from private travel in 'communist-controlled' countries. Like many other ill-informed people, I presumed that only China and North Korea would still fit the bill. Not so. According to the Foreign Office security department, Rumania, Bulgaria, Russia and other CIS states are still communist-controlled. Hungary and Czechoslovakia were only recently removed from the list. The very diplomats who have spent their professional careers endeavouring to bring down the Iron Curtain are the only British citizens (along with the army) prevented from enjoying the fruits of their labour.

All this might be funny if it did not betray an alarming lack of common sense. We have at present only one UK diplomat stationed in the CIS outside Russia and the Ukraine (there were two, but one fell down a manhole in Alma-Ata). Apart from the lost trading opportunities, it is particularly worrying that we are not keeping a closer eye on the nuclear weapon states of Belarus and Kazakhstan, especially with the latter being so close to the Middle East. The reason given is lack of funds, and recent cuts in the Foreign Office budget have not helped. But nor has the Foreign Office helped itself. The two embassies in which I served in Africa and the Middle East were both grotesquely overstaffed with people who could have been serving in the CIS. The Foreign Office recently sent two officers (one of whom speaks Russian but not Arabic) to fill the same post in the Middle East. I should know, because I was the one.

The Foreign Office feels particularly unloved at the moment. Its officials work ever longer hours for smaller salaries churning over an increasing mass of paper dealing with an ever more complex and uncertain world. Much excellent work is done. Yet its budget has been substantially cut. It remains an object of suspicion and dislike to MPs, the public and the press, for the simple reason that so much of what it does is shrouded in secrecy.

If the Foreign Office wishes to halt this demoralising decline it must change its antiquated culture. Essentially, this means opening up to the people outside the Government whose interests it ought to be serving, above all British exporters. If the MoD, DTI and Immigration Service place people in embassies, why should not the private sector, especially the wealth creators who ultimately pay for the Foreign Office anyway? The traditional security objections are no longer credible now that the Cold War has ended. Commercial and information work could be privatised, with each posting (as in the British Council) going to the best candidate, whether inside or outside the service, on a contract basis. International and EEC lawyers could be contracted into our UN and EEC missions; oilmen could be recruited to embassies in the Middle East and Kazakhstan; financial experts to Tokyo and so on.

The truth is that career diplomats, most of whom join straight from university, are simply not competent to deal with many technical and economic issues arising today; and the notion that diplomacy, like accountancy or law, is a profession demanding special skills is a fiction. Cross-fertilisation with the private sector should be encouraged by allowing diplomats to leave and rejoin the service with no loss of seniority, as in France. At present, British diplomats have no choice but to resign. Many of the best do just that.

The present system of jobs for life, which results in many posts being filled by expensive and inefficient old people and holds back the cheaper, younger ones, should change rapidly. This would make the Foreign Office more efficient and competitive, less cosy and collegiate – just like the outside world.

None of these ideas is new, and some are being more or less seriously considered by the Foreign Office itself. But change is agonisingly slow. If the Foreign Office culture is incapable of such flexibility, it can drop its claim to be a comprehensive and worldwide service. It should limit itself to its principal strength: negotiating with foreign governments and the major international bodies in the few places which matter – and forget the charade of global representation.

Either way, the Foreign Office must change to survive, or it will deservedly suffer the lingering fate of so many anachronistic institutions: death by a thousand Treasury cuts.

3 April 1993

IMPERATIVE COOKING:
FRYING TONIGHT

Digby Anderson

I have known for some time that university students are lazy and ignorant when it comes to cooking, wasting the generous grants we taxpayers are forced to give them on soggy pasta and ready-made sauces. But I was not aware that they had taken to forming gangs to terrorise the exceptional student who does cook properly. This happens, one of my correspondents explains, in the communal kitchens of Halls. He was quietly cooking a brace of pheasants when he was interrupted by a deputation demanding he should cease. A complaint had been registered with the Warden. The other students felt ill at the thought of trying to boil their ready-mix sauces while there were 'dead animals' in the oven.

I suppose it was bound to spread. Once government ministers, such as Mrs Peter Bottomley, make intolerance and hounding of other people's eating habits not only a virtue but a ten-year government policy, it is not surprising mere students should follow.

But there are other more subtle effects of health fascism in high places. The worst is that even those of us who know it to be nonsense find ourselves slowly falling into line. Thus I suddenly realised the other day that it was three weeks since I'd cooked any deep-fried food. Obviously, we Imperative cooks must watch our own behaviour to make sure we are holding the line. A self-examination, daily, is called for. Not before bed but around teatime, so that amends can be made at dinner.

But the deep-fried aberration gives me an idea. The letters I still receive from those wanting to join the Enemies of Mrs Peter Bottomley now have a common theme: what is the Club to do? Suggestions have included an annual dinner, protest marches and burning the Creeper in effigy. Let's start instead with ourselves and what we eat, making sure it stays uncontaminated by, indeed goes in the opposite direction to, the evil health of the nation plan. If, for instance, enough of us can up our fat intake, we will scupper any faint chance of the plan's targets being achieved.

So out with the deep-frying saucepan and off to the butcher to get as much beef fat, especially kidney fat, and pork fat for rendering as we can. Then make a list of all the wonderful dishes which depend on deep-frying and a resolution to go through them. Start simply. What better than fried bread, not only with breakfast every day – there's nothing better than hens' eggs on bread fried in chicken fat – but fried bread as the Frogs have it: fried bread with *rouille* and fish soup, fried bread with beef in wine stews or with spinach purées. Those wonderful French *beignets* – of brains or aubergines or potato with salt cod – are all deep-fried too. Then to Spain, above all Cadiz, for fish: dogfish, marinaded then deep-fried, deep-fried anchovies, whitebait, prawns; or to Italy for mixed fried fish. As you go, list the subtle differences in batters, oils and fats.

On then to the East, the true home of deep-frying. Start with Indian bhajis, onion slices dipped in a batter of egg and chickpea flour, or lentil vadees or mashed potato and spice balls. Even better, the twice or thrice cooking cultures of the Far East, where ingredients may be deep-fried then stewed or amalgamated in sauces, or steamed, sauced or marinaded then deep-fried. The best things, such as deep-fried, spiced crabs, are not one but several dishes with Thai, Indonesian, Chinese and Philippine versions. Pause for a while, a long while, with the Chinese books, count the number of recipes which involve deep-frying and consider the sheer mendacity of the food fascists who depict Chinese cooking as an endless steaming sauna.

Above all we must reclaim the chip. It is now attacked on all sides. The food fascists would ban it. The lower classes, in collusion with the chip shops using cheap oil and mushy, frozen chips, have ruined it. And the lazy British housewife demands bastardised versions of it – again pre-done and ready for the oven. Few things are better than eggs and chips or steak and chips for breakfast, but the chips have to be made from raw potatoes, cut fairly thin and twice deep-fried in beef fat.

I can only think of one thing further removed from the Bottomley vision of the world and that is home-made crisps. They absorb more fat and warrant more salt. You need a mandoline for slicing them and it's worth leaving the raw slices six hours or so in water to lose surface starch. Then dry them, deep-fry in beef fat and anoint with lorry loads of salt. If you put enough on, you will have to drink your Bottomley beer ration for a week in half an hour.

10 April 1993

DIARY

John Osborne

A few weeks ago I received, by special delivery, a scroll (I suppose you'd call it), framed and mounted, proclaiming that I had been 'nominated' (along with half a dozen others) for a Laurence Olivier 'Outstanding Achievement' award. I was invited to attend a luncheon with the other nominees. Since then I have been sent a letter from the BBC on behalf of the sponsors (Swet, the *Observer* and American Express) asking me to 'supply us with a copy of a biography regarding your career to enable us to compose a suitable eulogy should you win the Kenneth Tynan/*Observer* award for Outstanding Achievement for which you have been nominated. I look forward to your reply.' It was signed by the assistant floor manager for the awards. Who can enjoy being a supplicant candidate? The Big Night is this coming Sunday. Anyway, I threw the floor manager's letter into the bin. This may seem churlish, but I see no point in writing my own eulogy for an event I shan't attend in aid of a bauble I haven't a hope of winning. The gristle of fugitive instinct is about all I have left.

This present award reminds me of Ibsen. He was avid for medals, the 19th-century equivalent of our novelty-shop statuettes. He sought them out and put himself up for them like a touting film star. He was also in the habit, when inappropriately bemedalled at public celebrations, of becoming disagreeably drunk, cruelly abusive and having to be carried home. It all came back to me some months ago, when I accepted a gong from the Writers' Guild. It seemed a spontaneous, generous gesture on their part, didn't promote anything in particular, and would almost certainly go unnoticed. A disastrous miscalculation. The evening was not conducted by friendly scribes but commandeered by television bully-boys and moguls, lasted six excruciating hours, during which I snoozed off after a meagre distribution of drinks and, fatally, forgot to take my evening fix of insulin. Like Ibsen, I was carried from the platform, comatose. But sober. The following day, the Roundhead hoydens of opinion denounced my shame with all the primness the bilious old Norseman might have encountered from the bombazined daughters of the Oslo Band of Hope a century ago. As I was trying to borrow a large sum of money at the time, it seemed less damaging to my chances of escape from penury to allow my conduct to be interpreted as a drunken lapse rather than a diabetic hypo. Old Henrik was fortunate, living in an age of ironclad morality rather than maidenly priggery. I fancy he might have chucked his medals at the lot of them. I didn't get the loan anyway.

Another hand-out this week from the Daughters of Eve (West) – Boston post-mark, typewritten on University of Southern California paper – informing me of their programme for 1993. This one states that Sylvia Plath suffered Fatal Damage and that the Eight Daughters of the Council have decided to 'send a delegate party to the 30th anniversary ritual at the Plath grave in Britain and to bring earth from it for placement in the Daughters' Hearth and bury within the grove the citation of Honorary Daughter. This is now being crafted for Spring readiness.' Their main resolution is: 'The Daughters of Eve continue to research in the US and Britain charges of Fatal Damage against three male persons: Harold Pinter – fatal damage to Vivien Merchant, 1982. John Osborne – fatal damage to Jill Bennett, 1990. Ted Hughes – fatal damage to Sylvia Plath, 1963.' Tippexed over in bright green is the damning accusation: 'They showed no remorse, then or now.' If indicted, it goes on darkly, 'these persons will be tried by the Daughters' Jury. Witnesses will be called from Britain to bear testimony before the Daughters' Jury. In 1993 thirty years will have passed since Sylvia Plath suffered Fatal Damage ... And all Eve's Daughters shall be free.' All the latest American lunacies, from tooth-'n-claw feminism to political correctness, seem to be swiftly absorbed over here, so a transcript of the trial proceedings should make for a fruity evening at the Royal Court's Theatre Upstairs. With the accused *in absentia*, I would hope. Might the Dotty Daughters contemplate kidnapping? Perhaps I should look up the number of Special Branch. Or plead remorse?

I had intended to keep off the subject of the Theatre, partly because I know that it must be tedious to most readers of this journal (or why else would it consistently employ the most flaccid of drama critics?). But I am puzzled by the general antagonism to something few people, these days, choose to experience. The virulence of this antipathy is clear from the glee which has greeted the invention of the species *luvvies*. Now, I had all but given up resisting the contempt piled upon actors. Few of them are unspotted by ruthlessness and vanity. Some are little better than strolling psychopaths, and actresses, once baptised by fame, often come close to clinical madness. But the appellation 'luvvie' is a calumny, a journalist's jealous perception of something of which they know little and understand less. Enmity to success is ammunition to every British journalist's gunbelt. It is they who are largely responsible for the hysterical clamour of the Oscars, they who raise the drooling pitch to massed frenzy. The actors are merely the drafted clowns. Players may be excruciatingly silly, burbling about themselves on chat-shows, wearing idiotic Aids ribbons and making embarrassing acceptance speeches. But they often do express their affections openly, and sometimes genuinely, which grates on the newspaperman's sullen and frequently suburban heart. Actors are irredeemably tiresome when they bound onto the political stage, when they rival MPs or writers. They can be shrewd, kind, emotional, calculating, full of frailty and, occasionally, acute intelligence. They can become monsters, but not the very best of them. This is my 45th year in the trade, and I can count the number of 'luvvies' I have known on little more than the fingers of two hands.

17 April 1993

DOUGLAS HURD'S PUBLIC CONSCIENCE

Boris Johnson

In a building once intended to be a suburban Brussels maternity hospital, the biggest ever deployment of Nato troops is being planned. At Nato HQ, Evere, they envisage 75,000 troops for Bosnia, with about two thirds to be committed by America, Britain and France. The peacekeeping force for the former Yugoslavia would be the grandest thing, some would say the only thing, Nato has ever done. The troops have not gone yet. Indeed, the longer the West dithers, the longer Serbs mock western impotence, the less likely it is that they will. But if they were to go – and the martial hubbub is rising – it would be an extraordinary reversal of British foreign policy. Some would say it was absurd that Britain should even think about sending fighting troops to Bosnia; and not just because of the risk to British life.

Eighteen months ago, it was Britain which, seemingly single-handedly, blocked military intervention in the former Yugoslavia. Then, arguably, deployment was feasible. Ceasefires were evanescent, but existed. Then, the battle-ground was Croatia. Then, thousands, tens of thousands, of Bosnians now dead were still alive. Only now, when the dangers are so much greater, is intervention again being seriously contemplated. That is an irony which one would expect to surface.

And it does, not in Foreign Office briefs but in the extra-curricular writings of Douglas Hurd. In the last year, since Bosnia became a battle-ground, the Foreign Secretary has given us two vivid, workman-like short stories (and a fascinating Oxford speech, reproving the 'critics', or journalists, for their constant carping at 'achievers', viz. D. Hurd). They reveal an honourable mind ill at ease with what he has done.

These are not ordinary short stories. This is the British Foreign Secretary publicly meditating on the issues that underpinned his decisions – which were crucial – about the worst European war for 50 years, and, oh yes, justifying himself. For the student of Hurd, Europe and Yugoslavia, these texts read like a palimpsest of confessions and clues.

On 18 September last year, the *Daily Telegraph* published 'The Last Day of Summer', a 3,000-word tale by Hurd of how war spread to Bosnia, through the eyes of Borisav the Bosnian Serb. It is well-crafted, gripping stuff, with flashes of real humanity. Briefly: Borisav, a lowly forestry official, and his friend Tomic the Croat have together built a summer house. It is later symbolically mortared, with Tomic inside it. Borisav flees.

Hurd begins the tale one year before that tragedy, as Borisav stands gloomily by the local cemetery, pondering the still remote war in Croatia. Would it spread? The location of time is precise – 'The gnarled apple tree was heavy with unripe fruit.' This is the late summer of 1991. At exactly the time that Borisav was brooding, Hurd was in The Hague, arguing against European military intervention in Croatia.

On 19 September 1991, after the failure of sundry EEC ceasefires and the EEC monitoring mission, there took place the meeting of the Western European Union in The Hague, called by Herr Hans-Dietrich Genscher of Germany, at the urging of Mr Hans van den Broek, the Dutch foreign minister. Van den Broek wanted to send 50,000 men under the Western European Union, to enforce the stuttering ceasefire. The Germans were favourable, but – *Teufel!* – the constitution said they could not take part *themselves*. The Italians were favourable, but said they were ineligible because they were Yugoslavia's neighbours. The only countries that mattered that day were Britain and France, and possibly Holland.

'It was only the Brits that didn't want it', says one Dutchman, who attended the meeting. 'It was Douglas Hurd who killed that idea off. We still think we should have done it.' According to French officials at the time – and they may well have been lying – the French foreign minister, M. Roland Dumas, strongly supported van den Broek, making it two out of three. With 20–20 hindsight, military experts now say that this was one of the last few moments, when the Serbs were still travelling in convoys of tanks, when the style of battle was favourable to intervention.

Importantly, the WEU meeting took place just after the coup in the Soviet Union: the Serbs could no longer count on their great Slavic supporters to stymie western initiatives. It was a window of opportunity – and Hurd, so it seems, closed it.

Memories and reports of that meeting are perhaps unfair on Hurd; quite likely there was no appetite, in any country, for military intervention while there was the slightest whiff of a firefight. Maybe the continentals knew they had to make a gesture; and they also knew, cynically, that they could count on the intellectual honesty of Hurd to bat their suggestions aside.

And yet there will always be that element of historical doubt: not just whether the WEU option was really feasible, but whether it was right, in view of what was to come (which was hardly unpredicted), to close it off.

How could I have known? Hurd asks us in his short story. Back in

September 1991, he could see the future no more clearly than Borisav the Bosnian Serb. As Borisav contemplates a circle of first world war graves, with their split and illegible stones, all was perplexity in his mind. Would war really return to Sarajevo? 'Was history coming back?' asks Borisav-Hurd. It was.

By the end of January this year, the horrors had multiplied on television to the point where they were prompting renewed public calls for action. In 'Ten Minutes to Turn the Devil', published in the *Observer* on 31 January, Hurd's conscience drives him back to the theme of the European intervention force that never was. This time the hero is Richard Smethwick, the British defence secretary, who must convince a mutinous Brighton Tory party conference of the wisdom of having sent British troops to 'Caucasia'.

This time, Hurd asks us to imagine that he had gone ahead with the WEU force. (It is quite clear, incidentally, that he means the WEU, the putative defence arm of the EEC, so beloved of the federalists, which figured so largely in the Maastricht talks; the 'European Safe Haven Force' in the story comes from France, Germany, Britain, Spain and the Benelux; this is not Nato – no Americans here, no Canadians or Norwegians.)

Already, amid the alien guerrillas, British troops have sustained 96 casualties. Britain has been swept by a movement called 'TON' – Troops Out Now, whose supporters drape Brighton with banners showing a huge weight crashing down on the defence secretary.

Smethwick is the thinnest of masks for Hurd himself, from the stiffeners in his shirt collars to his knowledge of Ovid and even his political CV: 'He had served in Northern Ireland . . .' Like Hurd, he must face down the bloody-minded blue-rinsed Little Englanders (shades of Hurd's conference roastings over Maastricht, or capital punishment?), and, as he rises to speak, he is suddenly 'angry with the Party for the crude anti-foreign mood in the hall' – pure Douglas Hurd, at his prefectorial finest.

Mastering his doubts, waving aside the autocue, he shames the Little Englanders with statesmanship and an old-fashioned appeal to internationalism into support of the British presence.

Eighteen months after he blocked intervention in Croatia, Hurd, on this evidence, is still tormented by the dilemma of August and September 1991; increasingly tormented, in fact, as the chorus begins again for western military action, in far more perilous circumstances. In 'Ten Minutes to Turn the Devil', that dilemma is melodramatically pointed up in the last sentence, when Smethwick-Hurd learns, after receiving his standing ovation and the thanks of the prime minister, that his brother-in-law has been killed by a sniper while commanding British troops in the mud of Caucasia.

Mr Hurd lays it before us. You judge, he says: did I do the right thing? Far from finding his story self-serving, we are moved to admire him; for his candour, and for his doubt. We should also examine his motives.

That day in The Hague, 19 September 1991, a fierce scrap, however histrionic, appeared to have taken place. Against the WEU intervention proposal, seriously meant or not, the Foreign Secretary was forced to deploy the utmost vehemence. He appeared to the press in the evening in the basement of the bunker-like Dutch foreign ministry, tired and with the grimness of a pyrrhic victor. He had won the argument, but allowed himself to be painted as the spoiler.

His officials immediately circulated verbatim accounts of what he had said, a trenchant opposition to engagement, based on his own experience of Northern Ireland; that it was madness to send western troops to keep apart bloodthirsty bandits; that escalation was inevitable; that once committed, the troops could be there for decades.

Those are good reasons, ones that will satisfy most Tory MPs. But, in view of subsequent catastrophes which might have been averted, do they still satisfy Douglas Hurd? I believe there was a further reason for the British veto, one that preys on his conscience and may explain the literary searching of the soul.

When the Yugoslav crisis ignited in the summer of 1991, western Europe was halfway through the Maastricht negotiations, and at once there was a bizarre ideological contamination between Maastricht and Croatia. From the start, Jacques Delors and other EEC generalissimos saw not so much the threat to the lives of Yugoslav civilians as the threat to 'federalism' itself.

Pathetic inducements were offered to keep the Croats and Slovenes from splitting away – presumably to prove what Joe Brandt, in a paper for the Woodrow Wilson Centre in Washington, has called the 'federalist fiction', that monetary and political unions make intrinsically better sense; new EEC-Yugoslavia trade and cooperation agreements, new EEC-Yugoslavia financial protocols, studies showing the costs of 'non-Yugoslavia', all were dandled before the heedless separatists.

All they achieved, of course, was to convince Milosevic and the Serbs (the 'federal' government) that Brussels was somehow on their side in their murderous campaigns.

In fact, only one thing was more misconceived than the EEC's attempts to promote federalism in Yugoslavia. It was the miserable effort to use Yugoslavia to promote federalism in the EEC.

Jacques Poos, Luxembourg's bouncy-quiffed foreign minister, has earned immortal ridicule for his remark in June 1991, made in my hearing as we flew on a publicity-stunt mission to Belgrade: 'This is the hour of Europe!' Time and again, we were told that Yugoslavia was the 'laboratory', the 'melting-pot', the 'crucible', in which the new Maastricht Common Foreign and Security Policy was to be tested with fire. It was not just Jacques Poos.

Those were the high old days, remember, when Britain was 'at the heart of Europe', loyally playing along with the various fancies. Douglas Hurd himself said Yugoslavia was 'a European problem which had to be faced by Europe alone'.

As we know, the Community flunked it, tragically. It is a story riddled with flaccidity and lack of nerve. One could point to the fateful July 1991 decision of Jo ven den Valk, the EEC's chief 'ice-cream man', or monitor, to deploy his men only in Slovenia, leaving the Serbs to do what they would in Croatia. One could point to the complete inability to speak with a single voice over recognition, until 15 December 1991.

But mainly, one must point to the EEC's chronic failure, despite several lulls, several 'windows', to provide a credible military deterrent to Serb – or anyone's – aggression. As Warren Christopher, US Secretary of State, said to Hurd and others at Nato on 26 February this year, 'The West missed too many opportunities to contain the suffering, bloodshed and destruction when the conflict was in its infancy.

'The lesson to be learned from this tragedy is the importance of early and decisive engagement against ethnic persecution and aggressive nationalism.' *Touché.*

So the question is put again: Why did Hurd, who had *accepted* that Yugoslavia was a 'European' problem, block off Europe's only decisive means of intervention? Was it simply the risk of loss of British life?

Or were his calculations, like those of everyone else, contaminated by Maastricht? You have to remember that the body in question, the nine-strong Western European Union, was perhaps the biggest political football in the Maastricht talks. France and others were determined to build it up as an EEC-sponsored defence pact, independent of America, to rival and in time supplant Nato.

Britain, naturally, wanted to reinforce Nato, embracing as it does the advantages of American leadership, British lieutenantship, and a US presence in Europe; the WEU, in Britain's view, should be kept as a glorified talking-shop.

Now, as long as Yugoslavia was a 'European problem which had to be faced by Europe alone' (perhaps the root delusion of the whole disaster), a Nato force was out of the question. But to have sent a WEU force to Croatia in September 1991, or in the ceasefire in the New Year, would have suddenly incarnated the French dream; it would have been an irreversible victory for the federalist side.

My contention, therefore, is that Hurd had to say no, not merely because of the risk to British lives (had they not just been risked in the Gulf?), but because his veto was, apart from anything else, a move in the Maastricht negotiations.

Today, the Nato vs. WEU battle has ended decisively in Hurd's favour. Out there at the Nato HQ, the Americans are back in the saddle and the French, far from setting up their own Euro-defence pact, are virtually back in Nato's integrated military command, which they left in 1966. Whoever heard of the WEU, these days?

In the meantime, it has become convenient for the Foreign Office to blame the Bosnian conflagration, behind their hands, on Germany: apparently they should not have 'bullied' us into recognition of Croatia at the end of 1991. But the reality, surely, is that at several junctures before and after that date Europe failed to show either side, especially Belgrade, that aggression would not pay.

The war now having become so bad and so vicious, the West as a whole will almost certainly fail again – perhaps over Macedonia – whatever the preparations at Nato.

It is admirable that Mr Hurd's conscience should be so troubled; he emerges as the greater statesman for it, head and shoulders above his glib and insouciant colleagues. As he says of Hurd-Smethwick in his dark night of the soul, 'It was not as if in these small hours, he was sure that the policy was right.'

None of us can be sure. Nobody can know whether prompt and well-armed intervention to enforce a ceasefire in Croatia would have worked, or merely brought fresh catastrophe. But the truly tormenting possibility is that thousands of Bosnians may have died, thousands of lives been ruined, for the sake of a negotiating gambit in a largely defunct treaty.

17 April 1993

EXPLODING THE MYTH
OF CHERNOBYL

Piers Paul Read

Early in the morning of 26 April 1986 the fourth unit reactor of the V. I. Lenin nuclear power-station at Chernobyl exploded. Ever since, the name Chernobyl has become associated in the public mind with the pollution of a huge swathe of Europe and a lingering death for countless people. The accident delivered a fatal blow to the development of nuclear power, even though the Chernobyl reactor was of a design peculiar to Soviet engineering. In the United States, it confirmed the fears which followed the accident at Three Mile Island: no new reactors have been built since. In the Soviet Union itself, 40 reactors in various stages of development were either cancelled or converted to use coal and gas. Italy abandoned its plans for nuclear power. A public subscription in Austria raised the funds to mothball a brand-new power-station. The Swedes decided to phase out nuclear power by the year 2010.

Were these fears well founded? Seven years later, a chasm has arisen between the public's perception of the consequences of the explosion at Chernobyl and the assessment by the experts of its actual effects. The seriousness of the accident itself is not in question. Nor is the *ad hoc* approach to safety procedures in the former Soviet Union, in both the military and civilian nuclear sectors, resulting in a series of mishaps from the explosion in the nuclear waste depot in Mayak in 1957 to that in Tomsk last week.

However, it was precisely because of the earlier accidents like that at Mayak, and the contamination of territory around the weapons-testing grounds in Kazakhstan, that the scientists at the Institute of Biophysics in Moscow, who advised the Soviet government at the time of Chernobyl, probably knew more about the effects of radiation on human health than their western equivalents.

On 2 May, immediately after the May Day holiday, the Soviet Prime Minister, Nikolai Ryzhkov, went to Chernobyl and the juggernaut of the highly centralised state finally went into action. The 10-kilometre exclusion zone was extended to 30 kilometres. Because of the danger of caesium and strontium entering the food chain, other areas were either evacuated or became 'zones of strict control' where 'clean' food was shipped in. Two thousand medical teams were set up, and by the end of 1986 696,000 people had been examined, 215,000 of them children. Of these, 37,500 were sent to hospital for further investigation.

Few of these suffered from radiation sickness. This condition affects those who receive a dose of over 100 rems (roentgen equivalent man). The rem as a unit for measuring radiation has now been superseded by the sievert; however, it was the rem that was used at the time of Chernobyl, and the exposure of the victims can be compared to the average annual personal dose received in Britain from cosmic radiation, background radiation, medical treatment, etc. of around .25 rem.

After the accident at Chernobyl, between 200 and 300 men and women, principally power-station workers, firemen and members of the militia, were treated for radiation sickness in hospitals in Moscow and Kiev. The official figure for fatalities as a direct consequence of the accident was 31. It has been treated with scepticism but is probably accurate: and even among these some died as a result of falling masonry or straightforward burns.

Radiation sickness follows a pattern lasting around two and a half months. The deaths which took place in this period were particularly gruesome, but some survived doses that were hitherto thought fatal. Piotr Palamarchuk, a huge Ukrainian who carried a colleague from the wreckage, received an estimated dose of 780 rems. His hair and his fingernails fell out; he went blind. He received a bone marrow transplant but his body rejected the donor's marrow. However, he did not die. Five years after the accident, I met him in Moscow. He had recovered his sight. His hair and fingernails had grown again. Skin grafts had not been entirely effective: there were still open sores on his body; but he had survived.

Among the others I interviewed were General Pikalov, the commander of the Chemical Troops (estimated dose, 87 rems) and General Berdov, commander of the militia (estimated dose, 60 rems): both told me they had suffered no lasting ill effects as a result of their exposure to radiation. General Ivanov, the jovial deputy commander of the Soviet Civil Defence (estimated dose, 60 terms), thought that a small dose of radiation might be actually beneficial. He also espoused the common belief that the best antidote to radiation was vodka. Vladimir Chugunov, a senior engineer, was grievously ill after the accident: his hair fell out, he had atrocious burns on his legs, his weight fell to 88 lbs. He not only recovered but insisted upon returning to work at Chernobyl.

The Ukrainian scientist, Vladimir Chernousenko, who was one of the scientific advisers to the government commission after the accident and later contracted cancer, made headlines in the West by saying that several thousand of those who had worked at containing the consequences of the accident in the 30-kilometre zone – the so-called liquidators – had already died from diseases caused by radiation.

The retort that the death-rate would be the same for any equivalent group in the Soviet Union was impossible to prove because there were no adequate records. However, I found that Chernousenko's claims were treated with some scepticism by those who had worked at Chernobyl. Numerous power-station workers, like the chief engineer Nikolai Steinberg (now the minister responsible for nuclear safety in the Ukraine), received far larger doses than either the liquidators or the general population, yet continued to work at the power-station and remain in good health.

How, then, has it become accepted that Chernobyl has been responsible for thousands of deaths? The answer lies in the link between radiation and cancer. As with smoking, the dangers are statistical rather than certain, but since Chernobyl affected a large number of people theoretical estimates of final fatalities are high. Our National Radiological Protection Board has predicted around 30,000 cancers over the next 40 years in the affected parts of Russia and Western Europe, an 0.1 per cent addition to those anticipated in the same population over the same period of time.

Such an increase, however, is hypothetical. The margin of error in any survey is greater than the estimated increase, and so is not epidemiologically detectable against the high background rate for cancer, including radiation-induced cancer caused by radon gas, sunshine, X-rays, as well as cancer caused by the strong untipped cigarettes that almost everyone smokes in Russia. It is therefore impossible to say with certainty that any one case of cancer was caused by the accident at Chernobyl.

However, the risk of cancer – particularly leukaemia – was seized upon by the democratic forces in the former Soviet Union as a stick with which to beat their Communist foes. For example, the Soviet authorities were accused of genocide for allowing the May Day parade to proceed in Kiev despite the accident at Chernobyl. In fact, the level of radiation in Kiev was well within internationally accepted intervention norms and, because of rainfall over Bavaria, was no worse than in Munich. As the British nuclear expert Thomas Marsham said at the time, 'If you were to suddenly say everyone should get out of Kiev, you'd probably have two hundred people killed on the roads.'

The irony of the Chernobyl disaster is that quite possibly the nationalists, environmentalists and democrats did more harm than good to the victims of Chernobyl in their zeal to discredit the Communists. Between May 1990 and March 1991, at the request of the Soviet government, the International Atomic Energy Agency, the United Nations Scientific Committee on the Effects of Atomic Radiation, the World Health Organisation and the European Community organised the Chernobyl Project, sending a team of 220 western scientists to the areas of the former Soviet Union affected by the accident.

These scientists later reported that they could find no difference between the health of those living in the contaminated and uncontaminated zones. The chief mistake made by the Soviet authorities had been to apply *too strict* a criterion for evacuation. The harm caused by other pollutants in the industrially ravaged Ukraine – nitrates, pesticides, and so on – is probably greater than that caused by a low dose of radiation.

There was also the damage done by stress, taking peasants from pleasant wooden houses in ancestral villages and moving them to box-like flats in the suburbs of Minsk. Above all, the foreign scientists visiting the Ukraine thought it absurd for a state on the verge of bankruptcy to spend billions of roubles on evacuation when there were so many other more urgent calls on the public purse – not least the need for food.

This advice was rejected. By then, the party line had changed. The Communists had been ousted, the democrats were in power; and it had become part of the democrats' mythology that the Communists had left the people to die. New posts had been created for Chernobyl activists. There was now a minister for Chernobyl in each of the affected republics with a staff to enforce an elaborate Chernobyl law. Like the Trojan horse, the ecological movement had served its purpose (membership of the Ukrainian ecological movement, Green World, dropped from 500,000 in 1989 to 18,000 today) but its dogmas had to be preserved.

Given what they had suffered from Bolsheviks and their heirs, it is understandable that the anti-Communists should have used Chernobyl in this way. The attitude of the western press and television is less forgivable. On the fourth anniversary of the accident, the *Sunday Times* published a story saying that as a result of Chernobyl whole wards in 'hospitals in the Ukraine, Byelorussia and adjacent provinces of Great Russia . . . are lined with gaunt, dying and deformed children'. In Kiev, my requests to see these victims were met with embarrassment. A leading campaigner against official secrecy over Chernobyl, the botanist Professor Dimitri Grodzinski, told me that these stories

were nonsense. He showed me magazines that had used photographs of thalidomide children to illustrate articles on the consequences of Chernobyl.

The 220 western scientists of the Chernobyl Project reached the same conclusion. No statistically significant evidence was found of an increase in foetal anomalies as a result of radiation exposure. At the conference in Vienna held between 21 and 24 May 1991 to discuss these findings, the American expert, Professor Fred Mettler, was challenged by a Polish specialist, Professor Nauman, but only on the grounds that he had no real control group with which to compare the malformation rate. 'Isn't it true,' Nauman said, 'that genetic changes should be expected *only ten, twenty or thirty years later*?' (my italics). In other words, even a critic of the experts' findings did not suggest that *current* birth defects can be ascribed to Chernobyl.

Yet the stories persist. The *Daily Telegraph*, on the sixth anniversary of the accident, described a film made by a Ukrainian, Maria Obrazova, showing children born with fish-tails as a result of the disaster. More recently, on 7 August 1992, the *Telegraph* described a child with one arm as a 'Chernobyl victim . . . with deformities caused by radioactive fallout'. The *Independent* on 31 March 1993 showed a deformed and dying child 'in a Byelorussian hospital' and quotes a Dr Mary Brennan to the effect that 'the incidence of congenital malformation also increased dramatically'. On Monday 5 April 1993, *World in Action* screened a documentary, *Children of Chernobyl*, that is typical of those shown every April as we approach the anniversary of the accident. A gloomy commentary is intercut with sick and deformed children, their weeping mothers, and doctors who ascribe these afflictions to Chernobyl. No attempt is made to relate anecdotal evidence to the discoveries of the highly researched Chernobyl Project.

So, too, in the newspapers and magazines there are and will continue to be countless grainy photographs showing bald children with leukaemia which suggest that their hair has fallen out as a result of radiation from Chernobyl, when in fact radiation is frequently part of the treatment for leukaemia, a massive dose to kill off the cancerous blood cells. The leukaemia itself may or may not have been caused by radiation from Chernobyl.

Certainly, an increase in leukaemia and thyroid cancer is expected as a result of Chernobyl. But even here one must be cautious because of the absence of reliable base statistics. And the scale of the tragedy must be kept in proportion. A letter to *Nature* from Byelorussian specialists in September, 1992, reported that in the Gomel region of Byelorussia, the incidence of child thyroid cancer had risen from four cases a year between 1986 and 1989 to 55 in 1991. Sixty were expected in 1992. However, thyroid cancer can be treated: the cancer had spread in only six cases, and one child had died. One child.

Again, it is understandable that the doctors and hospital managers in Byelorussia and the Ukraine should look to the West for help. The bad health of the population and the lack of medicines and equipment in the hospitals make it irresistible for them to use the accident at Chernobyl to dramatise their appeals for much-needed cash. It is the same with the Chernobyl charities. Children, supposedly suffering as a result of Chernobyl, are sent for holidays in the West. Most are perfectly healthy. Andrew Ceelem, the director of a Dutch charity, Christian Care East-West, whom I met in Moscow, said that few of the children sent by the Russian charity, Chernobyl Help, were sick and what illness they found had nothing to do with radiation. In London, one of the children from Chernobyl was found to be the daughter of a former party leader living in Moscow.

Money and medical supplies sent to Byelorussia and the Ukraine have been known to go astray. Cornelia Wendt, the representative of the Bavarian Red Cross in Kiev, told me that she personally had to supervise the delivery of donated medical supplies to the hospitals (at the time she was dealing with 250,000 syringes) to prevent them disappearing into the black market. It is hardly surprising that people desperate for western goods and western currency should make the most of Chernobyl. Western journalists should know better than to fall for their tall stories.

17 April 1993

BOOKS

SEEKING AN AUDIENCE OF CHEERFUL ANGELS

P. D. James

DOROTHY L. SAYERS: HER LIFE AND SOUL
Barbara Reynolds
Hodder, £25, pp. 398

There are writers who hold such a perennial fascination for biographers that they are in danger of being as much read about as read. Evelyn Waugh is one, and Dorothy L. Sayers, who has little else in common with him, is another. But anyone tempted to question whether yet another biography is necessary can be reassured. It would be unreasonable to expect many new facts, but this well written, beautifully organised and perceptive biography brings both the woman and writer alive for me as has no previous study. Barbara Reynolds, Italian scholar and translator, is, of course, uniquely qualified for the task. She knew Dorothy L. Sayers as a close friend during the writer's latter years, completed the translation of Dante's *Divine Comedy* left unfinished at Miss Sayers' death, is chairman of the Dorothy L. Sayers Society and has had access to all the Sayers letters, which she is at present editing. The long-accepted portrait of the writer shows us, in the words of a 1979 reviewer, a woman who is

brilliant, erratic, rude and impatient, earnest, hard-
working, witty, eccentric, curious in appearance,
scholarly, a fighter who could be a worthy opponent in
any kind of controversy.

Barbara Reynolds emphasises Dorothy L. Sayers' less recognised qualities: her intellectual ardour, her courage, her capacity for friendship,
her funniness and her great practical kindness. After reading this
biography even readers who dislike the writer must surely respect the
woman.

The biography is also the study of a generation. Dorothy L. Sayers
was born in 1893 into a comfortable, middle-class, Oxford clerical
family. When she died, in 1957, that world had passed away for ever.
In 1897 her father accepted the lucrative living of Bluntisham in East
Anglia and we are shown the hierarchical life of a Fenland village
before 1914, the huge rectory, staffed by four maids but without electricity, where morning prayers began the day and the family invariably
dressed for dinner. We share the world of Oxford between the wars,
the struggle of a single woman to earn her living in the post-war
depression, the changing sexual mores which had not yet become a
sexual revolution, and the daily anxieties and privations of the second
world war.

Dorothy L. Sayers was a woman who found professional, but never
emotional, fulfilment. No wonder the centrality of her creed was the
almost sacramental importance of work. Sayers' professional life began
unpropitiously with a succession of jobs, including teaching, which
she disliked, before she found employment with Benson's Advertising
Agency and became a highly successful copy-writer, a job for which
her wit, imagination and verbal skill made her particularly suitable.
Then in 1923 she published her first detective novel, *Whose Body?*,
and embarked on the career which was to make her famous.

Stupid women often manage their sexual and emotional lives with
more skilful self-interest than do their intelligent sisters and Sayers
certainly mismanaged hers with spectacular thoroughness. She refused
to become the mistress of a man she passionately loved and desired
because of her abhorrence of birth-control and her hope of persuading
him into marriage. Then, on the rebound from his rejection, she had
an affair with a man she didn't love, used the abominated birth-control
ineffectively, and became pregnant. For her as a Christian abortion
was out of the question.

She gave birth to a son whose existence was a secret to her parents
and even to her most intimate friends, and placed him with her spinster

cousin, Ivy Shrimpton, who brought him up. Although Dorothy L. Sayers never acknowledged him during her lifetime, she supported him, gave him a good education, wrote to him and did her duty. For an unacknowledged child it was, perhaps, not enough; motherhood makes more stringent demands. Barbara Reynolds is reticent about their relationship in his adult life but, sadly, it seems unlikely that Dorothy L. Sayers' hope, expressed in a letter to her cousin, was realised:

> He is really a fine little chap, and I can't feel too bad
> about it myself now because it will be so jolly to have
> him later on. I am thirty now and it doesn't seem at
> all likely I should marry – I should have something for
> my latter age anyway.

Later she married a man psychologically wounded by war-service whose early zest for life deteriorated into self-pity, jealousy of her success and ill-humour. Her unconsummated affair with the man she loved, John Cournos, caused her years of deep anguish and physical deprivation, exacerbated by their masochistic habit of lying naked together. She took her small revenge in the portrait of Harriet Vane's self-regarding and unattractive lover who is murdered by arsenic in *Strong Poison*. Cournos gave his version two years later, in his novel *The Devil is an English Gentleman*. The Sayers novel is still in print.

Sayers wrote her detective stories for money – she had both herself and a child to support – but although she would doubtless have chosen to be remembered for her later religious plays and the translation of Dante, a task which was the great enthusiasm of her last years, she did not despise her more popular works. As a writer of detective fiction she was an innovator of style rather than of form. The 1930s mystery-reader demanded extraordinary ingenuity in the method of murder and those she devised were more bizarre than credible; some, indeed, would not have worked in practice. But she brought to her task a formidable intellect, a sure sense of place, a refreshing wit and humour and a prose-style which did much to lift the genre into literary respectability. Those of us who have followed her are in her debt. Lord Peter can be criticised as a creature of a snobbish wish-fulfilment, but he has a vitality and originality which has ensured his survival, and the fact that the novels are now period pieces has enhanced rather than diminished their appeal to new generations.

Sayers herself recognised the psychological dichotomy which dominated her life, the conflict between her essentially passionate nature and her intellect. It was a problem she explored in the most biographical of her novels, *Gaudy Night*, in the scene between her alter ego, Harriet Vane, and the don, Miss de Vine, who discuss the dilemma of people who are 'cursed with both a head and a heart', the difficulty of compromise and the imperative of choice. When Harriet Vane, later in that novel, says to Peter Wimsey,

> The reason why I want to get clear of people and feelings
> and go back to the intellectual side is that that is the only
> side of life I haven't betrayed and made a mess of,

she is speaking for her author.

This distrust of emotion characterised Dorothy L. Sayers' religious life. Mysticism held no appeal for her. She wrote that she had never experienced conversion or had any other spiritual experience and was incapable of religious emotion. After the great popular success of her radio drama on Christ's life, *The Man Born to be King*, and her theological plays, she was urged to commit herself personally to the task of presenting Christ to atheists and agnostics. It was a role she both deeply distrusted and felt herself unsuited for. She explained that the only presupposition of Christianity she could swear to from personal inward conviction was sin and the acceptance of sole responsibility for her own wrong-doing, and went on to set out her credo:

> Since I cannot come to God through intuition or
> through my emotions, or through my inner-light
> (except in the unendearing form of judgment and con-
> viction of sin), there is only the intellect left and that
> is a very different matter . . . The passionate intellect
> is really passionate. It is the only point at which ecstasy
> can enter. I do not know whether we can be saved by
> the intellect, but I do know that I can be saved by nothing
> else.

And to her friend and colleague, Val Gielgud, she wrote:

> When we go to heaven, all I ask is that we should be
> given some interesting job and allowed to get on with
> it. No management; no box-office; no dramatic critics;
> and an audience of cheerful angels who don't mind
> laughing.

I hope that she got her cheerful angels, and that she isn't wearying them with too much theological disputation.

24 April 1993

HE REALLY DID THE BUSINESS

Frank Keating

We were in Germany in the summer of 1979, in one of those swank Munich hotels. It was the day before the European Cup final and the hosts had hired this chandeliered ballroom for a press conference with the managers of the two competing teams. It was the sort of thing the Germans organise with punctilious efficiency – and take very seriously indeed. Waiters hushing around the deep-pile carpets with trayfuls of good Bavarian wine, and tables groaning with grub. An ideal preface to a press conference, and the place was packed with all the world's senior waffle merchants.

And we waited and waited, and then waited some more. The celebrity the press conference had been called for – nobody cared a hoot about the poor, fresh-faced, keen and punctual manager of the opposing team, Malmo – had neither arrived nor sent any message. The Suits of the German FA were in a state of tizz.

An hour and a half went by before Brian Clough made his entrance. He had been playing squash with his reserve team goalkeeper. He was in dishevelled shorts, scuffed gym shoes, and he was still dripping with sweat through his Aertex shirt. With no apologies, he took his place at the microphone and, brandishing his racket, blamed the German FA's driver for losing his way to the hotel.

'No wonder you guys lost the effing war. Doubtless this chauffeur you've given me was Head of Transport Command.'

The Germans were not amused. A few of us Brits looked at each other and smiled uneasily. We had heard it all before – and at least Jerry knew that Cloughie was in town.

Next day, little Nottingham Forest won the European Cup, of course.

And they kept it in style the following year, didn't they? He could produce football teams all right, could Cloughie. And they always played fair and clean, sometimes with a quite sublime simplicity and serenity, for if Clough had a tactical tenet he swore by, it was 'first time passing and keep it on the island'.

He did it, too, time and again, with what seemed at first a ragbag collection – a couple of exorbitant super-league stars, two or three old lag has-beens, a tyro or two from his youth team, a kid straight out of school, and two more seeming hobbledehoys he looked, at first, to have recruited off the public park. And all of a sudden they were top of the League and/or on their way to Wem-ber-ley. The late Jock Stein, esteemed eminence of soccer management, had no doubts:

> If you study every one of Cloughie's teams down the years you always whoop at the fact that players who look totally ordinary elsewhere take on a new quality when they go out and play for him. Not just because he can gee them up, but because of his innate genius at knowing which fellows go together and which spark off each other. He understands the game's 11-man collectivism like few others and that, plus his own turbulent inner rage for perfection, makes him so formidable.

Brian loved a drink (often in the most flamboyant plural). Once, on the train from Brighton, we got mutually sozzled through his buffet-bar generosity, so much so that by Clapham he was in tears – recounting how he had cried with rage as a boy every single Friday when his dad had given his Middlesbrough sweet-factory pittance to Mum to feed the family of nine; wept buckets when he failed his 11-plus; again when he started out as an ICI postboy at 15; tears for months when England dropped him after just two chances; and non-stop weeping for a year when he smashed his knee in his final match at Bury.

I had long admired him tremendously, and he knew that. Anyway, by the time we rolled arm in arm down the platform at Victoria that day I knew I should cash in with an exclusive interview the next week in Nottingham. 'Sure, pal, no problem,' he said. I rang to fix it: 'Hi, Bri . . .' 'The answer's No, shithead,' and he put the phone down.

I just pray he's not going to do a Citizen Kane, brooding at home, staring at his money, but in fact bitterly counting what he perceives as fractured hopes and unfulfilled dreams. For in fact Clough, as the game says, really did the business.

1 May 1993

ANOTHER VOICE

PEOPLE FIND IT EMBARRASSING THAT THIS MAN IS PRIME MINISTER OF THE UNITED KINGDOM

Charles Moore

On Monday Mr Michael Heseltine told the *Today* programme that in the 1930s the press had been wrong in calling for appeasement, and therefore the Government should not pay any attention to press criticism today.

The analogy does not seem terribly strong. In the 1930s, most of the press was supporting the Government's policy of appeasement, which was courageously opposed by between 20 and 40 Tory back-benchers. Today, the press is attacking the Government, and some newspapers are critical of the Maastricht Treaty, which is courageously opposed by between 20 and 40 Tory backbenchers. But the weakness of Mr Heseltine's comparison only helps to make clear what is the Government's one guiding maxim in these difficult times: don't do anything the press recommends.

This rule can be hard to follow. What it tends to mean in practice is that the Government does do what the press recommends, but only after a painful delay. Thus Mr Major keeps Mr David Mellor because the press says he should go and then sacks him when it has screamed the same message for a few weeks. Thus Mr Major kept Britain in the Exchange Rate Mechanism long after the press had said that the pound could not be sustained, spent £2 billion defending it in the markets and then pulled out of it after all. And thus Mr Major keeps Norman Lamont.

It might not be a bad rule of thumb. The press generally is wrong, and the more wrong the more unanimous. But one is surely entitled to ask for the Government to have some principles of action of its own. We, the press, are there to react to it, and not the other way round. Anyway, it was not the press which turned the Tories out of the shires, it was the voters.

But I think things will probably go on as they are because this Government is like a woman in a Kingsley Amis novel. It assumes that criticism is the same as malice, an assumption which tends to become self-fulfilling.

The entire debate about the ERM and Maastricht, for example, has been bedevilled by the idea that anyone who says both are mistaken is 'embittered', and simply wants to bring back Mrs Thatcher. It would not occur to Mr Major that people say those things merely because they believe them to be true. You cannot have a discussion with this Government about whether fixed exchange rates are a good idea, or what European Union means, or what should be the future of ex-Yugoslavia, because it does not understand the terms of such a discussion. It responds by saying things like, 'If the rate's fixed, we'll do well out of the Germans,' or 'European Union's just a phrase Kohl insisted on having' or 'Yugoslavia's not one we can sell to the punters.' None of those answers is necessarily wicked. You have to think about practical things like that in politics. It's just that it's *all* this Government thinks about.

Its attitude is all disclosed in that phrase 'the punters'. If you think of the voter as a man whose face you see only when he pays you money or, more rarely, collects it from you, you have spotted the first but surely not the only thing about politics.

Actually the press is being quite restrained. For what journalists say to one another in private is that Mr Major is absolutely no good at all; but they do not put it quite so harshly in print, partly out of residual kindness or fear, and partly because they realise that they may have him around for another four years and so they must keep up the fiction of interest in him. But now they are joined by politicians and by voters. It has reached the stage when people find it embarrassing that this man is Prime Minister of the United Kingdom, just as people feel about Dr Carey being Archbishop of Canterbury.

Amid the encircling gloom, I notice the political class turning to the Foreign Secretary. What a relief to see someone who is calm and dignified and can string a sentence together. Mr Hurd is like what a British Foreign Secretary is supposed to be like, not only because he is tall and distinguished-looking but because a first-class brain (itself a Foreign Office phrase) lurks behind the intimidating spectacles and

silvery hair. How we all commend his elegance whenever he comes
and tells the Commons that what he said about Maastricht two weeks
ago is now inoperative and that he proposes to do the opposite.
Wouldn't it be nice if he were Prime Minister?

I must admit to sharing this weakness, but weakness I think it is.
For this Government is not ruled by Mr Major alone, but by the 'Major-
Hurd axis'. This axis first came to prominence, readers will recall,
when it succeeded where the Lawson-Howe axis had failed and persuaded Mrs Thatcher to take us into the ERM. In its first action the
axis displayed its whole subsequent character, being (a) diplomatically
skilful; (b) conventionally minded and (c) mistaken.

Since then the axis has gone from strength to strength. The quality
of (a) ensured a good negotiation at Maastricht, while the quality of
(c) meant that the country has been plunged into 18 months of wran-
gling. The quality of (b) has prevented any reconsideration of errors.

And it really is an axis in that the one could not flourish without
the other. Look at the treatment of Denmark. When the Danes voted
no to Maastricht the first time Mr Hurd made it clear at once that
they would have to vote again to get the right answer. Then Mr Major
said how important it was that we all went ahead together. The second
Danish referendum arrives and Mr Hurd hints that Britain might,
despite previous promises, isolate Denmark, and Mr Major demurs,
but so softly that no one quite believes him. Or look at Bosnia. Mr
Major's folksy interest in Our Boys serves to conceal Mr Hurd's willingness to let Serbia win. Or Hong Kong, where Mr Major's chumm-
iness with Chris Patten hides the fact that Mr Hurd has forced the
Governor to back down. The Prime Minister does the matey bit for

home consumption. The Foreign Secretary does the posh bit which makes his master seem credible abroad.

Since this sort of thing is not Mr Major's bag, it is fair to guess that the Government's vision of Europe is Mr Hurd's. It is a modernised version of the Congress of Vienna. Talleyrand and Metternich and Castlereagh decide everything, and anything that blocks their power to decide – national feeling, democracy, parliaments, national laws – is 'unhelpful', 'tiresome', 'not sensible' or suchlike Hurd-words. This explains Mr Hurd's enthusiasm for giving so much power to the Council of Ministers in the treaty. His happiest model of efficient and enlightened decision-making is of a small body of people as civilised as himself. This is not a contemptible idea at all: it is conceived in the best interests of peace and stability. But it is an idea opposed to parliamentary government and I am sure the voters would reject if it were frankly presented to them, which is why the Government resists a referendum. Funny that it should be promoted by the most demotic Prime Minister in our history.

15 May 1993

BOOKS

A FULL REVOLUTION BRINGS YOU BACK TO WHERE YOU BEGAN

Julie Burchill

MICK JAGGER: PRIMITIVE COOL
by Christopher Sandford
Gollancz, £16.99, pp. 319

Whenever I am sent a new book on the lively arts, the first thing I do is look for myself in the index. Usually I am sandwiched between Anthony Burgess and William Burroughs – which, you may take it from me, is not the sort of place a girl likes to get sandwiched.

In Mr Sandford's book, though, I find myself stranded between Mr Paul Buckmaster and Mr Tito Burns; I have not come across them before, socially, and feel that this bodes ill for the entertainment value of the publication. Because so much of the Rolling Stones Story *is* boring; the pokey childhoods in the Home Counties (so different from the Beatles' amphetamine fuelled barnstorming around Liverpool and Hamburg; they always were the *real* bad boys), the half-hearted swotting at the LSE, the boring white blues clubs where spotty English teenagers pretended to be old, oppressed black men with names like Blind Lemon Shandy and sang phoney songs about waking up this morning and 'dusting my broom' – when you just know that the nearest they ever came to it was dusting their *room*.

No, the Rolling Stones Story never gets good until they're picked up by Andrew Loog Oldham – managers of pop groups are always weirder and smarter than the crooning cretins they boss – and he gets them to tart around in makeup and frocks long before Boy George was ever thought of. But he was only with them for three years, leaving in 1967; after that it's the same tired old bad marriages and interminable wrangles with managers and accountants who just might have done Mr Jagger out of 50p sometime in the Seventies.

A while ago I was sent Victor Bockris' biography of Keith Richards to review, and I remember leaving the proof closed on my desk until the last possible moment – not through dread, but because I knew that once I picked it up I would do nothing else for days but read it. The richness and strangeness of Keith Richards' life is so extreme that he now seems barely human. He is like the living earth, rich and loamy (and no doubt full of worms), layer upon volcanic layer of self-imposed suffering, relentless expertise and survivalism – like one of the ancient black blues players he loves so much. What is Mick Jagger by comparison? – a collagen car crash, a bank balance and a season ticket at Lord's. Well, he's so ancient now that it will take a miracle to keep him leaping around to 'Jumpin' Jack Flash'.

So I found my quote – a good one, too – and I defy any writer not to feel well disposed towards a book which follows her words with, 'She was right, of course.' But this really is quite a good book, and does as much as it can with a stringy sort of story which only really holds up in the context of ensemble Stones pieces.

From Satanic Majesty to Princes Trust, it is striking how little Mick Jagger has actually moved on. He still lives, for a large part of the year, in a south London suburb, and he still chases girls of 22, just like he was doing a quarter-century ago. From the obedient little boy who acted in his games-teacher father's P. E. films to the bloodless troubador described thus by his brother in his last official tour programme –

> Mick is basically about fun and he's never seen the
> music as anything much more. He likes to smile and
> laugh. He's worked hard on the preparations for this tour
> and the reward is seeing a lot of happy faces out there

– we are witnessing the career of a highly conservative Englishman
whose exhibitionism was somehow mistaken for rebellion. A common
mistake made in the Sixties, I believe.

Still, he had a shrewd eye for an original personality – as he would
later have for antiques – and made a point of picking friends and lovers
who added to him: Loog Oldham, Richards, Brian Jones, Marianne
Faithfull. Sandford comes alive when writing about them and shows,
with his collaborator Tom Keylock (a Stones tour manager in the
Sixties), a light and often comic touch. Here they are on Faithfull:
Sandford:

> A restless soul, doomed to wander forever down vistas
> of triteness, her only salvation the unconsciousness
> foretold by altered visions of reality.

Keylock:

> A right raver.

Further hilarity ensues when Jagger is elaborately courted by that
old phoney Tom Driberg, the famous friend of the Little Man who
loved tormenting servants. Like an Edwardian masher, Driberg laid
siege to Jagger for months, flattering him with suggestions of a political
career (a new twist to the stage-door Johnny's 'You're too good for the
chorus, my beauty – you belong on a bigger stage!'). Never one to turn
down a free meal, Jagger bore the bore gamely through long lunches
at – where else? – the Gay Hussar:

> To the direct question 'Why not stand for the local
> council', Jagger gave him a look of withering scorn.
> When next Driberg appeared for dinner at Cheyne Walk
> it was to be told by Faithfull that Mick was 'unexpec-
> tedly detained'.

On another occasion at the restaurant, Jagger interrupted a long mono-
logue on the post-feudal acceleration of the means of production to
ask for a glass of port. Albert Clinton, who waited at the Gay Hussar

for 20 years, remembers 'the elder gentleman doing the talking, the younger one the eating'.

While *International Times* urged him to join the revolution, Jagger joined the Country Gentleman's Association. While all around him were out of their heads, Jagger

> could always sit down to dinner and remember three
> hours later who had the scampi and who had the prawn
> curry.

Still, there were moments when his lack of couth had its comic side; on hearing of Brian Jones' death, he commented, 'I feel a bit shocked ... but the guy was unbearable.' I hope Mr Jagger finds it easy to forgive the frankness with which his ex-nearest-and-dearest talk of him here. It is Marianne Faithfull, always a woman wasted on the worlds she chose, who really sums it up. How did she feel when Keith first told her that Mick was in love with her? 'Disappointed. I preferred Keith.' Didn't we all? And this, above all, is Jagger's tragedy.

15 May 1993

'THIS IS BECOMING MOST DISCOURTEOUS'

Robert Cottrell

Paris

> Brezhnev is dying. The next general-secretary of the
> Communist Party will be Andropov. He is very
> efficient. Afterwards, it will be Gorbachev. I know him
> well. He is unique. He will bring about the triumph of
> the Soviet Union, both economically and ideologically.

Hard to imagine, really, a better illustration of the difference between good political information and good political judgment. The speaker is Jean-Baptiste Doumeng, late French billionaire of East-West barter trade and vendor of the Brussels butter mountain to Moscow. The listener is Jacques Attali, now head of the European Bank for Reconstruction and Development, but at the time – December 1981 – special adviser and amanuensis to the French President, François Mitterrand.

M. Doumeng is one of the many bit-part players in M. Attali's diary of his first five years inside the Elysée (from 1981–86; a second is promised), now published in the form of a 1,000-page volume called, nicely, *Verbatim*, and which squirms with the sort of juicy, living detail that in Britain might just about be authorised for release by the Cabinet Office after a decent interval of three or four centuries. M. Attali has been allowed to publish so soon not because the French government is so 'open' but because it is so arbitrary: a *fiat* from M. Mitterrand, who read the proofs, suffices.

Integral transcripts of conversations between M. Mitterrand and foreign heads of state are sandwiched between squabbling matches at European summits and briefing papers on the Strategic Defence Initiative, the day usually being rounded off by some suitably gnomic or cynical reflection from the French President himself. (Though a claim this week by a Paris publisher, Odile Jacob, that some 43 of these reflections have been 'borrowed' without acknowledgement from unpublished interviews with M. Mitterrand by Elie Wiesel, now promises a lively debate.)

M. Mitterrand's famous comment on Mrs Thatcher's charms is recorded here as: 'She has the eyes of Stalin, and the voice of Marilyn Monroe,' thus supplanting earlier and apocryphal versions of the remark which compared the eyes variously to those of Nero and Caligula.

Apart from her threat to cancel the Channel Tunnel if France were to falter in its support for Britain during the Falklands war ('How impolite,' notes M. Attali in his diary), the Elysian view of Mrs Thatcher is a generally sympathetic one: respectful of her determination to pursue closer ties between Europe and the United States ('The United States is just Europe across the Atlantic!'), if increasingly bored with her demands for a reimbursement of Britain's overpayments to the European Community budget. When, at the Fontainebleu Summit of 1984, Mrs Thatcher is finally compelled to accept a compromise budget formula:

> She cracks like glass, on the verge of tears.
> She wants a deal, no matter what. An astonishing
> sight . . .

Resilient nonetheless, here a year later is Mrs Thatcher at the Luxembourg Summit of 1985, arguing with the Italian premier, Giulio Andreotti, over factory law in the single European market.

> Thatcher: 'You are going to destroy businesses with all your regulations. I myself once worked in a three-person business, so I can tell you . . .'
>
> Andreotti: 'And what happened to the other two? They died of industrial diseases, I expect.'
>
> Thatcher: 'This is becoming most discourteous.'

Far harsher is the French view of Ronald Reagan, whom M. Attali introduces thus:

> Once past the obstacle of his charm, it is difficult not to remark on the extraordinary vacuum of his conversation. He is limited to reading small cards which he pulls out of his left-hand inside pocket. Often they contain just five words, ending in a question mark.

The scene shifts to the Ottawa Summit of industrialised nations, where Mr Reagan elects to open a session on North-South co-operation with a joke about garden hoses in Mexico:

> During this exposé, Suzuki sleeps with his mouth open. Mrs Thatcher powders herself. François Mitterrand signs his postcards. Spadolini chats with his sherpa. Schmidt shuffles through his papers and Trudeau verifies meticulously the angle of the red carnation which decorates his buttonhole.

Then on to the Oval Office of the White House, where Dick Allen, National Security Adviser, chats to M. Attali while Mr Reagan and M. Mitterrand are talking just six feet away. M. Attali records Mr Allen as saying:

> You know, that guy is a nothing. Have you noticed? All he does is read out loud the drafts that other people write for him . . . I'm writing at this moment his foreign policy speech for Congress. I'm sorely tempted to stick

one to him, to give him a speech which would go something like this: 'Ladies and Gentlemen, Members of
Congress, I want to talk to you about the Middle East.
In order to reflect deeply on the subject I have spent
the weekend in retreat at Camp David, and I want to
tell you that I have had an inspiration. I have come
back here with a solution to all of the problems – not
just those of today, but of the millennium yet to come
. . . The solution is so blindingly simple that I wonder
why nobody has ever thought of it before. It depends,
in fact, on the following three principles . . .'

And there, with the chamber hanging on his every
word, he will turn the page and read: 'Now, you son of
a bitch, you are on your own.'

At least the indiscretions here are mitigated, to the extent Mrs
Thatcher and Mr Reagan are no longer heads of government. The publication of *Verbatim* is likely to be far more irritating to Chancellor
Helmut Kohl of Germany, still in office, who is caught in a very large
number of unguarded moments. Here, for example, is Mr Kohl on the
situation in Poland in 1985:

We will have to help Jaruzelski. Everything that came
after him would be worse. The Poles have always had
eyes bigger than their stomachs and ambitions beyond
their means.

At least in this respect, Mr Kohl marks a continuity of sentiment
with his predecessor, Chancellor Helmut Schmidt, who says to M.
Mitterrand in 1981:

For Poland, I see only two solutions. The first is a
rational solution. Archangel Saint Michael intervenes
and puts everything to rights. The second is a miracu-
lous solution: the Poles start working again.

Yet despite some mischievous acts of selective quotation and the
predominantly feline tone of M. Attali's linking narrative, the driving
force of *Verbatim* does not seem, as might be held to be the case with,
say, Mr Alan Clark's memoirs, that of score-settling or the indulging
of an *ésprit d'escalier*. Rather, it constitutes an act of fealty towards

M. Mitterrand's obsession with history, and, more particularly, with the place which history will one day assign to M. Mitterrand's own life and achievements – an obsession in which M. Attali, the President's friend and confidant for the past two decades, is a fascinated accomplice. (And, lest M. Attali's memoirs should fail to impose, Mr Mitterrand has taken the precaution of engaging yet another loyal intermediary between himself and eternity: the political historian Georgette Elgey, who has been afforded unrestricted access to the presidential papers and archives.)

M. Mitterrand is said to have deleted only four words from M. Attali's manuscript and, considering what he has left in, it is hard to imagine what more they might have said. The echo, perhaps, of another presidential aphorism recorded by M. Attali:

> During the plane back from the [Luxembourg] Summit, I ask François Mitterrand what is, in his opinion, the most important quality for a politician. He replies: 'I would like to say, sincerity. But it is, in fact, indifference.'

22 May 1993

WE HAVE CHANGED, NOT THE QUEEN

James Buchan

Forty years ago this week, the Queen of England and Mount Everest enjoyed their moments of greatest celebrity: one was crowned, the other was climbed.

In the years since then, the Queen has aged, as human beings do. Her hair is streaked with grey. She loses her spectacles. Her children made bad marriages, as people do, though none is a junkie or in gaol or a sect. The Queen has changed her habits over 40 years: she no longer inspects the nubile daughters of the upper classes at court, she does walk in crowds, appears on television, sues the *Sun*. But her notion of herself and her function – of the British monarchy – has

'Hi, Honey. Shhh, I'm home.'

altered not at all. She's doing it because her father did it, it's what her family does: anything more precise would risk destroying all those 17th- and 18th-century political fudges that made Britain such a monarchical state.

Everest, meanwhile – well, everybody knows about Everest: South Col now resembles Piccadilly Circus during the winter of discontent. Whatever you think of the British monarchy in the second Elizabethan era, at least someone takes out the rubbish at Buckingham Palace.

We British are the Everest of this story. The Queen is now alienated from her subjects, not because she has changed but because we have. The Queen, and the whole circumstantial routine of monarchy, now appear to us as relics of a backward regional culture, a bit like whale-hunting in the Lofoten Islands or *foie gras* in Perigord: abhorrent to a prosperous and squeamish public avid for a conformist modernity. To understand the crisis in the monarchy, it's best to forget the Queen, who is the hole in our national doughnut, which is why people who write about her – from Tom Nairn to the editorialists of the *Times* – fall into airy abstraction. You concentrate on the people, the doughnut itself.

How have we changed? The conformist view of the 40 years since the Coronation is that it has been a period of national decline, of which the monarchy is the cause either directly or as the linchpin of a decadent and exhausted *ancien régime*. This view is, as far as I can tell, quite false. This country lost its empire and prosperity in and around 1941 and has made a good recovery, hampered by the loss of captive product markets and by bad and sometimes mad elected governments. The monarchy doesn't come into it.

If you take out the effect of 40 years price inflation in Britain and measure our prosperity in the prices of a single year – the measurement the Government likes to use – you see how well we've done. The national income per head in the month of the Coronation was £2,797 in 1985 money. Last year, and even after two and a half years of Majorite impoverishment, it was £6,013.

We all have far more things. In 1953, only 4 million people in Britain owned houses; now 16 million do. There were only 2 million private cars on British roads in Coronation year, less than are now registered in a single year; only 6 million telephones compared with 30 million; 2 million television sets against God knows how many. This accumulation of tat, rather than Trooping the Colour, gives our society its peculiar texture, and has occurred while the Queen has hung on to the same old things. When I was a child, only the Queen got to go to Barbados: this was the magic and mystique of monarchy (which were just good old British code-words for being very, very rich). Now lots of people can do what she does and, as de Tocqueville said in *Democracy in America*, 'the desire for equality always becomes more insatiable as equality is more complete'. In other words, when basic income tax was 9/6d in the pound, as it was on 2 June 1953, nobody minded that the Queen didn't pay income tax. Now it's less than 5/- in the pound, the middle class want the Queen to pay at the top marginal rate.

We have changed in other, less crude ways. I grew up snug in the memory of the wartime heroics not just of Britons but of British institutions: the armed forces, the imperial and domestic bureaucracies, parliament, the universities, business, the public utilities, the BBC, the institutional churches, the TUC and, on top of it all in some way, the monarchy as represented by the Queen's father. In the 40 years since then, these calm, hierarchical and condescending institutions have either vanished or become unrecognisable, or been challenged by new institutions (rapacious private monopolies, proliferating newspapers and omnipotent television) eager to justify themselves in terms of novelty. Only demoralised regiments, charities and learned societies still seek royal patronage. Poets run from the laureateship as if from plague.

These changes have not produced a variety of opinion on the monarchy, but a conformity as deadening as the old royalism: when 16 million people every Sunday read newspapers published from the same address in the republic of Wapping, how could it be otherwise? In 1977, the year of the Queen's silver jubilee, you couldn't find anybody with a bad word for her except Tom Nairn, Willie Hamilton and Johnny Rotten; in 1993, nobody will speak up for her. It is a conformity not so much of opinion as of reflex: the Queen is stale to us because she appears to us through the sickening monotony of television and the tabloid press. We hate the leaden royal 'bright' at the end of *News at Ten*. We are tired of old Trevor McDonald. We are tired of the Queen.

Here, the institutions of Empire and Commonwealth are a cata-strophic loss to the monarchy (and not simply because world dominion will excuse a horse as consul or a baboon as head of state). A monarchy designed for dominion over palm and pine has been driven back on a drizzly metropolis – and seems oversized and ill-content. Formidable royal energies, once exercised on irrigation schemes in Malawi, are channelled into planting bushes in Milton Keynes, and all before the fawning or spiteful eye of television.

The other big change is in the composition of British social class. The royalist fractions of society – the nobility and the traditional work-ing class – have disintegrated. The aristocracy always complained bit-terly about serving the royal household – oh, Her Majesty's stinginess, His Royal Highness's caprice! – but they were loyal. They knew that without a monarchy they'd lose their privileges and their point. They'd be like Italian counts. This class provided prime ministers as late as 1965, but they lost any hold on executive power in the Thatcherian purges of the early 1980s. Perversely, Margaret Thatcher also restored their wealth and left them free to indulge their footling and destructive hobbies. (How the Queen could have imagined this class would throw up suitable spouses for her children quite beats me, though people say the Queen Mother, who is from the Scots nobility herself, wanted company.)

At the other social pole, the royalist working class was simply destroyed. I never quite understood why a low income should make you pant for kings and queens, but in the jubilee year 1977, and at the Prince of Wales's wedding in 1981, I was exposed to scenes of prolet-arian enthusiasm of the sort that used to make Karl Marx weep during his London exile. In the 1980s, this class was broken up into a skilled section of home-owners and small-time speculators and an unstable and demoralised group of vagrants and thieves, for both of whom (for different reasons) loyalism was a painful and embarrassing memory. In retrospect, it was perhaps an error of the Queen to confine her hobbies to those fields where aristocracy and traditional working class met at extreme arm's length – racing, dogs, ceremonial, foreign pos-sessions – while ignoring the interests of the new Britons. The Prince of Wales, who might have restored the balance, has, like the Prince Consort before him, progressive ideas – but in such areas as land management, architecture and conservation, which are not much talked of in the Sierra-crowded lanes of the new model England.

These changes might not have mattered to the monarchy but for the seismic events at the turn of the 1990s: the revolutions in eastern Europe, the *putsch* against Margaret Thatcher and the devaluation of sterling last September.

The destruction of the Berlin Wall abolished at a stroke the privileges this country still enjoyed as a victor of the second world war and revealed the true relations of power in Europe: what use is one gross of nuclear weapons against the central council of the Bundesbank? It was not the end of history in any Marxist sense but a shuffling anew of all the cards in the historical pack, including a 1,000-year-old monarchy.

Margaret Thatcher's fall from power raised the terrifying prospect for the new Britons of a restoration of the old class relations, for which the monarchy appeared to be a symbol. Here the press, as the most successful estate of the 1980s, felt peculiarly vulnerable. Meanwhile, the devaluation of sterling, an event trivial in itself, was accompanied by such political hysterics that it appeared to be a national shame of epochal significance.

Other countries lived through these and similar shocks at the start of the 1990s. What did they do? The United States and France changed their governments. Italy, a little weary of this at the 52nd attempt, voted to restrict the patronage available to party politicians. We British have wittered about constitutional reform, insulted the Queen, blackmailed the Prince of Wales with adulterated tapes. A child could find the odd one out in this series.

In fact, we had a chance to change our government, in April 1992, during a period of intense and pointless deflation; but the offer from the Tories – Thatcherite policies at a lower level of vigour (Major instead of Thatcher) and intelligence (Lamont instead of Lawson) – captivated the electorate with results that were easy to predict. In September, the capital markets did the job we were too timid to perform and, in the process, robbed the Major Government of its legitimacy.

At this point of greatest national shame, the press and television did not just turn on the Government they'd persuaded us to elect; they also turned on the symbol of the nation, the royal family, and found a target-rich environment: the Queen's English, the Duchess of York's bosoms, Prince Edward's bachelorhood, the Prince of Wales's concept of married life. Yet the problems of this country have nothing to do with the head of state's family attributes, and everything to do with bad government, Tory and Labour. This becomes clear in a comparison with Germany, a successful state with a non-executive presidency much admired by the conformists. The truth is that the post-war German presidents have been yes-men (Heuss), clowns (Lübke), time-served party politicians (Scheel, Carstens) and prigs (Heinemann, von Weizsäcker); but they haven't mattered because Germany has had four outstanding chancellors (Adenauer, Erhard, Brandt, Helmut Schmidt). In 1983 and again in 1990, the Germans elected a mediocrity (Kohl) who has brought his country to a condition nobody even in Britain would envy.

I can see why the progressive forces should want one of their number as president of a German-style republic (perhaps a respected man of letters, like Martin Amis, or an elder statesman such as Edwina Currie or Gerald Kaufman), but it seems hardly worth the bother since the Prince of Wales is ready and very able to do the job, and as a king.

Speaking to the Commonwealth Parliamentary Association just before the Coronation, Winston Churchill said:

> The Queen can do no wrong. But advisers can be changed as often as the people like to use their rights for that purpose. A great battle is lost: Parliament turns out the Government. A great battle is won – crowds cheer the Queen. We have found this a very commanding and durable doctrine. What goes wrong passes away with the politicians responsible.

It would never have occurred to the old boy that the British would be so enfeebled and so mesmerised that they would be incapable of changing the composition of parliament, and instead flail out at a frangible institution and break it, as a child breaks a watch. The crisis of the monarchy is nothing but a crisis of the British administration (or, if you must be fancy, of the recruitment of party political élites): to be resolved not through News International conferences on constitutional change, appeals to Bagehot or Shakespeare or Queen Beatrix on a bicycle, but by the hard graft of politics. The rejuvenation of politics is the challenge of the remains of the century: it's a matter not of our monarchy – which we can, after all, do without – but of our democracy, which we can't.

29 May 1993

RESTAURANT

PLANET HOLLYWOOD

Nigella Lawson

While we understand that the *Spectator*'s is a church so broad as to make the general synod seem positively sect-like by comparison, there are some activities which we guess to be beyond the interest of even the most catholic reader. A club made up of *Spectator*-reading acid house partiers or motorcycle sidecar racers or home brewers would, I imagine, be a small club indeed. And it was on this basis that I thought long and hard before braving a table at Planet Hollywood on your behalf. But – *O tempora! O mores!* – it turns out that the Trocadero, that purple and chrome excrescence on Shaftesbury Avenue where a perfectly elegant building used to be, has become something of an up-market Brent Cross, and just as the teenagers of Hendon and Edgware hang out at the former, so have the sons and daughters of Mayfair and Belgravia – you get a better class of lout these days – adopted the Troc as a sort of youth-club-cum-coffee-bar.

I am presuming that you are already acquainted with what its owners, investors and publicists like to call 'the concept', since even the broadsheets deemed the opening of a new hamburger joint in Piccadilly to warrant press coverage. And if you do not know that Planet Hollywood is part-owned by Bruce Willis, Sylvester Stallone and Arnold Schwarzenegger you are lucky indeed, and luckier still if you don't know who Willis, Stallone and Schwarzenegger are, or that hereabouts we know them as Bruce, Sly and Arnie.

So let me pass over all of that and sit down to eat. Not that Planet Hollywood is about food; it is, rather, about the American-born, globally shared, fascination with celebrity. This goes beyond star-gazing fans. It is a characteristic of famous people everywhere to feel nervous around those untouched themselves by fame. In New York, film stars open restaurants, you could almost think, just so other film stars have somewhere safe to go at night. Planet Hollywood, at least in its cisatlantic incarnation, is not quite the same story. Not least because Bruce, Sly and Arnie are merely playing the parts of restaurant owners. They are investors in the business, but it is Mr Robert Earl's baby. And if people really are prepared to queue outside for hours (as so far they seem prepared to do) in the hope of catching sight of someone famous, then they really are gullible saps.

The real point of Planet Hollywood is merchandising. Jackets, T-shirts, baseball caps, the usual, are piled up for sale and punters are piling up to buy them. This at least has a nice appropriateness for a cinema-themed restaurant; Hollywood films – *Batman*, *Teenage Mutant Hero Turtles*, *Dick Tracey* and so on – have become something of a merchandising exercise themselves. But not everything is for sale. Exhibited 'free of charge' are, among the garland of movieland memorabilia, the icepick from *Basic Instinct* the handcuffs from *9½ Weeks*, the axe from *The Shining* and, on a more salubrious note, the dirndlish garment in which Julie Andrews sang 'I Have Confidence in Me' in *The Sound of Music*.

The pandemonium that greets you – employees in psychedelic shirts shouting at each other by walkie-talkie – is a fair indication of what is to follow. The place is crashingly noisy, and thus ideal for covering up the embarrassed silences of divorced fathers having their fortnightly Saturday lunch with their offspring. Now, I have no doubt that children will love it here (but then, like old people, children have such bad taste), but if you want to give your darlings a treat, be prepared for sacrifice.

The food is vile. I love American food as eaten in America, but if you served a London Planet Hollywood burger in the US of A, you would probably find you were in contravention of the Constitution. Desiccated and bready and nuked within an inch of its life, it is a shoddy piece of work. Ribs were like cardboard. Fajitas TV-dinnerish. Texas nachos rather enjoyable in a junky kind of a way. Caramel Crunch pie ditto. Drinks made one shiver. How about 'The Terminator', which is 'a cyborg's mixture of vodka, rum, gin, Grand Marnier, Tia Maria, Kahlua, sweet and sour, splashed with cranberry, then topped with draught beer? This one will leave you saying, "I'll be back".' I'll say – can you imagine a more instant emetic?

The fact the food's bad won't, I imagine, deter many people, but I feel the prices might. Dinner, admittedly a self-sacrificing and dutifully sampling three-courser, for three of us came to £73 without tip.

Planet Hollywood, Unit 75 Trocadero Centre, Coventry Street, W1.
Tel (no booking): 071 287 1000.

29 May 1993

THE JUDGMENT OF OTHERS

Edward Leigh

A couple of weeks ago a taxi-driver was taking me home from a radio station in Hull, just across the Humber from my Lincolnshire constituency.

'Some kind of politician are you?'

'Yes.'

'What's your name?'

'Edward Leigh.'

'Never heard of you!'

I doubt whether even now, following my summary dismissal from John Major's Government for lack of political correctness, he has heard of me. The fate of a junior minister is only important to himself, his family and perhaps his diary secretary. But my departure does serve to give an inkling of the style of this Government.

The summons to the Cabinet room in Downing Street came just before lunch last Thursday. Once I arrived, I felt a short burst of panic as I entered the room where, two and half years earlier, I had waited at 6 o'clock in the morning in a vain attempt to persuade Mrs Thatcher to fight the second ballot.

I walked in and went to sit opposite the Prime Minister across the long table, in the seat where the Chancellor customarily sits. However, the Prime Minister asked me to sit beside him, in the long line of empty chairs; perhaps, I remember thinking, so that he could pat my knee.

He started off: 'A painful business, reconstructing the Government . . .'

I knew then: this was it. I was determined to show no emotion at my execution, to behave (in a pre-classless society phrase) like an officer and gentleman. I expected some emollient words, and that that would be that.

Then something extraordinary happened. The Prime Minister's natural honesty took over.

'You're a man of conviction,' he told me. 'I would admire you less if you weren't. You can't change. There's no question of your competence. Quite the contrary. But in the Westminster hot-house your criticism of policies and personalities in the Government are well

known. It has come winging back. In difficult times it's better to have
a united team. Perhaps you can come back later.'

That was it. I was sacked for speaking my mind too loudly to too
many people; I was sacked for my principles. I reflected on the irony
that, during the Thatcher years, ministers had survived acts of disloyalty far worse than anything I had ever perpetrated. Some of those
ministers now occupy the highest offices of state. Today, though, we
have a régime unwilling to tolerate dissent, and afraid of views different from its own. There is little respect for the judgment of others,
and I was one of the others. As I walked out of Downing Street I heard
a hurried whisper from the doorman. They knew I was coming. The
door of No 10 opened. Daylight flooded in. A mass of photographers
had gathered beyond. I thought not of them, but of my freedom.

Funnily enough, I like John Major even more. I don't feel an ounce
of bitterness. His natural courtesy and honesty are enormous. It clearly
hurt him much more than it hurt me. Of course he was entitled to
sack me, to have his own team.

So what had I done to deserve this?

For months I had been thinking of resigning over Maastricht. I consulted my ministerial friends, even some priests. The advice was all
the same. 'You'll achieve nothing . . . keep fighting from within . . .
never resign.' It would, they said, look temperamental, quixotic and
pointless. So I didn't. At least I had the satisfaction of knowing I didn't
walk away from the fight. They walked away from me. Anyway, as a
good Catholic, I cannot subscribe to the political equivalent of suicide.

But I know now what suicides feel like. Every morning I wake at
dawn with a black miasma of despair sweeping through me. Not at
losing my puny job, since I care nothing for that. My despair is at
having voted for Maastricht and against my conscience out of party
loyalty; because I didn't want to rock the boat publicly in difficult
times. I even asked the whips if I could quietly be somewhere else and
miss the vote on Third Reading. No one would have noticed. They
refused and had me shot a week later instead, having strung me along.

Never again will I vote against my conscience. What Maastricht's
cynical protagonists do not realise is that for us it is a matter of conscience. We feel, rightly or wrongly, that we are betraying our country.
That is why I suggested months ago to the Prime Minister that a free
vote of a free parliament would unite not divide the party, and not
open wounds. But I know now that Sir Thomas More was right. One
should always put one's conscience before the interests of government,
because ultimately nothing, certainly not position, is more important
than one's soul.

While I was in the Government, I argued my point of view. I organised meetings of ministers – making sure always that the whips had been informed. Following one such meeting, before the actual negotiations for the Treaty were complete, I went as the spokesman of 14 junior ministers, setting out direct to the Prime Minister our worries over the threat of the European Court and governments eating away our opt-outs. After the first Danish referendum I organised another meeting. The word was passed back to Downing Street that, in our view, legally the Treaty was dead. I wrote to the Prime Minister suggesting a free vote to unite the party. At the paving motion I played for time, suggesting the delay of the Third Reading till after the second referendum. But all along delay was our only weapon. We never had a majority.

My disagreement with Government policy was not confined to the European question. I expressed my concern that the abolition of the poll tax would erode our ability to control local government spending. I also questioned our abandonment of our traditional role as defenders of property rights on the Leasehold Reform Bill. I protested about our loosening grip on the public sector deficit. I questioned our defence of existing benefits and rates and opposition to workfare.

Inside the Department of Trade and Industry, I put the dreary Post Office Citizen's Charter proposals in the bottom drawer and went for privatisation. I convinced – just – Michael Heseltine, then the officials, and finally most backbenchers. Finally I was nagging a cautious Prime Minister. A decision will soon be made. At the time of my going we were working on exciting plans to ensure maximum employee and public involvement in any flotation, and giving sub-postmasters what they have always wanted: the power to compete. If our plans can be fulfilled, they will be running thriving financial centres in our villages and on our street corners.

I was trying to break the cosy cartels in telecommunications that artificially inflate the cost of international calls. Competition is the best regulator for British Telecom. Cable companies must be given opportunities in the mobile phone sector. Abroad, I sought to promote free trade. Our firms must be allowed into America in return for AT&T coming here. I hoped it was a grand strategy for telecoms to promote competition and choice – or as Michael Heseltine kindly told me, 'knocking the civil servants around'.

As Technology Minister I had met 250 companies to work out new programmes competitively delivered locally to small companies, rather than centrally allocated to large companies. I was also trying to interest the European Space Agency in an eventual merger with Nasa, and to persuade the Russians to create a World Space Agency and to revive Hotol, the long-range ultra-high-speed aircraft. In Europe I had, to Dutch and French fury, resisted a massive £600 million subsidy to High Definition Television. Commissioner Andriessen had actually complained about me, no doubt contributing to my fall.

But those plans and programmes must now be discharged by somebody else. It is a relief that I can now speak my mind, even if no one wants to listen. It is better than people listening but not being able to speak one's mind. The Prime Minister is right. Men of conviction as junior ministers are a danger to themselves and government. I'm glad to be free.

Meanwhile, the Left of the Tory party has now achieved its ambition to control economic, foreign and industrial policy. The Right sits beleaguered in isolated fortresses in the Home Office, Social Security and Wales. But we on the Right must fight back. I, at least, can now stand up for what I believe in: a Europe of full independent nation states co-operating, not bound together in a community structure; a balanced budget; a society of opportunity not dependence; sound armed forces; and increasing private sector involvement in the delivery of public services, with the state as enabler, not provider.

In the interests of good government that has some respect from the people, we must try to do these things. My taxi-driver, as he drove off, said to me: 'I'll never bother to vote again. You're all the same. You don't believe in anything.' And I don't believe he is alone.

Edward Leigh is MP for Gainsborough.
He was Under-Secretary of State for Trade and Industry from 1990 to 1993.

5 June 1993

BOOKS

ROYALTY AND ROYALTIES

John Osborne

Not since the Great Lisbon Earthquake of 1755, when 30,000 people were killed and 11,000 buildings destroyed within six minutes, has a natural, if freakish, phenomenon caused such apocalyptic hysteria as the collapse of the Royal Heir's marriage. The reason for this monumental upheaval has been confidently located as the Windsor Fault. Seismological theory has it that this is partly due to irreversible atmospheric cooling. What is above becomes too large to fit the interior below and must then collapse. The scars then heal and, the theory adds significantly, 'the process repeats itself *with failures* at intervals'.

In the aftershock of Lisbon came firestorms of perfervid prophecy, intimations of wickedness and divine intervention. The first confirmation of the Windsor Fault, with the Abdication in 1936, might be interpreted on the One-to-Twelve Richter scale as Six. 'Felt by all. Some heavy furniture moved. Damage slight.' The next faulting, the divorce of Princess Margaret, scarcely scores more than Two. 'Delicately balanced objects may swing.' The subsequent uncoupling of Princess Anne and Prince Andrew pushed the graph upwards, and the present glum and gleeful forecasts for the Prince Charles Faulting are needling erratically towards Twelve. 'Damage total. Waves seen on ground surfaces. Lines of sight destroyed. Objects thrown up into the air.'

The tidal waves from this turmoil have brought with them a

relentless drizzle of Windsor-Richter almanacs, almost blotting out the already dark, recessionary skies, as they buffet and blind the tabloid conscience of a sullen democracy, uneasy with its palpable mediocrity, manifest ignorance and dismal achievement. Fanning the epidemic are what the film producer, Sam Spiegel, used to call his 'opinion-makers'. In his case, a bunch of Hungarian comfort-stooges who unfailingly read out the runes he wished to hear. This lot are mostly upstart journalists and academics of the dimmer sort.

Opinion-making is this country's most virulent growth industry. Everybody has opinions and everybody wants more. The market is insatiable. Newspapers and television pour out opinion, urged on with the frenzy that stepped up the production of Spitfires during the war. Phone-ins proliferate, choked with calls from the semi-literate, bigoted and barmy. Opinion polls, the entrails of despotic democracy, are picked over for prophetic insights. We are becoming a nation of babbling back-seat cab drivers. 'What are you giving up for Lent?' I asked my wife. 'Opinions,' she said, adding, 'Permanently.'

At this moment, we are deluged by a cloudburst of opinion-making Windsor books. It's amusing, I suppose, to be told that when Diana informed her puzzled mother-in-law that she needed 'space', the matriarch replied, 'Kensington Palace isn't bijou, is it?' Or that, if you get a gong, the Palace will offer you a £55 video of the great occasion. Your 30 seconds of glory stitched into a standard 25 minutes of routine ritual.

But only one is readable, let alone honourable (an attribute inimical to what is known in the earthquake trade as 'seismic prospecting',). The exception, astonishing, considering the below-stairs tattling banality, the seedy snobbery and suburban hypocrisy of this factitious genre, is A. N. Wilson's *The Rise and Fall of the House of Windsor* (Sinclair-Stevenson, £14.99, pp. 211). It is written in a cool, amusing, plain-dealing style, devoid of the malignity which informs the solipsism and crass speculations of all the other grubbing prospectors. It is not without prejudice but, as Dr Johnson possibly said, 'One good prejudice is worth twenty principles.'

'What's it all in aid of – is it just for the sake of a gloved hand waving from a golden coach?' I gave these lines to a naïve but bewildered girl in a play I wrote when I was 26, and was generally reviled for it. Later, in a volume of essays by up and coming opinion-makers, I put in my bit by describing the monarchy as the 'gold filling in a mouthful of decay'. In 1961, I presented *The Blood of the Bamburgs*, a light-hearted lampoon about the trappings of monarchy, and royal weddings in particular. No one realised that this was not mockery of the institution, but of the lunatics who were using it to shore up the debilitating inertia and conformity that dominated life at the time.

My complaints then were against those whom I thought were exploiting something of poetic and symbolic value for their own sentimental and cynical ends. I was not to know then that those whom I regarded as their victims would ever make the suicidal error of yielding to the alligator smiles of the Fourth Estate and, later, put their heads in its mouth with the expectancy of not mere connivance but loyalty and friendship. Thirty years on, Mr Wilson's harsh and personal judgment on individual members of the Royal Family, particularly Prince Charles (whom he dismisses as a non-runner for the throne) and the Queen, who is damned with the ambiguous praise of being 'uninteresting', will not receive a porchful of excremental tributes as I did. Nor, I suspect, will he be 'targeted' by shooting threats from military men in Bagshot.

Where were all these reckless heretics and seditious opinion-makers when a minor character in a stage play put the plain question about a gloved hand waving from a golden coach? Asleep or unborn, I suppose. Anyway, Wilson provides some eloquently honest responses and, blessedly, without any presumptuous claims to privileged access or inspired insights. We can know little enough of the interior life of our closest friends. Only Art can penetrate the guesswork of daily intimacy, and kingship is probably immune even to such inspired scrutiny.

The beauty of the British Monarchy lies in the fact that it requires no damned merit in its unchosen head. As Wilson points out, there is no perceptible onus on its holder even to be liked. Queen Victoria was popularly detested. The no-neck little widow spent most of her 60 glorious years skulking behind closed portcullis doors, leading a life of ineffable dullness, snapping at her huge family, foreign relatives and patient ministers. Her husband was convinced she was mad.

The reigning monarch may be drunken and adulterous, cruel and clever like the Tudors, pious or libidinous like the Stuarts, dim and wilful like the Hanoverians, or prosaically worthy-bourgeois like the Saxe-Coburgs. The succession is a constitutional roulette wheel. Sometimes you win, mostly you don't. Consider the reign of Charles II, one of the most glittering periods of English history. Charles is portrayed as lazy and indulgent, but he was a ruthless, articulate, cultured and sexy man. When asked why he found it necessary to have 39 mistresses, he replied: one for each Article of Faith.

He was responsible for Christopher Wren becoming an architect, for John Bunyan publishing *Pilgrim's Progress*, for the foundation of six of the original thirteen American colonies and the encouragement therein of religious freedom. When he ascended the throne there was £114 in the kitty. He transformed a bankrupt state into the richest and most feared nation in Europe. He was also directly responsible for the patronage of Henry Purcell. Mr Wilson reproves Prince Charles for unseemly intervention in the GATT negotiations. What matter if he should have said a foolish thing? Why should he yet not find the opportunity to do a wise one? We could do with a Purcell or two, and, most of all, a Wren.

Wilson's final paragraph restores common kindliness and sanity to its lost place in this lunatic debate:

> More than the House of Windsor will fall if the Monarchy is allowed to be hounded out by the bullies and brutes. It will be a symptom of the coarsening of life in Britain today, in which the brashly new inevitably defeats the old, in which the ugly always overcomes the beautiful, and everything of which the British used to be proud is cast down and vilified. Is it too much to hope in modern Britain – filthy, chaotic, idle, rancorous modern Britain – that sweetness and light could ever triumph over barbarism? The Queen is the only individual in British public life who has held out some hope for that.

Even after reading some 200 pages of such detached intelligence, I was beginning to feel that I had been colonically irrigated with the firm's famous brown soup, and a further flip through the housemaid's dumb twaddling of professional snoopers and barking professors is enough to turn the bowels. Nigel Dempster, as you may know, is an Australian coxcomb who assumes the airs of a floor-walker lately fired from Fortnum's for colonial chippiness and demoted to the counter of a Jermyn Street shirtmakers, from which he jumped into the arms of a Duke's daughter: a bizarre alliance of patrician beauty and fawning braggart.

Together with Peter Evans, he has produced the glossily packaged *Behind Closed Doors* (Orion, £16.99, pp. 264, no index). This one will be the parvenues' pick, and it is by some lengths the most sleazy. Viz Charles: 'He is shy, he is sensitive, he is even sometimes desolately lonely, but he is also a shit,' says a 'polo friend'. An unnamed source claims that 'the girls' talk was that he wasn't a great lover, not even a very good one.' As for Diana, she can take it or leave it, preferably leave it. How different from the home life of our own dear Queen.

Dempster claims that the Duke of Edinburgh found 'Sex without Elizabeth had been wonderful. Sex with Elizabeth had been a revelation.' Anyone who can stomach some six pages of Dempster-speak deserves a straight-cucumber republic.

James Whitaker is the jovial hack they call the big red tomato, and he would clearly rather be a peach. In *Diana v. Charles* (Signet, £14.99, pp. 237) he is pro-Di, sort of. His royal opinion-monger's CV is impeccable. He was there at the Wales's Majorcan holiday in 1986:

> They read, they sunbathed, they chatted to others, but never once did they address a single word to each other. *I watched through my fieldglasses* [my italics] completely mesmerised . . . I have since been told that following this week in the Majorcan sun the Prince and Princess never slept together again.

End of Fairy Tale. Anthony Holden's *The Tarnished Crown* (Bantam, £16.99, pp. 320) is a loftier number. Bagehot is Holden's man, and his guns are trained on the Windsors' venality. Holden is *very* pro the sainted Di, who chooses to fly economy in a seat next to the loo.

> The coy, blushing teenager married in front of 700 million people now holds the rest of the world in thrall, and the future of the thousand-year-old British crown in the palm of her elegant hand.

Cor

> To the British people, their wronged princess is more than ever an object of adoration.

Cor.

Tom Paine is mad professor Stephen Haseler's man (*The End of the House of Windsor*, I.B. Tauris, £14.95, pp. 208), and the 'royal-state' his target, but there is not much of the zealot's flame in his belly, or prose. This is a sad, mean book. 'The culture of pseudo-mediaeval kingship bears down upon the hapless British subjects in their very daily routine.' Would your tax demand be more bearable if it wasn't marked On Her Majesty's Service? 'The monarchy has added little to the development of Britain as a serious country.' What is a serious country? Don't ask. Or the potty prof. will explain.

Whatever the interpretations of the Windsor Fault, it has brought ignominy and humiliation upon the heart of tolerance, irony and kindliness of the country in which I grew up, a land where the modesty of heroes is now despatched with the same derision and contempt as the most wickedly ambitious. The seismic prospectors, the malign opinion-makers, have thrown up a generation to whom the word 'honour' is forgotten, meaningless currency. In the face of this aftershock of concerted brutality, I can only cry: 'God Save the Queen', and confusion to her enemies, for they are mine too. May God rot the tyrannies of equality, streamlining, updating; the deranged dreams of chimerical classlessness and, most of all, absurd, irrelevant relevance. And God help the Prince of Wales.

5 June 1993

IT'S YOUR MOVE, PEKING

Dominic Lawson

The simplest way for the Conservative Party to reduce its bank over-draft of £19 million would be to recall Christopher Patten from the governorship of Hong Kong. One of the leading lights of the British business community in the colony, Mr Philip Tose, has let it be known – not entirely in jest – that he would guarantee a £5 million donation to the party, if only John Major were to find Mr Patten another job. Mr Tose's animosity to the 28th Governor of Hong Kong is shared by almost every other rich white settler, and the reason is plain: they are worried that Mr Patten's confrontation with Peking over democratisation in Hong Kong is doing their investments in the colony no good at all.

'One of these businessmen even threatened to shoot me,' Mr Patten told me last week. But he is monumentally unruffled. 'These self-serving Cassandras have been proved hugely wrong. The Hong Kong stock-market is up 30 per cent since I put forward my proposals in October. Of course, I can understand that some businessmen think that, if they want to do some deals in China, it does them no harm to badmouth the Governor. And surprisingly few of them understand the relationship between Hong Kong's prosperity and the rule of law. And they don't understand that part of the rule of law is a free press and a credible legislature. But many of these same people, in the last year or two before the 1997 handover, will be knocking on my door saying, "What guarantees have you got that the Chinese will behave as they say they will in the Joint Declaration? What are you going to do about the rule of law after 1997, Mr Patten?"'

But for all the Governor's confidence – and he does not look at all like a worried man – there are signs that his patron in Downing Street is losing patience with the political deadlock over Hong Kong. Since April, when the Chinese finally agreed to discuss the colony's electoral arrangements, there have been five rounds of Sino-British talks. On each occasion the British delegation has left Peking (the Chinese only play home matches) with next to nothing. Now John Major has recalled Chris Patten to London, for a meeting on 1 July of the Cabinet's Hong Kong Committee, to decide whether there is any point in continuing the dialogue of the deaf with Peking.

'There are those,' Mr Patten told me wearily, the day after the fifth round of talks had ended, 'more accustomed than I to negotiating with the Chinese, who think that they are moving, but it's not like negotiating with any other country.' He rolled his eyes. 'It requires the patience of the aeons.'

China insists that Mr Patten's proposals for the widening of the franchise for the next elections to the Hong Kong Legislative Council infringe the Basic Law, the Chinese statute that will govern the 'Hong Kong Special Administrative Region of the People's Republic of China' after 1997. Mr Patten, to their fury, quotes back at them chapter four, section three of the Basic Law: 'The ultimate goal is the election of all the members of the Legislative Council by universal suffrage.' The Chinese then quote in return Article 158, which states: 'The power of interpretation of the Basic Law shall be vested in the Standing Committee of the National People's Congress.' In other words: we decide what the Basic Law means, not you. And so it has gone on for months.

In the relative sanity of his office at Government House, Mr Patten hilariously describes the 'Kafkaesque' predicament in which he has found himself, by giving me the edited highlights of his talks with the Chinese in a style more Pinter than Kafka: 'It usually goes like this: "Mr Patten, you have broken the Basic Law." "I haven't broken the Basic Law." "Yes, you have." "Show me where I have broken the Basic Law." "You must have broken the Basic Law because we wrote it, and we are telling you that you have broken it." "Here is a copy of the Basic Law. Point out to me where I've broken it." "Well, you've broken

the spirit of the Basic Law." "What is the spirit of the Basic Law?"
And so on, *ad infinitum*. They haven't been able to demonstrate in
any sense that what we are proposing contravenes the Basic Law. But
the trouble is that negotiating with the Chinese is like playing chess
with an opponent who suddenly moves a knight along a diagonal, and
when you say, "How can you do that?" he says, "There are different
rules for us."'

Had I, too, not had an encounter with the officials of the Chinese
foreign service the day before, I might have thought that Mr Patten
was exaggerating. I had sought an interview at the New China News
Agency, whose Hong Kong office is effectively Peking's embassy in
the colony. I was granted an audience with the deputy director, Mr
Zhang Junsheng. I awaited Mr Zhang's entrance in the company of
four of his colleagues, all of whom rose as he entered the room. Every
word that Mr Zhang subsequently uttered was furiously scribbled
down in quadruplicate; even when, which was most of the time, he
was merely answering my questions by declaiming from a bound copy
of the Basic Law, which I imagine all the cadres present knew by heart
anyway.

At times, however, Mr Zhang improvised, by switching from reading
out aloud from the Basic Law to reading from cue cards. One went:
'Mr Patten refused to consult with China, although we asked him to
do so. We asked him not to publicise his policies. We told him it would
give rise to public debate. But he wouldn't listen to us.' 'But,' I asked
Mr Zhang, 'if he had consulted you privately about his proposals,
would you not have rejected them anyway?' The senior cadre looked
up from his notes as if he was answering a question too stupid to have
been anticipated. 'Yes. But it would have been more correct if he had
done so.'

The legalistic row over the Basic Law, which Mr Patten cannot win,
masks the essence of the dispute, which is simply that China, whatever
it professed at the time of the drafting of the Basic Law, cannot tolerate
the idea of democracy, or anything resembling it, in Hong Kong. Some
of their more honest apologists admit this. As Mr Tsang Yok-Sing,
leader of the openly pro-Peking Democratic Alliance for the Better-
ment of Hong Kong, told me with disarming candour, 'Mr Deng Xiaop-
ing does not believe very much in this western idea of democracy.'
While maintaining the pretence that his paramount leader was not
anti-democratic, Mr Zhang made it clear that his government regards
the British habit of installing democracies in colonies they once admin-
istered as nothing less than deliberate sabotage. 'When Britain with-
drew from her former colonies she always left a lot of problems and

contradictions. I need only mention Israel[!] and India. We are now wondering whether Britain is going to produce a lot of contradictions in Hong Kong. We'd like to tell Britain that it's impossible for her to create contradictions in Hong Kong.'

I put Mr Zhang's argument to the Governor. Wasn't it understandable that the Chinese should see the last-minute introduction of democracy into Hong Kong by a departing administration as a scorched-earth policy?

'This is part of the intellectual infrastructure – if I can dignify it with the expression – of their abuse. *Wen Wei Po* [the Communist-run Hong Kong daily newspaper which has variously called the 28th Governor 'a prostitute', 'a serpent' and 'a criminal down the ages'] has been publishing a series of dusty old articles on the history of the British Empire. They even produced a special pull-out section on the subject – the contention is that introduction democracy into developing countries is a British attempt to wreck them after we've departed. It's an argument that some of them, preposterously, have tried to put, and Lee Kwan Yew gives them a certain amount of intellectual support. Well, it's true that we have had a fairly familiar routine: put them on the launching-pad with the rule of law, a clean civil service trained at St Antony's, a Westminster model of democracy *à la* Sir E. Jennings; then we'd throw in a Speaker's chair, light the blue touch-paper and send them off into outer space. Sometimes it worked. Sometimes it came crashing down to earth, as in Uganda. But it wasn't our fault when that happened. The dismantling of our colonial empire is something we've done honourably.'

I pointed out that there was a crucial difference in Hong Kong. We are not preparing it for independence but for a resumption of Chinese sovereignty. 'That,' said Mr Patten, 'does not make it any the less honourable an enterprise.'

That is not altogether the view of Martin Lee, the leader of the United Democrats of Hong Kong. China is far more scared of Mr Lee than it is of Mr Patten. It was Mr Lee's courage that brought out one million people in protest onto the streets of Hong Kong on the day after the Tiananmen massacre. It was Mr Lee's party that swept the board in what passed for elections in Hong Kong in 1991. It is Mr Lee's party that, the Chinese fear, will take control of the Hong Kong legislature if the franchise is widened. In Peking's eyes, that is tantamount to Hong Kong's being taken over by subversives.

I arranged somewhat tactlessly to meet Mr Lee at the exotic China Club, a remarkable celebration of communist kitsch and cuisine on the 13th floor of the Bank of China building, from where, at the height of the cultural revolution, Bank of China employees shouted down on the people of Hong Kong to overthrow the Governor. 'I almost refused to meet you here,' said Mr Lee, casting his eyes over such glittering attractions as 'The Long March Bar'. Mr Lee cannot understand why Mr Patten, having announced his proposals last November, has still not presented them to the Legislative Council, and instead has kept Hong Kong's fledgling parliament waiting for months while the British and Chinese foreign services attempt to come up with a diluted version of Mr Patten's democratic heresy. 'Mr Patten holds himself as a champion of democracy in Hong Kong, and has thus gained adulation from here to Capitol Hill. How can he back down? On the other hand, how can China make huge concessions to a "prostitute"? The talks are doomed to fail.'

Mr Patten is, in fact, quite prepared to see his proposals amended. 'You could produce – I could do it now – all sorts of arrangements which would achieve the same objective of clean elections, elections that can't be rigged, that produce a credible legislature, and not a rubber-stamp legislature. My bottom line is that whatever emerges from the talks must produce that result.'

Originally, the British set a private deadline of July for the talks to succeed. As that deadline approaches, Mr Patten's problem becomes acute. Does he dare put his proposals to Hong Kong's legislators, and risk an almost certain retort from Peking that it will not recognise the new parliament when it takes over in 1997?

Mr Patten appears to be preparing for confrontation while hoping it will not come to that. 'July has been mentioned as a reasonable time to get our legislation in place, and to prepare for free, open and fair elections. I don't want our negotiators to feel contained by the calendar but plainly there comes a point beyond which you can't reasonably delay.'

'And what happens at that point?'

'At that point we would have to carry out the responsibility of government.'

The mayhem this – pressing ahead in the teeth of China's most bloodcurdling threats – would cause could add new chapters to the colourful history of Sino-British diplomatic insults.

On the face of it, Mr Patten has no cards to play. China, as one of the members of the British negotiating team told me, 'can do whatever it likes to Hong Kong, and we can't stop them'. But Mr Patten is not entirely bluffing. He knows that any major confrontation between London and Peking would devastate the Hong Kong stock-market. And who has been the biggest single investor in that market in recent months? The Chinese government. Last week, for example, Citic, a Chinese state investment arm, bid almost HK$10 billion to take over the Hong Kong hotel company Miramar. This year alone, the Chinese government plans to float nine of its companies on the Hong Kong stock-market. Such desperately needed refinancing plans would be completely scuppered by open diplomatic war between Britain and China. Quietly, almost silently, Peking's leaders have become as dependent on the financial markets as any democratically elected western government.

But all this means is that we are relying on China to put its financial self-interest ahead of its – rather horrifying – political principles. And, I asked the Governor, didn't the Tiananmen massacre show that Mr Deng's mind, however decreasingly lucid, did not work like that? 'I don't believe that history is likely to repeat itself.'

Old Foreign Office hands, such as Sir Percy Cradock, the architect of the existing Sino-British political settlement in Hong Kong, believe Mr Patten fatally underestimates the Chinese capacity for brutality, and that he would be acting in the best interest of the people of Hong Kong if he did not risk provoking such repression after 1997.

The mention of Sir Percy seemed to irritate the Governor far more than the names of any of his Communist opponents. 'I must say that the people who have been giving me this wise advice don't seem to have delivered much for the people of Hong Kong in the recent past. But I don't want to be as obsessive about Sir Percy as he seems to be about me. There is a view which some diplomats, though not the best, adhere to, that diplomacy is about using words cleverly in order to finesse matters of substance. I don't happen to believe that . . . if we hadn't been prepared to stand up for Hong Kong before 1997, there was bugger all chance of seeing anybody stand up for it after 1997.'

After 1997. The Governor, like everyone else in the colony, is a tenant at the smouldering end of a burnt-out lease, at the mercy of a capricious freeholder. I left Mr Patten at his desk. On the wall behind him hangs a bleak terracotta crucifix. The wall in front of him is equally austere, decorated only by a large, plain clock. If ever there was a man trapped between things spiritual and things temporal, that man is the last British Governor of Hong Kong.

26 June 1993

IS THE UN
REALLY NECESSARY?

Anne Applebaum

There are certain places in the world which remain frozen in another time or another era, certain places which never change, no matter what great events – political or climatic, economic or military – shake the world around them. While the Acropolis deteriorates and the pyramids sink into the sand, these places continue to exude the aura of the past. The United Nations headquarters is one such place: when one enters the tall, glass building on the East Side of Manhattan, one is immediately transported backwards – to a time before peace-keeping missions, a time before blue helmets, a time when the UN was a place for talk, not action.

Since the cornerstone was laid in 1949, UN headquarters has been international territory – a no man's land, in other words, where national bigotry is loudly denounced, and national fictions are accepted without question. In the gloomy hallways outside the Security Council meeting-room, a gift from Iran is still framed in plexiglass: it is the world's first human rights declaration, carved on a stone, and it symbolises Iran's ancient and ongoing commitment to human rights (regardless of sex or religious belief).

Nearby hangs a carpet donated by the Ukrainian Soviet Socialist Republic, a relic from the days when Soviet Ukraine, although not independent, had its own seat at the UN (thereby giving the Soviet Union more votes in the General Assembly). Along with the gifts, there are displays dedicated to Decolonisation, World Peace, and the Search for a Solution to the Question of Palestine, all causes which the UN continues to advocate. In the corridors upstairs, there is a Centre Against Apartheid, an Outer Space Affairs division and a Peace Studies unit, all of which the UN continues to fund.

Times have changed since these gifts were given and these programmes were founded, but the culture of the UN has not. Although now expected to carry out large and difficult tasks in the real world – to keep peace in various unpeaceful places, to distribute food where people are starving – the UN Secretariat in New York is still a place whose political arms have withered away into symbolism, whose energy is wasted on outdated programmes and superfluous publications. While one would imagine from the headlines that the UN now devotes a large part of its time and energy to peace-keeping, this is not the case. Of the $7.8 billion spent by the entire UN system in 1991, a mere 10 per cent went to peace-keeping and political affairs, while nearly 90 per cent went to UN economic and social programmes. Of the 10,000 people who work for the UN in New York, only 25 of them now work in the peace-keeping division.

Far from devoting themselves to security issues, the denizens of the upper floors of the UN Secretariat dedicate themselves, among other things, to various committees and commissions on apartheid (I counted three at least), although apartheid no longer exists. They serve on the Committee on Decolonisation, issuing report after report (recent meetings have discussed Gibraltar and established an International Decade for the Eradication of Colonialism), although decolonisation is largely over. They work on the UN Economic Commissions for Europe, Africa, Asia and Latin America, each with its trade and technology division, its natural resource division, and offices in places like Luxembourg and Addis Ababa, where they continue to commission studies which duplicate the work of the EEC, the OAS and other regional organisations. Richard Thornburgh, who was briefly Undersecretary General for Administration and Management, has called the UN's budget-making process 'surreal', but 'immortal' is a better word for the endless committees: once born, they never die, and their longevity is precisely what gives the UN the feeling of a place locked in the past.

The explanation for the endless growth of programmes and projects lies in the bureaucratic culture of the UN, which is peculiar to the nature of the institution. Populated on the one hand by idealists who believe everything they do is valuable, and on the other hand by time-servers who are there to get what they can, the UN has degenerated into a place where symbolism is reality, where people believe that saying something can make it true, where discussing a problem is thought to amount to solving it.

Take, for example, the UN official who spoke to me on 'deep background' (all UN officials, no matter how insignificant, speak on 'deep background') of the World Summit for Social Development. The Social Summit, as it is known in UNspeak, is a conference of world leaders which is scheduled for 1995. Although it is being planned along the lines of the Environmental Summit in Rio, its goals, the official said, are much broader: the elimination of poverty, the reduction of unemployment and the ending of social disintegration – 'or rather the beginning of social integration, we like to accentuate the positive'. That means, apparently, that minorities like women must 'have a voice' too.

Within the world as UN bureaucrats see it, events like the Social Summit are not just optional icing tacked on to the political cake: they are the substance of politics itself. 'Talking about these problems will help solve them,' this particular official told me, 'we need to put these issues back on the international agenda,' meaning, presumably, the UN agenda, since she knows no other. This is, after all, a woman who joined the UN over ten years ago, will probably never be made redundant, will almost certainly be promoted: it is in her interests to have as many conferences as possible. This is a woman who also complains that her department is understaffed, which is probably true. Due to budgetary strains, the UN has had a hiring freeze for the past year. Like everyone else who works at the Secretariat, she also grumbles about 'certain big countries' not paying their dues, which is not as true as she thinks. In fact, member states paid nearly 94 per cent ($976 million out of $1.04 billion) of last year's regular budget, discounting peace-keeping and other agencies.

She is correct in saying that the UN is plagued by a perpetual financial crisis, however, although she does not make the connection between wasteful projects like the Social Summit and the need for budget cuts. In fact, the Social Summit – along with the Global Conference on Sustainable Development of Small Island Developing States, the World Conference on Natural Disaster Reduction, and the Ninth UN Congress on the Prevention of Crime and the Treatment of Offenders – is one of nine international conferences which the UN is sponsoring over the next three years.

Each one of these needs publicity, advance planning, and a secretariat (with offices and computers) to organise it. Each one requires international travel – a senior UN executive flies first-class and receives up to $300 per day expenses – and each one forces government officials to take time away from other duties. Some, like the Fourth Conference on Women, are follow-up conferences which will require further follow-ups; others are simply gifts given to small countries which could use the extra hard currency. While it is true that these conferences do not take up a huge proportion of the UN budget, it is fair to say that the budget targets would be easier to meet without them.

UN waste, of course, has not escaped everyone's attention, and the nine conferences are not the only example of it. Reform is a constant topic among the UN's top bureaucrats, 'efficiency' and 'management skills' are the new buzz words. Yet from year to year, little seems to change. According to one western diplomat, Secretary-General Boutros Boutros-Ghali has found himself unable to fulfil promises of staff reductions, and has therefore refused to publish an official staff list for the past two years. 'I find myself counting names in the phone book when I want to know how many people work here,' she complained. The member states themselves made one recent attempt at restructuring the General Assembly. It collapsed at the end of June, partly because no one could agree on how many seats of a particular committee should be given to developing countries.

It is true that the UN has an auditing system and a budgetary oversight committee (whose members also speak only on 'deep background'), but these bodies look for corruption and waste within departments which have already been set up, and do not ask, say, whether an international conference is required to solve the problem of social disintegration. In a bureaucracy which is responsible to everyone and no one, even press scrutiny has little impact. Last year, the *Washington Post* pointed out that the UN Centre on Transnational Corporations had spent 15 years drafting a 'code of conduct' for multinationals investing in developing countries (for 'code of conduct' read 'restrictions on foreign investment'), at a yearly budget of $6.4 million. To date, that centre has yet to be dissolved.

As for individuals who try to reform the system from within, they risk ostracism and loss of their jobs. In an office building not far from the Secretariat, I met a UN official who had been hired from the private

sector in order to bring management techniques to a particular department. After a year in the job (during which time he recommended more
management training for UN employees and merit-linked promotion,
among other things) he found himself accused of racism: calling for
higher standards, apparently, was tantamount to discrimination
against employees from developing countries. The director of the
department apologised, and transferred the man to a lower-level job.
Alas, he too spoke on 'deep background', and would not be quoted by
name.

For too many UN bureaucrats from poor countries, a New York
posting is not a job but a reward for good service, something they feel
they deserve; for too many others, it is a place to go when one's party
falls out of power or one's leader falls from grace. For some, it is even
a frightening experience. After all, bureaucrats hint, the ex-communist
countries once filled their bureaucratic quotas with KGB operatives –
few of whom have seen fit to retire. Much weirder are the stories about
Sri Chinmoy, a guru who conducts readings and meditation sessions
inside the UN building, and has allegedly organised many mid-level
bureaucrats into a secret brotherhood within the UN.

Now, there is nothing so terrible about gurus, and it even makes
sense that lonely people living in a foreign city band together for company. But the UN is a secretive place, the kind of place where even
the simplest piece of information is hard to elicit. I went, for example,
to four departments to find out the cost of the Social Summit. One
told me the information was unavailable for 'security reasons', another
said that it was 'impossible to know at this time'. A third told me to
send a fax which would be forwarded to someone in Vienna (whose
phone number could not be revealed). Only the fourth, the press secretary of the Chilean ambassador – who is not a UN employee – would
tell me that the UN has put up $2.5 million for start-up costs. In that
atmosphere, it is no wonder that rumours of gurus and organised cabals
seem oddly terrifying: one never knows what anyone is really up to.

Of course none of the problems described here – nor the secret-
iveness, the resistance to reform, the weirdness or the waste – is very
new. As long ago as the early 1980s, Jeanne Kirkpatrick, the American
ambassador to the UN, described the organisation as nothing more
than a place for nations to let off rhetorical steam. She called this the
'Turkish bath syndrome'.

Since 1989, however, the 'international community' (Britain,
America, France, and Russia, that is, with China abstaining) has been
gripped by collective amnesia where the UN is concerned. Long reviled
as a 'talking shop', the UN was suddenly called upon to perform incred-

ible tasks. The same bureaucrats who were considered incompetent in the past were immediately asked to organise food and weapons for armies in Bosnia, Cambodia, Somalia. The same institution which had always been described as corrupt and ill-managed was asked to make difficult military decisions at very short notice. And yet the world is surprised when the UN reveals, as it did last week, that eight top officials involved in the Cambodian peace force have been suspended for corruption, or that commanders in Somalia disagree about tactics, or that some of the UN battalions in Croatia arrived without weapons, training or any clear idea of what they were supposed to be doing there.

In fact, many of the problems which have appeared abroad merely reflect difficulties which have always plagued the UN's New York headquarters. Thanks to poor organisation, for example, the Department of Peace-keeping Operations and the Field Operations Division report to different authorities: when the two units disagreed in Cambodia, no one ranked lower than the Secretary-General himself had the authority to reconcile them. Thanks to lack of trained staff, the UN military operation in Somalia was called 'essentially dysfunctional' in a report prepared for the American Senate. It would have failed entirely without American administrative support.

Given the UN's institutional flaws, the failures of recent peace-keeping efforts are not extraordinary: what is extraordinary is that anyone ever thought they would work in the first place. Leaving aside the fact that the UN is not, as many pretend, a sovereign state which can command soldiers and expect them to obey, it was simply unfair to ask the institution to carry out the tasks now required of it. At the end of 1991, the UN peace-keeping budget was $700 million and the number of peace-keepers, soldiers and civilians hovered around 11,000. Now, the costs are closer to $3.5 billion, and the number of peace-keepers around the world has soared to 90,000. Giving huge new projects to an old-fashioned, unreformed bureaucracy was always going to be a recipe for disaster.

This is not to say that the UN needs vast new resources, as Boutros-Ghali has claimed. It only took three people to negotiate the recent cease-fire in El Salvador, the UN's most successful recent project. But if we want the UN to continue sending blue-helmeted policemen into far-flung parts of the world, the institution itself needs reform. Many of the UN funding agencies have proved their worth in the past, but do we still need a UN Committee on Trade and Development, or a UN university in Tokyo, or a Social Summit?

If efficient policing is what we now expect the UN to provide, better to disband these projects immediately and spend the same time and the same money building a serious international police force from scratch, with its own supply systems, its own intelligence networks, and its own training schemes. If peace-making is what we want the UN to occupy itself with, we should place a moratorium on pointless economic studies, and hire 15 well-paid professional negotiators instead. Simply attaching expensive new departments to the existing organisation will produce more of the problems we have now, and will not cure the institution of its fundamental bureaucratic ills.

Most of all, western politicians should not continue to speak of 'breathing life' into the UN. For the UN is not a 'dead' organisation; we only thought it was dead because we were not interested in its fate. In fact, it has been alive and even growing for a long time – living and breathing according to the fashions of another age.

31 July 1993

DESIGN

TWEE ARE NOT AMUSED

Nicky Haslam

It turns out that all the uniformly chic black London railings were so painted as one of those myriad marks of respect to the Prince Consort on his death in 1861. Before that, the capital's ironwork was rainbow-hued . . . imagine! But, in a reversal of this 130-year-old habit – even though less than a mile away Prince Albert's multi-coloured Memorial stands mouldering, encased in a scaffold nearly as expensive as the apparently unfundable repairs to the Memorial itself – London is about to be treated to an eyeful of glitz whose glare not even the blackest Raybans can diminish.

Created, one would swear, by the makers of My Little Pony, based on a design by Norman Hartnell's embroiderers with additional artistic input from Dame Edna, and forged in Elfland, the Queen Elizabeth Gates now bestride (well, not bestride exactly, as there is something infinitely twee about their footfall) the South Carriageway in Hyde Park, within spitting distance of Decimus Burton's classical screen and mellow, manly Apsley House. From every angle of approach, this restrained backdrop of appropriately citified architecture is infringed by the raucous sprawl of John W. Mills ARCA FRBS's latest Disney-esque gentility.

The Queen Elizabeth Gates were conceived as a timely and touching tribute to his Majestic and Imperial aunty by Prince Michael of Kent, who was absolutely right to believe that the country should honour her with a memorial in her lifetime. Some of the costs having been met by public subscription, it says a lot for Prince Michael's powers of organisation that these gates were created at all, let alone erected in comparatively record time (it would have been even quicker, but apparently the contractors put the pier foundations a few feet off the designated spot and were made to relocate them). But did Prince Michael or anyone else, myself included, when looking at the model, foresee that the reality would be quite so out of keeping?

If a memorial is meant intrinsically to reflect its subject, this one should contain some classic reference to the Queen Mother's matriarchal qualities, her stoicism, her steadfastness. But no. It's all whoopsy pipe-cleaners of bent chrome, adorned by (easily vandalisable) knots and twiddles, and interspersed with youthful 'symbols' – and some not so youthful: even that naughty, throat-catching fish is there.

Furthermore, the name of the Queen Elizabeth Gates is a worry. To most people outside the most intimate royal circles, Queen Elizabeth means the Queen, and her mother is the Queen Mother. These gates will surely be thought by the public to be a memorial to the Queen herself. When they both unveil the gates next week, might they not wish the appellation clearer, the memorial itself more suitable? Less like a wedding tiara for Mandy Smith, or Raine Spencer?

. . . Oh, perhaps that's it – if the royal heir's marriage hadn't gone adrift, the new gates could have been dedicated more aptly to the Queen Stepmother-To-Be.

3 July 1993